The author

Ann Hoffmann has spent the greater part of her professional life working with or for writers. After a first job in publishing, she travelled widely in Europe and, on returning to England, spent four years as secretary/researcher to the well-known writer, the late Robert Henriques. In 1966 she established a research service for authors, which she ran until 1987. She now devotes the bulk of her time to researching and writing her own books; these include *The Dutch: How They Live and Work*, *Bocking Deanery*, *Lives of the Tudor Age*, and *Majorca*.

In this expanded and revised edition of RESEARCH FOR WRITERS, Miss Hoffmann writes knowledgeably from personal experience on a variety of sources of information, on research methods, on some of the pitfalls to be avoided by the 'novice' researcher, on the particular problems facing writers of fiction and non-fiction and on the impact of the new technology on research.

Research
for Writers

Research
for Writers

5th edition

Ann Hoffmann

A & C Black · London

Fifth edition 1996

Under the title *Research for Writers* the third and fourth editions were published in 1986 and 1992 by A & C Black (Publishers) Limited, 35 Bedford Row, London WC1R 4JH

ISBN 0-7136-4269-6

Previously published under the title *Research: a handbook for writers and journalists*
First edition 1975 Midas Books
Second edition 1979 A & C Black (Publishers) Limited

Typeset in 10 on 11pt Sabon by Florencetype, Stoodleigh, Devon
Printed in Great Britain by Redwood Books, Trowbridge, Wilts

Contents

Principal Abbreviations used in this Book

AGRA	Association of Genealogists and Record Agents
Aslib	Association for Information Management (formerly called the Association of Special Libraries and Information Bureaux)
BAC	Business Archives Council
BALH	British Association for Local History
BBA	*British Biographical Archive*
BBC	British Broadcasting Corporation
BFI	British Film Institute
BHI	British Humanities Index
BL	British Library
BLAISE	British Library Automated Information Service
BM	British Museum*
BN	Bibliothèque Nationale
BNB	*British National Bibliography*
BoB	Bibliography of Biography
CD-ROM	Compact Disk-Read Only Memory
CSO	Central Statistical Office
DNB	*Dictionary of National Biography*
FFHS	Federation of Family History Societies
HMSO	Her Majesty's Stationery Office
ICA	International Council on Archives

* On 1 July 1973 the former library departments of the British Museum were incorporated in the British Library Reference Division. Subsequently other collections, principally the old India Office Library and the National Sound Archive, were added. The collections are currently housed in 18 different buildings throughout London, but principally at the British Museum in Great Russell Street, WC1, where it is now known as the British Library Humanities and Social Sciences Service. A new purpose-built British Library nearing completion at St Pancras, North London, is scheduled to open at the end of 1997. Scholars and *habitués* of the Bloomsbury Round Reading Room and the Students' Room of the Department of Manuscripts still use the old affectionate term, 'the BM'. Once the collections are transferred to St Pancras, this will fall into disuse.

IGI	International Genealogical Index
ITC	Independent Television Commission
KIST	*Keyword Index to Serial Titles*
LA	Library Association
n.d.	no date
N.S.	New Style (dates)
NSA	National Sound Archive
OED	*Oxford English Dictionary*
OPAC	Online Public Access Catalogue
O.S.	Old Style (dates)
PCC	Prerogative Court of Canterbury (wills)
PCY	Prerogative Court of York (wills)
PRO	Public Record Office
SRIS	British Library Science Reference and Information Service
WWW	World Wide Web

Note: For the sake of brevity and to avoid the clumsy repetition of 'he' and 'she' throughout the book, writers/researchers are referred to by the one pronoun, 'he'. No offence is intended to the female person.

Author's Note

When I embarked on this project in 1975 it was with the idea of setting down, for freelance writers faced with the daunting task of researching for publication for the first time, some practical notes on methods and sources that would start them off along the right lines and at the same time help them to avoid some of the pitfalls. Although the book has grown in the process, and this fifth edition enables me to revise the text once again, it was never intended to be – nor, considering the vast sources available to the modern writer, can it ever be – more than a guide. No one researcher can do more than scratch the surface, let alone compile a comprehensive research manual. Even with a team to assist me and the almost unlimited space of a CD-ROM it would be a thankless task, given the need to keep it up to date with the thousands of new reference works, electronic as well as printed, that are published each year. Not only would such a manual have to be priced beyond the means of the very people my little book is intended to reach, it would defeat my prime purpose, which has always been to point the way and to encourage the researcher to *research*. The danger of making too much information available too easily and too speedily is that the recipient may be tempted to sit back, accept what is offered as gospel and not bother to delve further.

Researching, like writing, is an individual, creative and selective process. It cannot be 'taught'. In his quest for original material – and who does not dream of stumbling upon a cache of hitherto unknown, unpublished papers or the answer to a problem that has baffled scholars for several generations? – the writer never ceases to learn. All the time he is probing, absorbing, adding to his store of knowledge of sources of information largely by trial and error. Either he has a 'nose' for it or he has not. If not, unless he has time on his hands, he would be well advised to use the services of a professional. An elementary grasp of sources can of course be gleaned from a textbook and a few days' intensive study in a good reference library; this has immense value as a springboard. After that he is on his own. Invariably he will find himself, at different stages of his research, thrust into the unaccustomed roles of student, librarian, interviewer, detective and private investigator, and much else besides.

Throughout the compilation of this and previous editions, therefore, I have kept in mind the many time-consuming problems likely to be encountered by a novice writer/researcher, whether he is concerned with fiction or non-fiction. I have dared to suggest, from my own experience, ways in which these problems may be tackled. Like all craftsmen, I have my favourite tools – principally those tried and trusted reference works that served me well during my years as a professional researcher. Over the last decade I have taken on board many of the newer, electronic aids. Laying these out alongside one another on the work bench, as it were, for fellow craftsmen to pick up, handle and use as they see fit, has been a joy and a challenge. They may not constitute the particular assortment that a colleague would select, being drawn in the main from my own research activities and thus inclined more to the factual, historical and biographical than to the scientific or technical. But I can vouch for them absolutely as loyal and steadfast helpmates, and I am confident that they will go on for some time yet to help others to solve some of those alarming and often seemingly insoluble conundrums that have the nasty habit of cropping up at the worst possible moment in a writer's working day. If, in the long term, there may result books and features and theses that are not only better researched, but researched with less strain and less burning of the midnight oil on the part of their authors than was once the norm, then the putting together of this book, the fifth time round, will have achieved its purpose.

Gradually, over the past quarter of a century, writers have become accustomed to the 'information explosion'. Terms such as 'database', 'online', 'CD-ROM', 'Internet' and 'email' are in everyday use and no longer need special explanation here, although when you come to use them you find you have to master a new language. The present generation, computer-literate from its early schooldays, takes for granted speedy access to information worldwide and the facility, when armed with little more than a mouse and a modem, to communicate and exchange ideas internationally at relatively low cost. Never before has so much source material been so instantly accessible. And with the world hurtling at breakneck speed down the 'information superhighway' of the late 1990s, we can be confident that more 'miracles' are on the way.

I feel very strongly that it is up to each individual to harness from the new technology only that which he personally can put to good use. No more. Whenever we enter a bookshop or library we all benefit from online cataloguing. Most researchers make full use of the photocopy, the microfiche and the microfilm. Some use library computer services to search a database or two. But let us be realistic: does the average novelist or dramatist need to surf the Internet?

I do not wish to belittle the new technology. The invention of Xerox relieved us of the tedious task of copying long texts by hand; the computer enables our academic writers to get the benefit of recent research anywhere in the world far sooner than was previously feasible. It is not surprising that the present generation of writers cannot conceive how anyone got by without photocopy and microfilm, let alone without CD-ROM and email. I do however question whether some of these wonderful new techniques, in banishing the tedium, may not also have shed a good deal of the 'magic'? Is it possible that bringing up a text on screen can genuinely match the thrill of holding in one's own hands a medieval charter complete with original seal or the handwritten letter of a Queen Victoria or a Winston Churchill? Perhaps accessing a database the other side of the globe generates its own particular brand of magic. If so, I have yet to experience it. Speaking for myself, I shall always be thankful that I was able to do the bulk of my professional researching at a time when nearly always you were entrusted with the original newspaper, the original document. Today, understandably, in the interest of preservation of our national heritage, 80 per cent of the time the closest you get is a microfilm. Thus has the researcher's job been totally transformed.

As I prepare this new edition I am rather in the dark as to the proportion of my readers who use the new technology and those who, for financial or other reasons, do not. I would like to re-assure those who belong to the second category. For a long time to come most writers are going to carry on using the method and sources outlined here. The majority will continue to do the bulk of their research in the library and archive centres for many years yet. Books and journals will continue to be published in printed form. The old techniques of note-taking and face-to-face interviewing will still be practised. Those who have tried to use a computer and decided it is not for them – yet – are not going to be outlawed overnight. Nor will any sane editor reject a well-researched, well-written work purely because it is submitted on A4 paper and not on disk.

Mark Twain, the first writer known to have delivered a book to his publisher in typescript, purchased one of the early Remington typewriters in 1874. Five generations on, in 1996, some bestselling authors still choose to write in longhand and to pay a professional typist. The message is clear: the age of electronic authorship – and, it follows, electronic research – may have arrived, but you are still free to suit yourself.

One of the problems I have had to resolve in compiling this new edition is to judge which of the older titles to drop in order to make room for more recent works. Inevitably, with so much new material to hand, some have had to go. I am of course only too well aware that in the present economic climate libraries are being forced to cut down on the renewal and purchase of their reference stocks, which means that researchers without easy access to a copyright or university library may be at a disadvantage. To this end I have taken the middle road, discarding what I person-ally consider to be 'dead wood' (titles that have been superseded by more up-to-date, improved works), while retaining as many as space permits of the well-established or one-off reference books that still rank among the best on their subject. If this time round I have inadvertently axed one or two of my readers' favourites, I ask their forgiveness. May I suggest that before they chuck out the earlier edition they make use of the blank pages provided at the back of this one to keep a note of such titles?

As before, books mentioned in the text are listed alphabetically by title at the end of the relevant chapter rather than in one long bibliography at the end. (Listing by title rather than by author runs contrary to recognised bibliographic practice. Its continuance in this edition is, I hope, justified for reasons of quick reference: the works themselves are referred to first by title in the text and users of earlier editions will have become familiar with this method.) Microform and CD-ROM editions have been included where most relevant. Publication on film, fiche and CD being such a fast-growing industry, to have attempted more would have been at best incomplete. It would also have added considerably to the bulk (and thus the cost) of this book. A researcher who is 'on the ball' will ask at the library information counter; even if he does not, the competent librarian or archivist will usually bring such editions to his attention. Regrettably, it is not possible always to indicate those books which are out of print, as the situation changes constantly and reprints or new editions may become avail-able during the lifetime of this book. Most of the out-of-print titles mentioned will be found in the larger public libraries or may be borrowed through the public library lending service; but researchers needing to use such books over a long period are recommended to 'shop around' for them in secondhand and antiquarian bookshops (and even jumble sales), or to ask a book-finding service to try to locate them (see page 42).

The need to deliver the manuscript some months before publication makes it impossible to be fully up to date, but readers who follow my guidelines for using library catalogues and bibliographies should have little difficulty in tracing recently published material or new editions of existing works. Addresses and telephone numbers are a different matter, changing as they do, it seems, with unpredictable frequency. This means that, depending on the month of publication, even annual guides may be to some extent out of date by the time they appear. This aspect – or hazard, if you like – of modern living is one we simply have to learn to accept.

I should like to take this opportunity to express my gratitude to the many librarians, archivists, curators, press and public relations officers and others who have so efficiently and courteously dealt with my enquiries on a multitude of subjects over the years, and most especially the staff of the British Library. I am also indebted to several fellow writers, research colleagues and librarians who made constructive comments on the first four editions, some of whose suggestions are now incorporated.

My mail-bag since the appearance of the first edition makes it clear that *Research for Writers* has been of use not only to the amateur and student for whom it was intended, and even on occasion to those who make a hobby of entering competitions, but also to the more experienced 'diggers' who – so they tell me – sometimes suffer from extraordinary lapses of memory or mental blocks which may result in their wasting precious time searching for information that in fact is close at hand in their own reference collection or in a local library. To all these people I dedicate this fifth edition. In return, the greatest compliment they can pay me will be to *use the book as a working tool, to annotate it profusely, and to up-date it as their research requires*. For this purpose my publishers have again included a few blank pages at the end for personal notes. If, by the time these pages are filled, the book is starting to come apart at the spine through constant usage, hopefully there may be a sixth edition in the pipeline. As before, comments and suggestions for future editions will be most gratefully received.

A.H.
Tunbridge Wells, 1995

1

The Writer as Researcher

Every writer, unless he is creating a work of pure fantasy, has to do research. The nature and depth of that research will vary enormously, according to the subject of the work, the field of writing (factual article, novel, biography, history, thesis, children's story, etc.) and whether it is intended for the academic, popular or juvenile market. Whereas the scholar may have comparatively unlimited time (and probably also a research grant) which allows him to follow up pretty well every relevant line of enquiry in detail, the journalist's 'copy' must be on the sub-editor's desk at a given hour, and he is always pressed for time. Both texts must be correct, up to date and original – in other words, properly researched and well written.

In the end-product the academic work, with its notes and references, bibliography and index, may look to be the more meticulously researched, but this can be a deception: the thousand-word newspaper or magazine article, in order to present its data in a convincing, accurate and readable way and to show that its author is fully conversant with the latest events and/or published studies on the subject, may well involve as much, and sometimes more, research in proportion to its length. Whatever the field of authorship, the writer has to know a great deal more than he actually puts into words if what he writes is to ring true – and this applies as strictly to fiction writers as to journalists and historians and biographers. Ernest Hemingway, in an interview published in *Paris Review* (Spring 1958), put this very well. 'I always try to write on the principle of the iceberg,' he said. 'There is seven-eighths of it under water for every part that shows. Anything you know you can eliminate and it only strengthens your iceberg. It is the part that doesn't show. If the writer omits something because he does not know it, then there is a hole in the story.'*

---

* The same author, in *Death in the Afternoon*, expounds on this theme at greater length in a memorable passage worthy of framing and hanging above every writer's desk. It will be found at the end of chapter 16, in the current paperback edition (Arrow Books, 1994), at pages 168–9.

In ideal circumstances an author would write only of what he knows. No one, however, can have first-hand knowledge of every trade or profession in which he wishes to place his characters; few can afford to visit all those far-off lands that they are tempted to use as 'local colour' in their work. In most short stories or novels or plays, therefore, there are bound to be some people, some situations, and some settings that are beyond the personal experience of the writer, and for which he must rely to some extent at least on secondhand material – that is to say, on what others before him have observed and recorded, on printed statistics and factual data, and often on the recollections of third parties. The writer of history or historical fiction has no choice but to rely on documentary sources, either in print or in manuscript. In all these instances the research done must be thorough and, as far as possible, undertaken *in the round* (i.e. from more than one angle, avoiding reliance on any one source), or the result will be cardboard people, cardboard backgrounds and a loss of credibility in what may otherwise be an excellent piece of writing.

The prime importance of researching thoroughly before going into print cannot be over-stressed. Once his reader's confidence has been lost, the author will have an uphill battle to regain it. All too often a disillusioned reader or bright schoolchild will write and tell him where he has gone wrong, or – which is worse – may write and tell his editor or publisher, which in turn destroys their confidence and is likely to influence their attitude to the author's future work.

It is dangerous to rely on only one source for a given piece of information, however authoritative that source may seem to be. Mistakes occur all too frequently in even the most erudite book. They may not be the original author's fault at all, but the result of slipshod proof-reading in the editor's office or a printer's error that occurred at a later stage, such as when the type-setter re-sets a line to incorporate the author's or publisher's corrections. The sad thing is that once they are in print, mistakes are bound to be copied in good faith by someone else, and that person's work in turn may well be used as source material by another, and so on, so that even if a correction is made in subsequent editions of the original work, the misprint in that first edition may be perpetuated *ad infinitum*. By 'misprints' in this context is meant the mis-spelling of a proper name, a mis-quotation or a wrong figure – the sort of error that would not necessarily be spotted by a reader. The other kind of mistake, known as a 'literal' in publishing and printing, which may be a character set up in the wrong fount, or upside down, or two characters transposed, and the more obvious spelling mistake are more likely to be spotted at proof-reading stage.

Such are the hazards of authorship that the writer of non-fiction would do well to keep constantly in his mind's eye as he works the image of future trusting generations of students and researchers relying on his text as an authoritative source.

For most modern writers time is a precious commodity. Gone for ever are those halcyon days when Samuel Johnson could speak of a man turning over half a library to make one book; since his day millions more books have been written and published, and our libraries, archive collections and record repositories now house a bewildering and ever-increasing conglomeration of printed, manuscript, microfilmed, recorded and electronically produced material; there are also vast databases worldwide. More than ever before has it become essential for the writer/researcher to organize his working hours to the best advantage. He must know where and how to get at the information he requires in the quickest, as well as the most efficient and economical, way. As the great Dr Johnson also said: 'Knowledge is of two kinds. We know a subject ourselves, or we know where we can find information upon it.' While the specialist must know his pet subject inside out, there is no question but that for the general writer the knowledge of *where to go* to find what he needs is of the greater value. Quite apart from the fact that no one would want to become a walking encyclopaedia, even if it were humanly possible to carry a mass of information on a variety of subjects in one's head all the time, most professional writers would agree that a sound knowledge of available sources (or, failing that, a reliable researcher on whose services they can call) allows them more time to concentrate on the creative activity. Nothing can be more distracting or more paralyzing to the flow of ideas and their shaping into words than a nagging worry, 'Where on earth am I going to be able to find out about *that*?'

Seeking information implies curiosity, a characteristic inborn not only in the feline species but in the whole human race. We have all been researchers since we were in the cradle. Long before he can speak or read or write, a baby is obsessed by the desire to find out about the things around him. Attracted by the colour of an unknown object, he reaches out to touch it and, having seized it and found it pleasing to hold, usually puts it into his mouth. What does it feel like? Does it taste good? What is it made of? *What* is it? He has taken the first step along a path of discovery and enchantment that will last a lifetime. From that first childish desire to learn about objects, he progresses to curiosity about himself and his body, and then to other people and animals; from the happenings he observes in his immediate circle to those of history; through history to religion, and then to science and speculation about the future. He will never know it all, but if as he grows older he keeps alive his youthful sense of curiosity he will – especially if he becomes a writer – have endless resources on which to draw, and he will never be bored.

It is a well-known saying that a writer may be angry, disgusted, amused, uplifted or almost anything in between, and his work will be the better for it, but if he is bored it will be reflected in his writing. Robert Louis Stevenson held that life would be only a very dull and ill-directed theatre unless we had some interests in the piece. 'It is in virtue of his own desires and curiosities that any man continues to exist with even patience,' he wrote, 'that he is charmed by the look of things and people, and that he wakens every morning with a renewed appetite for work and pleasure. Desire and curiosity are the two eyes through which he sees the world in the most enchanted colours: it is they that make women beautiful or fossils interesting . . .'*

Because a writer's raw material is derived principally from a study of other human beings, their complex relationships, their strengths and weaknesses and idiosyncrasies, as well as their history, he can probably get away with being more openly curious than any other group of people – provided always that he does not offend by his looking or probing. The arts of observation without seeming to observe and of probing without seeming to probe are skills that can – and should – be acquired.

While most writers are also researchers, not all researchers are talented as writers. The prime function of the researcher is to seek information; that of the writer is more complicated, for his duty is both to impart knowledge and to give pleasure – in other words, to entertain as well as to instruct his reader. And just as a factual book can give pleasure to the reader by the manner in which it is written, so the most absorbing and entertaining of stories can impart knowledge. The one thing a writer must never do, under any circumstances, however, is to distort the truth for the sake of a good story.

Everything that comes within the writer's own experience is grist to the mill and should be stored away, ideally in note form or on tape or computer, for future use. Ideas, an unusual turn of phrase, a gesture, a conversation overheard, brief descriptions

* From the essay 'El Dorado' in *Virginibus Puerisque*.

of people or places, on-the-spot reports of events, even pain suffered (you think at the time you will always remember how it felt, but you rarely do): these will be of immense value, provided that they are kept in such a way that they can be turned up quickly when required. (Some practical suggestions for filing and storage are discussed on pages 16–22.) Naturally it is not possible to predict years in advance what you are going to need, so that how much or how little is noted and filed must be a decision for the individual writer, but it is a fact of life that once you throw something away, you need it. The Preface to Somerset Maugham's *A Writer's Notebook*, first published in 1949, makes interesting reading on this score, for the author admits that there were many years in which he made no notes at all, that he kept no record of his meetings with famous people. 'I never made a note of anything that I did not think would be useful to me at one time or another in my work,' he states, 'and though, especially in the early notebooks, I jotted down all kinds of thoughts and emotions of a personal nature, it was only with the intention of ascribing them sooner or later to the creatures of my invention. I meant my notebooks to be a storehouse of materials for future use and nothing else.' So spoke the short story writer and novelist. It would be unthinkable for a diarist or biographer to fail to record his meetings with famous people.

In the course of his researching life a writer will be faced with a variety of tasks. These may range from the simple checking of facts (dates, quotations, spellings, statistics) to the tracing of a contemporary account of some historical event, or the more complicated unravelling of someone's ancestry, or an authentic setting for a novel or play. The best-selling author Frederick Forsyth reckons to divide his research into four categories: *geographical* (which necessitates visits to places); *historical* (checkable in source material); *procedural* (which involves contacting and talking to 'inside' people); and *technical* (checkable facts). It will be obvious that there are wide differences, both of skill and approach, between the four, and that some of the categories overlap or merge.

In *factual research* (statistical, historical and technical), the enquirer knows precisely what he is looking for and what he expects to find, so that, provided he knows where to go for the information, he should encounter no great difficulty. Knowing where to go is the key here.

In pure *historical research* the scope is much wider, as regards both the material available and the use that is made of it. As no two writers, given the same plot and the same set of characters, will come up with an identical story, so no two researchers, confronted with the same documentary sources, will use those sources in an identical way. The basic facts – the skeleton – will be similar, of course, but whereas one researcher will explore a certain avenue in more detail than another and quote extensively from a document that in the eyes of his colleague merits no more than a passing reference, the second may be less selective on one aspect of the search but obsessive about detail on another, depending upon the angle from which their respective works are to be written and on the market for which they are intended.

Background research (which includes the geographical and procedural), usually required for a work of fiction, modern or historical, generally demands less discipline but, as a result, may lead the enquirer down some unforeseen channels and possibly end by radically changing the shape or character of his story.

Thus both historical and background research fall into the category of *creative*, as opposed to *factual*, research. In these fields the researcher, not knowing beforehand what he is going to find, must be alive to each and every clue he comes across, any one of which could lead to some vital discovery that could bring his work to life in an exciting and original way.

In general, an article or thesis will require either factual or historical research, or both, whereas most books will demand a mixture of all three types of research, in varying proportions according to their subject and what the writer already knows. In a biography, for example, some factual research will be necessary to substantiate a quotation from a letter or diary of a certain date; historical research to fill in the detail of an event in which the subject of the biography played a leading part; background research to permit the author to describe, say, the environment in which that person grew up. In an historical novel, dates and names and events must be factually correct, while background research will be important in order to bring it to life, to add accurate details of costume, food, manners, etc. of the relevant period. In a modern short story or play, the setting must be authentic and the characters must speak the right language (slang, dialect or technical idiom related to their occupations and age). Some of the problems and pitfalls, as well as the sources of information appropriate to each of these categories of research, are outlined in later sections of this book.

Whatever the subject or nature of the search, the procedure is roughly the same. You may begin with one solid fact or several – this may be a date, or an event, or a name, or sometimes merely an idea – and you build up your dossier rather like the Criminal

Intelligence Service officer tracks down his suspect: with patience, persistence, and (hopefully) the occasional lucky break. You make full use of modern technological aids but do not eschew the conventional methods. It may take you months to ferret out one vital clue, or you may chance upon it straight away. Often it is just when you have returned despondently to square one from yet another in a series of blind alleys that you stumble on the missing link – and curse yourself for following up so many red herrings on the way. All professional researchers know the elation such an unexpected discovery produces. Nowhere is it more aptly described than by the university professor quoted in Dr A.L. Rowse's *A Cornish Childhood* as saying, '. . . I felt that curious thrill, the authentic sensation of the researcher . . . It is as if you were to sit down and find you have sat on the cat. The thing comes alive in your hand . . .' Peter Fleming, discussing the art of research with the late Joan St George Saunders of Writers' and Speakers' Research, the first professional research service in this country (there are several others now), likened it to fox hunting: 'The horns sound, one races for the first covert – then a halt while the hounds snuffle around in the undergrowth. Here the cunning hunter circles around the wood and knows instinctively which way the hounds will break. Off you go again and by the end of the day you are still there – perhaps to be blooded with success!'*

One of the researcher's greatest problems lies in deciding when to call it a day. It is always possible – and tempting – to go on delving just a little further – provided, of course, that time and adequate funds are available. But he must keep in mind the terms of reference of his work and discipline himself accordingly. Only experience will enable him to acquire the 'feel' of the job, to know when he should follow his hunch and go off at a tangent, when to replace the reference books on the shelf and pick up his pen. The temptation will nearly always be there to continue researching 'for a little while longer'. All too easily the writer can slip into the comfortable routine of a perpetual student.

It is a bad thing to postpone indefinitely the real creative process. Indeed, to prolong researching unduly is regarded by some academics as an indication of a fear of the actual writing. Therefore once a certain stage in the research has been reached, it is best to press on with a first draft. A modest amount of further research will almost certainly be necessary, and possible, at a later

---

* Letter to the author from Mrs St George Saunders, 15 August 1975. Quoted by kind permission of Sir Alan Urwick.

stage, when you will know more precisely what you need or in order to up-date, to fill in any gaps or to explore aspects of your subject which you may have ignored at the outset but now wish to include. Very often an editor or agent, after a first reading of the author's typescript, will suggest modifications or additions; in the case of a book, it will be the copy editor who will query with the author certain spellings or statements, some of which may involve extra research.

Modern society is constantly on the move, new studies appear every week, and since it now takes an average of between nine and twelve months from delivery of manuscript to the date of publication of a book, unless a writer is submitting an article of topical interest for almost instant publication in a newspaper or journal, it will be impossible for his work to be fully up to date. Modern typesetting procedures and the current practice of going straight into page proofs instead of first into galleys and then into page have made it prohibitively expensive for any but the most essential corrections and up-datings to be incorporated at this stage – apart, of course, from printer's errors and 'literals'. You should not allow this to worry you unduly: it is the same for everyone, and a well-researched, well-written work will always achieve recognition as such.

In the fulfilment of his work, whether it be long or short, fiction or non-fiction, the author will surely have experienced the deep sense of satisfaction that is the reward of a thorough job of research. If it has not been altogether too traumatic an exercise, he may even go along with the view of the poet Robert Herrick:

> Attempt the end, and never stand to doubt;
> Nothing's so hard, but search will find it out.

2

Organization and Method

The writer's first task, when embarking on a new project, is to survey and organize the material already in his possession. By the time you have done this, you will have a pretty good idea of how much additional research needs to be done. Then, and only then – and always bearing in mind the intended length and complexity of the end-product, as well as the time and funds available – are you ready to move on to tap other sources.

At this stage you should make a preliminary list of everything you need to find out and where you think you will have to go to get it. The key here is to *plan ahead*. Books you want may be in use by other readers, so that you will have to wait a few weeks for them; the people you hope to interview may be busy or away; information you send for may take longer than you anticipate to arrive. You will be surprised also at how much time and money you will save by taking the trouble to write down all those people and places you envisage having to visit: with the aid of a good map and gazetteer you can plan itineraries that take in several assignments on each trip.

Just as it is false economy to skip the amount of time necessary for a thorough study of basic material and sources, so it is foolish to neglect to give proper thought to setting up a system for the storage and easy retrieval of that material, remembering always to make suitable provision for material still to be acquired. Since both these operations cost money as well as time (time = money being a constant theme throughout this book), this is an appropriate place in which to outline some of the financial aspects of research.

Costs of Research

The first thing to remember is that it will always cost more than you expect. Leaving aside the question of working time, outgoings will include stationery and equipment, travelling and motor expenses, search fees (charged by some private libraries and by clergy for inspection of parish registers), the purchase of books, periodicals and newspapers, photocopying, photography, computer and fax supplies, telephone and postal expenses (these can be unexpectedly heavy). Meals away from home when researching can be expensive, and you should not forget the lighting, heating and cleaning of a room used as office or study, since over the years this too can mount up – and if you are making an income from writing most of such outgoings can be included as legitimate expenses to set against tax. The fees of a professional researcher, if employed, will be another major item, as will those of an indexer, and, at the end of the day, unless you are a good typist, you should allow for the cost of producing the final typescript in two or more copies. Computer-owners should remember to include the cost of the print-out from disk.

It is an excellent idea to make a list of every conceivable expense you think you are going to incur – and then double it. Costs are rising all the time, and if a book takes four years to complete instead of the eighteen months you envisaged at the outset, this will play havoc with your budget. However, you will not have to fork out the total amount in one go, but as you proceed.

If you are fortunate enough to have a book or article commissioned, explain to the publisher or editor before you negotiate the contract or settle the fee just how much research expenditure is likely to be involved, and, in the case of a book, try to negotiate an adequate advance against royalties; this will probably be payable in instalments. Journalists may be able to arrange their assignments on an expenses-paid basis. In all cases, it is wise to keep a record of every item of expenditure, from a packet of paper clips to the hotel bill, and to ask for receipts for all major payments: you may not be a published writer when you start out, but if you end up as the author of a bestseller or even a writer with a modest regular income from his work, you will need to justify your expenses to the tax inspector.

It is always dangerous to state prices in print, especially in these days of inflation. As a guideline to the uninitiated, however, it should be borne in mind that at the time of going to press (autumn 1995) freelance researchers and record agents are charging between £12 and £25 an hour, depending on the special skills involved. Typing costs vary: most agencies and home typists now offer a word processing service, with inkjet or laser printing. (Consult advertisements on the back page of *The Author*.) If you type your own work, remember that paper, ribbons, floppy disks, and ink or toner cartridges for the printer are not cheap.

(Members of the Society of Authors may order stationery through their fringe benefit scheme – provided they can collect the goods from the Society's office in Kensington.) By shopping around locally you may find an outlet selling office and computer supplies at discount prices. Do not overlook the need for servicing your equipment from time to time: keeping even the faithful old manual typewriter up to scratch can cost in excess of £50 a year.

Photocopying varies from as little as 10p to 30p a sheet, plus VAT, according to size, to as much as £1.50 plus VAT for A3/A2 size copies from newspaper pages. The cheapest are those you make yourself on a coin-operated machine. 'Enhanced' photocopies and copies from microfiche or microfilm are more expensive. Bear in mind that applications by post will be subject both to a minimum charge and to a handling fee. Some libraries offer an express service at additional cost. Genealogists and family historians constantly bemoan the fact that photocopies of birth, marriage and death certificates now cost £6.00 apiece if applied for in person or between £12.00 and £15.00 when ordered by post (see chapter 7, pages 126–7).

One major expense so often overlooked by a writer is the cost of quoting from copyright material: fees are liable to be charged for anything more than a few lines, although in practice some agents and publishers will be content, in the case of a short passage, with a suitable acknowledgment or possibly a free copy of the book. Reproduction fees for illustrative material, on the other hand, vary according to the size of the reproduction and the nature of the rights sought (i.e. British Commonwealth rights, world rights, etc.), but are normally not payable until the date of publication. Sometimes a publisher is willing to bear all or part of such expenses, and an author wishing to quote extensively from copyright material or to use pictures from private photographers, picture agencies or libraries would be well advised to ascertain the costs in advance and to discuss the financial division of responsibilities prior to the contract being drawn up for signature.

'Hidden' expenses will include the number of free copies an author is expected to hand out. Normally he will receive six free copies of his book and may buy additional copies at a substantial discount. It is courteous to give signed copies to those who have helped to prepare the book for the press, such as the professional researcher, translator, indexer or proof-reader (where these are not taken care of by the publisher), and to the typist; copies should also be presented to anyone who has provided a substantial amount of material or granted the author access to private papers. The publisher is responsible for sending out review copies.

Equipment

No one would dream of taking up a sports or leisure activity without the proper equipment; nor should a writer or journalist embark on his researches lacking the few essential tools of the trade. It is true that pen and paper, the rudiments of shorthand or speed-writing, access to a good library, and an unlimited amount of time were once all that was needed, and although one might still 'get by' with these, today, when time is money (a recurrent theme of this book, for which I make no apology), it is both sensible and practical to make full use of all that modern technology provides to help us obtain the information we seek as speedily and as inexpensively as possible.

The basic equipment required can be divided into three groups: 1) the tools you take with you in briefcase or car when researching outside the home; 2) equipment for use in the writer's study; and 3) equipment that is 'desirable' (i.e. where funds permit) or for special assignments.

The suggested items are (excluding normal stationery):

To take out 'on the job'
Large briefcase and/or shoulder bag
Portable PC (laptop or notebook type)
Mini cassette recorder/pocket memo/electronic note-taker, with plenty of spare cassettes and batteries (take twice as many as you *think* you will need)
Tape recorder (with or without detachable microphone), good supply of tapes, preferably C90s, and batteries
Camera (if the job requires it), with generous supply of film, flashbulbs and batteries. N.B. The 'instant' or disk camera is quite adequate if pictures are for research, but a good SLR at least is essential if for reproduction
Filofax/personal organiser, or failing that a pocket diary/telephone and address book
Clipboard (useful for writing on as you walk around or when interviewing)
Plenty of notepads
Pocket magnifier
Mini-stapler
BT or Mercury chargecard and/or Phonecard
Plenty of ballpoints and *pencils*, with sharpener and rubber. (Local record offices and most manuscript departments of libraries permit note-taking only in pencil)
Ruler

Envelopes and stamps (Royal Mail ready-stamped envelopes)
Map of area to be visited
Local bus/rail time-tables
Small cash book (for noting tax-deductible expenses)
Spare pair of reading glasses (if used)
Torch
Loose cash (coins), for cloakroom lockers and self-operated photocopying machines (also useful for tea and coffee vending machines)

N.B. For security reasons many libraries and record offices require visitors to deposit briefcases or bulky packages before entering the search rooms. (Ladies are at an advantage here, if they have the kind of briefcase that doubles as a handbag!) Be sure that all your papers are securely fastened or in document folders so that you do not scatter them along the corridor on the way.

For the study
Typewriter/word processor/personal computer (preferably with hard disk and CD-ROM drive)
Printer (inkjet or laser)
Fax machine
Good desk lamp
Transcriber for cassette recorder, with foot pedal
Filing cabinet or other storage system
Card index system
Large magnifying glass
Stapler/punch (better than paper clips for fastening notes)
Paper guillotine (for trimming half-used sheets of paper and enabling you to use offcuts for notes and/or bookmarks)
Letter scales, leaflet with current postal rates and good stock of stamps in varying denominations (to save queueing at post office)
Highlighter felt pens in different colours
Soft pencils
Generous stock of yellow 'post-it' notepads

For the professional researcher and those on special assignments (in addition to the above)
Sophisticated type of tape recorder, as used by most radio and TV reporters (essential if interviews or recordings are to be broadcast)
Telephone answering machine

Video recorder

Shredder (especially if you handle confidential documents)

Photocopier capable of copying from bound volumes

Microform reader (to enable you to use microfiche/microfilm at home)

Modem for connecting to Internet and other databases, plus all the necessary cables and software

N.B. It is wise to have a back-up computer in case your main one goes down (if this should happen, it will invariably be at the most critical moment). Keep your old one when you up-grade or buy a secondhand one cheap. Make sure it is compatible.

Computers

Most professional writers and a high percentage of as yet unpublished writers now use word processors. More and more are going online in order to access the vast databases worldwide, to use the Internet, and to send and receive email. Electronic publishing, with its increasing list of major reference works on microfiche and CD-ROM, is a growth industry.

It does not fall within the scope of this book to discuss the finer points of word processing or to recommend any particular equipment or software. It would be irresponsible of me to do so, since the new technology advances at such a pace that anything I write today is likely to be superseded within a very short space of time and out of date by the time this edition is published. For the same reason I understand that authors who previously wrote about word processing for writers (and whom I have mentioned in earlier editions) are now reluctant to up-date their books. This does not mean that you cannot get help: a first-time buyer should look at the article on word processing in the current *Writers' & Artists' Yearbook* and at the Society of Authors' *Quick Guide*, 'Buying a Word Processor'. Dealers are notoriously ignorant – or unwilling to grasp – the special needs of writers. The best advice you can obtain will come from a fellow author or journalist. You will find up-to-date articles on word processing for writers in Gordon Wells' two regularly revised titles, *The Book Writer's Handbook* and *The Magazine Writer's Handbook*.

If you are the kind of writer who does a great deal of research you should invest in a word processor with the largest possible RAM ('random access memory', which means that stored information may be called up out of sequence); this is measured in 'bytes'. If you intend to use the word processor only for writing and storing your texts, you can probably get by with a modest floppy disk system and a good printer. The standard 'floppy' is 3.5 inch. The writer who needs to set up his own database of stored reference material or research notes, or who is thinking of running one of the latest more complex programs, however, must splash out on a PC with a hard disk. Naturally, this is more expensive, but it will enable you to store a great deal more data and to access that data more speedily. You should buy the best printer you can afford: an inkjet or laser type gives better results than the older daisywheel or dot matrix. You will also want a CD-ROM drive, so that you can make use of the numerous reference works now being published in this form. The latest range of computers are 'multimedia', with internal CD-ROM drives and stereo speakers. Unfortunately, in order to get the sophisticated facilities you need, you may have to take on board all sorts of other options that, in your writing life, you will never use.

There are many interesting packages and discounts on offer, and it is wise to take the time to shop around. Talk to your local dealer, browse through some of the computer magazines. Best of all, consult a knowledgeable friend (preferably a writer). When you do take the plunge, make absolutely sure that what you get is PC compatible so that you will be able, if required, to deliver on disk to your publisher or, if an emergency should arise, to print out on a friend's equipment. The book and magazine world seems to be divided in its preference for PCs or Macs (Apple Macintosh). Macs run the Macintosh operating system and can read or convert PC disks; PCs run the DOS and Windows systems.

Later on, should you decide to go online, you will need a 'modem', which you plug into the telephone socket and then connect to the computer, plus the appropriate communications software. (Most modems come with the necessary cables and software.) You then subscribe to one or more of the network providers through whom you can have access to email and to the Internet, which is the fastest-growing information resource in the world. Add some browser software and you will be able to navigate the World Wide Web (known as WWW or 3W). You pay a monthly subscription to the provider and also telephone costs: charges levied for entering and searching a database vary, but you are billed only for the time you are linked to it.

To the uninitiated all this may appear at first sight as a bewildering, impenetrable maze, not least because of its strange vocabulary and (in the case of email) absence of capital letters. Once you join the thousands of scholars and other professionals who now exchange information and communicate with one another worldwide on a regular basis, you may become addicted yourself. You will revel in the speed with which you can obtain information. But be warned: it does not come cheap. Unless you are an academic or a professional author, it may not be cost-effective. Do your sums before you embark.

Inevitably in the wake of the Internet and email 'explosion' there has come an avalanche of literature. A good introduction to the subject is William J. Martin's *The Information Society*. The *Keyguide to Information Sources in Online and CD-ROM Database Searching* by Chris Armstrong is one of the best international guides. Other recommended titles for the writer include Jane Dorner's *Writing on Disk*, *Database Systems and Historical Research* by Charles Harvey and Jon Press, *Going Online and CD-ROM* by Phil Bradley and Terry Hanson, Sue Schofield's *The UK Internet Book*, and *Surfing on the Internet* by J.C. Herz. An information sheet entitled 'Email for Authors' is available from the Society of Authors, whose members automatically receive *The Electronic Author* twice a year (this may be purchased by non-members).

Photocopiers

Unless you do a great deal of photocopying, it is not really worth-while purchasing a machine. Some of the cheaper desk-top models copy only from loose sheets, and not all those that take bound books give satisfactory results, especially if the volume to be copied is thick or tightly bound. Eager salesmen may promise copies at a fraction of the commercial cost, which can be tempting, but when you take into account the cost of materials, electricity, servicing charges, annual depreciation of the machine *and* operating – your valuable working time – there may not be a great saving. The value of having a photocopier at hand is the *convenience* of being able to run off copies instantly, without the need to make a special trip into town. Much depends, therefore, on how close you live to the nearest copy shop. Remember that you can use a fax machine to make a working copy of the odd sheet.

Organization of Material

There are few hard and fast rules in research, but it is wise to establish at the outset, and to adhere to, some systematic method of note-taking and data storage. There is little point in accumulating a mass of notes, press cuttings and other material unless you also devise a fairly foolproof system which will enable you either to bring up on screen or manually locate what you want *when you want it*. Those who store manually should get into the habit of replacing any documents they have extracted immediately after use so that they can find them again later. (This will take only a minute or two at the time. It could take two hours, or more, if the document has been mislaid.)

Storage methods will differ according to individual circumstances and taste, and according to the type of material involved. Computer owners who set up personal databases will find them ideal for the storage of research notes and other information. The rest of us, soldiering on manually, divide into two camps: those who favour card indexes, and those who prefer notebooks, pads or loose sheets of paper, with a filing cabinet or cupboard large enough to house them.

Electronic storage

Building and maintaining a database on your PC is not difficult with the aid of your manual and the appropriate bibliographic software. Follow instructions, and try to keep it as simple as possible. Remember that the object of the exercise is to be able to access speedily everything you store. Remember too that in order to keep your database up to date you must regularly key in your research. If you do this when you are tired after a day's concentrated work, you may well make errors of transcription (we are all human). With a manual system you could have filed that same material, in the original, within minutes of getting home.

No one system is ever perfect. There is the problem, if you are storing electronically, of what to do with the photocopies, the newspaper clippings, the photographs. Or, for that matter, your original notes (which you must keep, in case you need to double-check something). The ideal solution is quite clearly a compromise: a database *and* a filing cabinet. (You will of course create a key index, suitably cross-referenced and regularly updated.)

Card indexes

The principal advantages of a card index are its flexibility and portability. It need not be expensive. All sorts of cartons, from shoe boxes to cereal packets, can if necessary be converted into filing receptacles; and for the one-off job a local printer may be persuaded into supplying slips of paper cut to size, which you can use instead of cards (but they must not be too flimsy). For permanent filing I recommend the commercially manufactured type of box in metal or plastic. You should only buy the kind of guide cards which have plastic or reinforced alphabetical tabs, as the cheaper variety will not stand up to hard wear. Record cards (ruled or plain) will withstand constant fingering better than slips. (For real economy, the researcher can always do what some professional indexers do, and once a particular job is finished, re-use the cards or slips by writing on the other side – preferably using a different coloured ballpoint so that there is no danger of confusion should the odd one be accidentally turned over.)

Cards or slips may be carried to and from the reference library or other place of research, as required, either in envelopes (clearly marked in subjects or whatever divisions best fit the job in hand) or in small packs secured by rubber bands. They can be sorted into alphabetical, subject or chronological order, either in one continuous series or per chapter and, if necessary, re-grouped as the work proceeds; coloured cards and coloured stickers (available in various shapes) may be used to denote different subjects or periods within each main division, and slips bearing brief cross-references can be inserted as appropriate. The value of such a system is that its permutations are so great.

Loose sheets and notebooks

Many writers prefer to make their notes on larger sheets of paper. For them the shorthand reporter type of notebook is recommended, or there are various sizes of ruled pads, with or without punched holes for fitting into loose-leaf ring binders or spring binders. Keeping notes in exercise books is not a good idea, unless a separate book is used for each section of the research, and even then it is advisable to number the pages and make a simple index in the front of the book, otherwise it may be difficult to locate the exact subject-matter when it is required.

For filing purposes it is best, when using sheets of paper rather than cards or slips, to note each item on a separate sheet or at least to leave a good gap between each item so that the notes can be cut up at home and each one slotted individually into its right folder or envelope. Although this may sound extravagant, writing on both sides of the sheet, unless it is on the same subject and clearly indicated by a bold 'PTO' or arrow at the bottom right-hand corner of the first side, is false economy – much valuable material has been 'lost' in this way. It is all too easy to gather up notes and file them without checking to see what is written on the back; nothing is more frustrating to the writer than to *know* that he has made a note of some vital fact or quotation or source – but *where?* It is also a good plan to get into the habit of putting material away as soon as possible after returning from the library, or after use. Otherwise the telephone may ring, there is nothing else handy on which to jot down a message, so the sheets lying on the desk are turned over, scribbled on – inevitably, sooner or later, something will go astray.

Working chronologies

Some writers engaged on an historical study or biography find it helpful to make themselves a working chronology to keep at their elbow while they work. This can be a straightforward listing of events or, in the case of a biography, may consist of a loose-leaf ring binder with the sheets arranged so that when the book is open the left-hand page lists the happenings in the life of the biographee and his family, while the right-hand page lists outside events of approximately the same date. Ample space should be left between dates for subsequent insertions as research proceeds, to avoid the necessity of retyping pages. The time spent on the preparation of this simple working tool will be amply repaid by the ease with which the writer will be able to see his subject in perspective as he works.

Another useful system for the non-fiction writer is a small card index containing, on separate cards, a brief note of all the important points that must be covered, chapter by chapter. Before starting each chapter the writer can cast his eye over the cards and re-group them in the order in which he intends to deal with them, and when that chapter is finished anything that needs to be mentioned again later can be transferred on to the relevant section, so that he will not lose sight of it when the time comes.

Filing

If the documentation is not vast, the most convenient form of storage may be in large manila envelopes, clear plastic or multi-coloured document wallets, numbered or clearly marked as to subject or content; some researchers prefer the 'concertina' type of file or the folders secured with elastic that have up to nine divisions. For all but the simplest research collections, however, a steel filing cabinet will be a worthwhile investment. There are some small trolley-type cabinets on castors, which will suit the

19

writer who likes to have his material at his elbow, at desk or armchair, wherever he works; otherwise the single- or multi-drawer cabinet, with or without suspension filing, is the best buy. As each book or writing project is completed, the material can be cleared out, parcelled up and stored elsewhere to make space for the next assignment.

So far as the storage of used material is concerned, the cardboard cartons obtainable free from wine shops and supermarkets are most useful; but photographs and manuscripts are best kept dust-free and flat in the kind of boxes usually supplied with good-quality typing papers. For the perfectionist, or the writer who envisages the need to have quick access to his old material, there are excellent lightweight storage containers, ranging from collapsible box files to the more rigid corrugated board storage cabinet complete with drawers. Simple parcels wrapped in brown paper and clearly labelled may be adequate. It is worth remembering that cardboard and brown paper allow documents to 'breathe', whereas metal does not; valuable archive material (e.g. original letters) should not be kept for any length of time in a closed filing cabinet.

Whatever system you adopt, there are two essentials that will prove their worth over and over again: the establishment of a key for quick reference, and a system of clear labelling. Notebooks with alphabetical divisions or the most compact of desk-top card indexes are recommended for the former, a supply of labels and felt marker pens in various colours for the latter. The card index, which may be kept in a box or in a rotary filing unit, should be as simple as possible, containing just sufficient information – either names and telephone numbers, or titles of books and periodicals, with page references and/or dates, or any suitable code of reference numbers – to send the user directly to the required source material.

A word of advice now to those who are setting up a new storage system – THINK BIG! As work progresses, you are bound to accumulate at least twice as much material as you planned for, and you should bear in mind, too, that a four-drawer filing cabinet takes up no more floor space than the single-drawer model. Few writers will be like the well-known historian and biographer who has admitted to having taken four years to decide to buy a proper filing cabinet and another four years to fill it – but those who do find themselves with empty drawers at the outset can always put them to good use. (Think of the peace of mind it will give you when you go away to research or on holiday to know that the one and only copy of your unfinished manuscript is securely stowed away, comparatively fireproof and out of the reach of vandals!)

The same goes for original material loaned to the writer. This is a big responsibility, and it is advisable always to make a point of photocopying or taking notes of what you need and returning the originals to their owners without delay. If this is absolutely not possible, at least keep the material in a safe place. Newspaper cuttings will go brown if kept in the daylight for any length of time, and photographs can be easily damaged and rendered unsuitable for reproduction if left lying around on the desk. Some picture agencies require the borrower to pay substantial costs for the loss or damage of negatives or transparencies.

Books should always be treated with special care, whether they are loaned by private individuals or borrowed from the library. If they are to be handled a great deal, it is a good idea to cover them with plastic film or brown paper. *Never* write in the margins or turn down corners to mark a reference (unless of course the book belongs to you and you regard it as a working copy); and be very careful when photocopying that you do not bend it in such a way as to damage the binding.

Take special care to write on the backs of photographs only with a very soft pencil; anything else can do irreparable damage. It is best to keep all illustrative material in a separate drawer, box file or filing tray, with each print inside a plastic folder or stiffened envelope. Elementary advice, maybe, but it is a fact that many photographs suffer through being left lying about unprotected; even if they are stacked underneath other papers they may sometimes inadvertently be scribbled on, and once that kind of damage is done it cannot be undone.

For those who handle original documents, there is an excellent booklet, *Caring for Books and Documents* by A.D. Baynes-Cope, published by the British Library. A free leaflet, 'The Care of Records: Notes for the Owner or Custodian', is available from the British Records Association, 18 Padbury Court, London E2 7EH (tel. 0171–729 1415).

Three final tips:

1 Having set up the system that suits you and your project, do make an effort to keep the filing up to date, or the whole purpose will be defeated. If it is not possible to slot material away as it comes in, it is a good idea to keep some kind of 'pending' box or file, or a nest of filing baskets, into which you can put it until you have the time.

2 Remember that every good filing system has a 'Miscellaneous' file, and get into the habit of looking there for anything you cannot find instantly. As the 'Miscellaneous' file grows – and

21

it is wise to allow plenty of space for it – new subject headings will suggest themselves and the appropriate material can be extracted and filed separately.

3 NEVER THROW AWAY ANY NOTES without keeping a record of the sources.

Research Methods

Having established his storage system, the writer is ready to go out and seek the additional material he needs.

Use of libraries

Finding your way round the library or libraries where you intend to do the bulk of your research is half the battle for the writer. The first thing to remember is that the librarian's job is to guide the researcher or reader to the right books; he is not paid to do original research for you. It is nevertheless astonishing how much a cooperative, interested librarian *will* do, and it is always politic to take him into your confidence about the scope of your research and what you are writing. Similarly, it is advisable to contact the librarian of a special library, either by telephone or letter, before making a first visit; provided he is given due notice of your interest, the librarian or one of his assistants will usually then prepare a preliminary selection of titles, and you can begin work without delay. If you do not do this, you may find that the librarians are tied up with other readers when you arrive, and you can easily waste half a day of valuable researching time.

In public libraries, the reference departments of most public libraries and the majority of special and private subscription libraries, the reader has access to the stacks and will be free to browse among the books arranged on the shelves related to his subject; where this is not the case, he should ask a library assistant to explain how the catalogue or subject index is organized and how to order books. At the major copyright and university libraries a certain number of reference works are on what is known as 'open access', that is to say on shelves where they may be consulted by the reader or from which they may be taken to the reader's desk (but not of course out of the reading room); all other titles must be applied for either on the library requisition slips or on the computer terminals provided; this involves looking up the relevant shelf-marks in the general catalogue. As it may be anything up to two hours before the books are delivered to the reader's desk, it is wise to order what you need at the earliest moment, if not a day or two in advance, and to fill in the waiting period by using works that are on the open shelves or by looking up shelf-marks of books for the next phase of your research. Because of lack of space, many libraries today 'out-house' selected classes of books; these may take twenty-four hours or more to arrive.

Researchers wishing to use the British Library or other copy-right libraries, those of the Imperial War Museum, National Maritime Museum, Royal Botanic Gardens and most university and museum libraries must obtain a reader's ticket, and it is advisable to do so in advance of your first visit – although temporary day tickets will normally be issued on demand. Write to the Admissions Office of the relevant library for full details and application forms.

On your first visit to a library, you will need to devote a little time to familiarising yourself with the layout and cataloguing system. Ask one of the library assistants to explain any unusual features, and how to look up anonymous works, yearbooks and directories, or the proceedings of learned societies. Some major libraries display a map showing the layout of the reference shelves, or there may be a printed leaflet available. Most have separate card indexes arranged under authors and subjects, but occasionally you will come across a 'dictionary' type of catalogue which combines author, subject and title in one alphabetical listing. Nowadays the catalogue after a certain date is most likely to be on microfiche; the up-dating of these by computer is a godsend to researchers, as it keeps the listings constantly up to date. You should be meticulous in replacing all microfiches in their correct numerical sequence after use, for the sake of subsequent researchers (and long-suffering librarians).

In smaller libraries the catalogue is usually cumulative, but in others there may be separate drawers or cabinets containing cards for acquisitions within a stated period. This 'Recent Acquisitions' section should not be overlooked. The trap here for the inexperienced lies in the word 'acquisitions', for although this section of the catalogue will consist of mainly new titles, it will also include books that have been purchased or otherwise acquired recently – some of which may have been published some years ago. When you fail to find the book you are looking for in the general catalogue, therefore, always turn to this section.

The majority of libraries in the United Kingdom have adopted the Dewey Decimal Classification, which divides human knowledge into ten classes, each sub-divided to accommodate subjects within each class. Try to memorise the main divisions, as follows:

000 General Works
100 Philosophy
200 Religion
300 Social Sciences
400 Languages
500 Science
600 Technology
700 The Arts and Recreations
800 Literature
900 Geography, Biography and History

The *British National Bibliography* (*BNB*) also uses the Dewey classification, and if you are seeking a published work on a certain subject, and do not know the author or precise title, you should go straight to the relevant class listing, as you would do in the library.

A word of advice here for the uninitiated who find themselves confronted by an unfamiliar array of 'new technology' equipment. DO NOT PANIC! There is bound to be an instruction manual – probably very dog-eared as a result of frantic searching by other users in need of assistance, and usually pretty incomprehensible to the lay person! (To be fair, they *are* nowadays becoming more 'user friendly'.) This manual will tell you which keys to press and in what order. Once you have pressed the first key, step-by-step instructions will appear on screen to guide you through the next phase, and if you do something wrong a message will appear instantly on screen to that effect, with instructions on how to remedy the error. If all else fails, put yourself in the hands of a trained library assistant, who will do it all for you the first time. (In my experience, far from resenting such demands on their time, librarians are quite keen to show off their newly acquired skills and to play with their 'new toys'; but this attitude will not last for ever. Watch very carefully: you will not be popular if you have to ask for help a second time.)

Note-taking

There are three 'golden rules' of researching:

1 *Copy accurately*
   Care must be taken to retain original spellings in quoted matter, using an editorial *sic* in square brackets if necessary. It is a

good idea to get into the habit of double-checking all figures and proper names immediately they are written or typed. For example, the date '1943' can so easily be copied as '1934' when one is tired (or more easily, because one's mind is on the current year, '1969' as '1996'!), and whereas it takes only a few seconds to verify the figure at the time, such a mistake can take hours to correct later – or may not be discovered until the work is in print. Writing unusual proper names and place names in block capitals in the researcher's notes also helps to avoid error and will save a lot of trouble if, several weeks later, the writer is unable to decipher his own hurried scribbles.

2 *Check, double-check and, if in doubt, triple-check all facts*
Primarily where verbal recollections are given to the researcher by private individuals, but whenever and wherever possible in all other cases, especially if any doubts are entertained as to the accuracy of facts (even if printed facts), these should be verified in another source. Where confirmation of a fact or figure cannot be obtained and the writer remains in doubt, it is best either to avoid using it or, if you must, to state the source or sources relied on. The problem of 'conflicting authorities' is discussed in chapter 4 (page 74).

3 *Keep a note of all sources*
The importance of keeping full reference notes cannot be over-stressed. Valuable time may be wasted if, for example, when your first draft is written, you wish to examine a particular source in more detail but cannot turn up instantly a note of the author, title, date and relevant page number, and prefer-ably also the shelf-mark of the library where you originally saw it. Even more time will be wasted if you have omitted to follow the recommendation under (1) above to check page references on the spot and, failing to find what you are looking for at, say, page 241, you must thumb through a hefty tome, possibly without the help of an index, only to discover the right passage at page 421. (Whenever this happens, the short cut is to try first all the permutations for the number origi-nally written down.) Making brief cards or slips for each refer-ence as you go along will halve the work when it comes to compiling a 'notes and references' section or the bibliography (see chapter 10, 'Preparation for the Press', pages 162–70). Press cuttings and photocopies should be clearly marked with the book title, newspaper or periodical, plus volume number, date, publisher and page number where appropriate. Remember

to do this before you hand in the volume or microfilm or replace it on the shelf.

What should you do when you come across an incorrect date or figure in a library book, perhaps a wrong page entry in an index? In the interest of future users, the temptation is to amend the text – in pencil, of course – but is it worth the risk of being expelled from the premises for life? The duty librarian is probably too busy to take much heed. My opinion is that if it is a modern title, provided you have the time and the inclination, you should write to the publisher asking him to make the correction in any reprint or new edition. If it is an old book, sadly there is nothing to be done.

Photocopying

All reference libraries and most other libraries and record offices operate a photocopy service, subject to the usual copyright restrictions and a ban on old or rare editions that might be damaged in the process. Microfilms and the type of photocopy suitable for reproduction can usually be obtained only from major libraries and record offices, and may take several weeks, but the electrostatic print or 'rapid copy' or 'xerox' as it is sometimes called, which is the most useful to the researcher, is often available while you wait or within twenty-four hours. Some libraries have installed coin-operated machines and expect you to make your own copies.

With material that is out of copyright there is no problem, but unless the copyright owner has given permission in writing, copying of all other printed matter is restricted to one article from any one issue of a newspaper or periodical, at any one time; or to a total of one-tenth of any one book in copyright. In all cases the applicant will be required to sign a statement that he has not before obtained a photocopy of the same extract, that he requires the copy purely for the purposes of research or private study and that he will not use it for any other purpose without the permission of the copyright holder. The cost is modest when one considers the amount of time it takes to copy a text by hand. Another factor to be borne in mind is that the photocopy is an *accurate* copy. When ordering photocopies from a library, it is essential to keep a note of the author, title, date of publication and edition of the source material, since these will not always appear on the photocopied sheets and the originals may not be returned to you; write these on the photocopies as soon as you receive them, and always before filing.

Commercial photocopying services abound in every city and major town these days, with self-operating machines at some railway stations, department stores and supermarkets. The quality of copies varies considerably, as does the cost; some places offer a substantial discount for a large number of copies made at any one time. These 'copy shops' are not usually worried about copyright and will often copy a complete book without demur, although in so doing both they and the purchaser are breaking the law. Anyone planning to copy a large amount of text still in copyright should first apply for permission to the publisher.

Infringement of copyright by reprography is an international problem. The British Copyright Council's recent booklet *Photocopying from Books and Journals* clarifies the present law.

Copyright

Writers and researchers should be aware that the law on copyright in member states of the European Union will change, following the EC Directive which came into force on 1 July 1995. Before the Directive becomes law, however, each member state individually must pass the necessary legislation. At the time of writing (summer 1995) the instrument has not yet been laid before the United Kingdom Parliament. The main change affects the duration of copyright, which will be extended from the present fifty years to seventy years after an author's death. There are transitional problems involved, such as those concerning works that were out of copyright but will now come back in, and where original copyright owners have passed their rights to other people. Once the new law is enacted, we can expect a crop of books and leaflets to clarify the position. In the meanwhile the current law stands, as outlined below.

The Copyright, Designs and Patents Act 1988, which came into force in the United Kingdom on 1 August 1989, replaced all previous copyright statutes and sought to re-state the law of copyright in this country. The Act forbids 'unfair dealing' in all works still in copyright, i.e. during the author's lifetime and for fifty years after his death. It also confers certain moral rights on the copyright owner. In practice this means that anyone wishing to quote substantially from a work in copyright must obtain permission from the owner of that copyright, normally the writer of the work in question, if he is still alive, or, after his death, his heirs and/or literary executor or anyone to whom he may have assigned the copyright. It sometimes takes quite a while to trace the copyright owner, and it is prudent therefore to make application to use such material in good time, through the original publisher of the relevant work. Biographers and historians should remember that although a letter *belongs* to the recipient, the copyright in it is vested in the writer of the letter and, after his death, to his estate; this applies also to letters published in the press.

British copyright law is immensely complicated. While the quotation of short passages for the purposes of criticism or review is deemed to be 'fair dealing', in all other cases involving more than a short phrase or a couple of lines of poetry it is advisable to seek permission. It used to be held that quotations totalling less than four hundred words from any one work did not require special clearance, provided that acknowledgment was made to the author, title and publisher; but most literary agents and the Society of Authors now recommend formal clearance. A fee is sometimes payable, the amount depending on the length of the passage or passages it is intended to quote and on the nature of the rights sought (i.e. British only, or British Commonwealth or world rights). Foreign rights are frequently controlled by publishers or literary agents abroad, but the UK publisher should be able to provide a name and address to write to. It is most important to allow adequate time for the clearance of all such requests before going to press.

International copyright is safeguarded by two separate conventions: the Berne Convention and the Universal Copyright Convention, to which different countries adhere. For details of these and of the new Copyright Statute of the United States, which came into force in January 1978, see the articles on British and US copyright in the current *Writers' & Artists' Yearbook*.

So far as the United Kingdom is concerned, the Society of Authors' *Quick Guides*, 'Copyright and Moral Rights' and 'Copyright in Artistic Works, incl. Photographs', set out the present position very clearly. Other recommended titles are the *Handbook of Copyright in British Publishing Practice* by J.M. Cavendish and Kate Pool, and Raymond A. Wall's *Copyright made easier*.

Use of typewriters, cassette recorders and portable PCs

Most major libraries have special typing rooms for students or set aside a portion of one search room for those who wish to bring typewriters or portable PCs. Portable cassette recorders are not usually permissible, except by special arrangement with the librarian – this will depend on whether or not a private room can be made available so that other readers are not disturbed.

Dictating into a recorder undoubtedly saves time and fatigue, in the library, but can create problems of transcription unless proper names are spelled out and punctuation indicated; nothing at all will be saved if, at the end of the day, it proves necessary to go back to the original to check a quotation. The researcher will find a small recorder of real value, however, where a good deal of interviewing or travelling has to be done: even if there are objections to using such a device during an interview, a quick dash to the car or hotel afterwards to record one's impressions while all is fresh in one's mind is very worthwhile, and so is a recorded on-the-spot description of buildings and scenes to be portrayed in a writer's work. For this purpose the small battery-operated hand-held type of machine known as a 'pocket memo' or 'electronic note-taker' is ideal. A larger machine with separate microphone and facility for longer-playing tapes is more suitable for interviewing or sound recording, and here it is best to choose a model which will run both on batteries and on mains. If you intend to transcribe your mini- or micro-cassettes, you will need the appropriate transcriber, with foot pedal; most of the larger machines have a socket for plugging in a pedal (essential for tape transcription).

The use of microform readers (for microfiche and microfilm) baffles some novice researchers. The machines do vary, and it is wise in the first instance to ask a library assistant to show you how to operate one. It is very important never to touch the film with greasy fingers or to get it twisted, and always to re-wind the film onto the original spool before returning it to the issue desk. (Nothing is more exasperating to the next user than to discover that the spool must be rewound!) Similarly, it is most important – for the sake of the next user – to replace all microfiches after use in the box provided *in the correct numerical order.*

In libraries where there are a number of microfilm readers installed, often close together, some people find they cannot do more than an hour or two's work at a time, partly because of the noise of other users constantly winding and re-winding and partly due to eyestrain. Some professional researchers tackle these difficulties by wearing earplugs and/or tinted spectacles.

Interviewing

Interviewing people, and getting the maximum information out of them, is a skill that is acquired with practice. There are no hard and fast rules, but here are a few tips from personal experience:

Always write or telephone in advance, stating clearly who you are, why you need the information, and precisely what it is you seek.

If time permits, take 'two bites at the cherry'. People are naturally on the defensive at a first interview, but when you go back a second time they already know you and will welcome you as a 'friend'.

Never ask a crucial or controversial question right at the start. If necessary, put the person being interviewed at ease, make some social small talk first. It can be quite productive sometimes to bring out your 'key' question almost at the end of the interview, as though it were an afterthought and not all that important – the interviewee will be relaxed by that time and much more expansive.

Don't assume that you can use a cassette recorder. A lot of people are nervous of being recorded and will 'freeze' if you insist. A good plan is to have your machine tucked away in your briefcase and then, when the interview is well under way, you can say something like, 'This is tremendously good stuff, I can't get it all down accurately in my rusty shorthand . . . would you mind very much if I put it on tape?'

Offer to let interviewees see anything you intend to quote in print, and ask them how they wish to be acknowledged. And always write afterwards to thank them for sparing the time to talk to you.

The question of how far to trust information given to you from personal recollection is dealt with in the chapter on Biography and Autobiography (see pages 115–16.)

Up to a few years ago Eve McLaughlin's *Interviewing Elderly Relatives*, written primarily for the guidance of genealogists and family historians, was the only handbook on the subject available in the UK. Now I am able to recommend three recent titles. *Interviewing Techniques for Writers and Researchers* by Susan Dunne offers a step-by-step approach, from the research and planning that are necessary beforehand to getting the best out of the interview and (increasingly important nowadays) avoiding libel. Sally-Jayne Wright's *How to Write and Sell Interviews* contains other valuable advice on the technique: how to talk to anyone, from the man-in-the-street to the celebrity; how to ask the questions that get results; body language and telephone manner; even what to wear. *Interviewing for Journalists* by Joan Clayton is equally strong on practical advice.

So much for search procedures and storage of material. Throughout the writing of this chapter I have tried to keep in mind the needs of the novice writer of fiction, the amateur family historian and the biographer. Hopefully I have included one or two tips that may be of use to the more experienced. Students preparing theses and writers embarking for the first time on academic work are recommended to read Roy Preece's *Starting Research*.

There are many ways of researching. Methods that work for others may not come naturally to you. At some stage you will probably want to consider storing your notes electronically, setting up your own personal database. Give it time. Never let yourself be pressurised into taking on board in one go all that the new technology has to offer, simply to keep up with other writer friends. And *never* when you are already launched into or about to begin a major work. Go for the way of working that *you* feel most comfortable with, the one that intrudes the least on your creative skills. You will certainly save yourself a lot of unnecessary stress – and possibly also an unnecessary overdraft.

The Author, quarterly journal of the Society of Authors, free to members, £6 per issue to non-members

The Book Writer's Handbook 1996–7, by Gordon Wells, Allison & Busby, London, 1995

'Buying a Word Processor', *Quick Guide No. 3*, Society of Authors, London, rev. edn, 1990*

'The Care of Records: Notes for the Owner or Custodian', British Records Association Memorandum 22, available free from the BRA, 18 Padbury Court, London E2 7EH

Caring for Books and Documents, by A.D. Baynes-Cope, British Library, London, 2nd edn, 1989

'Copyright and Moral Rights', *Quick Guide No. 1*, Society of Authors, 1989*

'Copyright in Artistic Works, incl. Photographs', *Quick Guide No. 11*, Society of Authors, London, 1990*

Copyright made easier, by Raymond A. Wall, Aslib, London, reprinted 1994

Database Systems and Historical Research, by Charles Harvey and Jon Press, Macmillan, London, 1995

The Electronic Author, published twice a year by the Society of Authors, London; available to non-members at £2.50 per issue

* The *Quick Guides* published by the Society of Authors are free to members (with s.a.e.) or otherwise obtainable at £1.50 each, post free, from the Publications Department, Society of Authors, 84 Drayton Gardens, London SW10 9SB.

'Email for Authors', information sheet (1995), available from Society of Authors, London; free to members (with s.a.e.), £1 to non-members

Going Online and CD-ROM, by Phil Bradley and Terry Hanson, Aslib, London, 9th edn, 1994

Handbook of Copyright in British Publishing Practice, by J.M. Cavendish and Kate Pool, Cassell, London, 3rd edn, 1993

How to Write and Sell Interviews, by Sally-Jayne Wright, Allison & Busby, London, 1995

The Information Society, by William J. Martin, Aslib, London, 1995

Interviewing Elderly Relatives, by Eve McLaughlin, Federation of Family History Societies, 3rd edn, 1993; available from FFHS Publications, 2–4 Killer Street, Ramsbottom, Bury, Lancs BL0 9BZ, and local family history societies

Interviewing for Journalists, by Joan Clayton, Piatkus Books, London, 1994

Interviewing Techniques for Writers and Researchers, by Susan Dunne, A & C Black, London, 1995

Keyguide to Information Sources in Online and CD-ROM Database Searching, by Chris Armstrong, Mansell, London, 2nd edn, 1995

The Magazine Writer's Handbook 1995–6, by Gordon Wells, Allison & Busby, London, 1994 (new edition in preparation)

Photocopying from Books and Journals: A Guide for All Users of Copyright Literary Works, by Charles Clark, British Copyright Council, London, 1993

Starting Research: An Introduction to Academic Research and Dissertation Writing, by Roy Preece, Pinter Publishers (Mansell), London, 1994

Surfing on the Internet, by J.C. Herz, Little, Brown, London, 1995

The UK Internet Book, by Sue Schofield, Addison Wesley, Wokingham, 1994

Writers' & Artists' Yearbook, published annually by A & C Black, London; articles on word processing and on British and US copyright

Writing on Disk, by Jane Dorner, John Taylor Book Ventures, Stevenage, 1992

3

Basic Sources of Information and their Location

A writer's raw material will normally be derived from a combination of the following sources: personal knowledge, experience and observation; printed, microfilmed or electronically-stored material (books, newspapers, periodicals, etc.); unpublished documentary, recorded or filmed sources (manuscripts, family papers, theses, archive collections, tapes, photographs, etc.); and other people's knowledge, experience and observation. Of these the most important must be the first-mentioned, since it is a writer's own viewpoint, drawn from his personal knowledge, experience and observation, that above all else puts a stamp of originality upon his work and distinguishes it from the work of every other writer.

Except where the work in hand is one of pure reminiscence – and even then certain statements will probably need to be substantiated by fact – it is however not enough to rely solely upon your own knowledge. As soon as your original material has been studied and sorted according to the shape of the projected piece of writing, you must consider what are the other sources of information to be tapped.

Printed Sources

Books

Printed books and information about books are obtainable primarily from bookshops, publishers and libraries. When you are engaged on a specific project, you will always find it worthwhile to acquire copies of the standard works on your subject, which you can keep at your elbow and either annotate in the margins or interleave with narrow strips of paper or markers on which you write some basic headings or other indications. It goes without saying that library books and books belonging to other people should *never* be marked in any way; but 'working copies' are a writer's essential reference tools and should be used to the best advantage.

New books may be purchased from booksellers or, in case of difficulty, direct from the publishers. A good bookseller will be aware of what has been published recently on a particular subject and, through *The Bookseller* and other trade papers, and his contact with publishers' representatives, of what is forthcoming. He will look up titles for a customer in one of the Whitaker bibliographies, normally the CD-ROM *Bookbank* or *Global Bookbank*, or the microfiche *Books in Print*, *Books now OP* (out of print titles), *ISBN Listing*, or *New and Forthcoming Books*. If the title is not in stock, however, delivery may take a couple of weeks or more, depending on the publisher, and it is sometimes quicker to telephone one of the larger bookshops in London or one of the big provincial cities rather than wait for your local shop to obtain a copy.

A most useful and inexpensive publication for the book-buyer is Peter Marcan's *Outlets for Specialist New Books in the UK*, which lists not only bookshops and mail order businesses, but practically every book supply source in the country; it also contains a great deal of other related information.

You will probably be able to obtain most of the books you need for your research through your local public library or, if you are a member, a private subscription library or institution library. If you want to obtain a new title reasonably quickly, be sure to put in an application as soon as you see it announced in the press. A modest reservation fee is payable at the public library, and normally you will not be allowed to retain a new book after its initial borrowing period if it has been requested by another reader. However, two weeks or so should give you ample time to make some notes and to decide whether or not you need to buy the book. At other libraries you may be able to retain the book until someone else asks for it.

So far as not-so-new titles are concerned, if your public library does not stock what you need, you should be able to borrow them through the inter-library lending scheme. The British Library Document Supply Centre at Boston Spa, Wetherby, West Yorkshire LS23 7BQ, will loan books, film, fiche and other types of documentation from its own collection; it also supplies photocopies. Requests for such material should whenever possible be channelled via the local library or the British Library in London; but if this is not possible occasional users may use the easy order LEXICON service direct (tel. 01937 546138; fax 01937 546210). For full details of a wide range of services available from the

Centre, contact the Customer Service (tel. 01937 546060). There is a special arrangement for British Library readers, who may search the DSC Monograph Catalogue on the Online Public Access Catalogue (OPAC) terminals in the main reading room and order material on a 'next-day delivery' service from Boston Spa. Items supplied in this way cannot however be taken out of the reading room; material required on loan for use at home must be applied for as outlined above.

It happens sometimes that you cannot afford to wait even a few days for material – you may need it for one chapter before you can proceed to the next – and then it may be worth the expense of travelling to your nearest copyright library or other major reference library. Remember, however, that you cannot count on seeing a very recent title there: acquisition and cataloguing processes take time.

Copyright and reference libraries

Under the provisions of various Copyright Acts that have been passed since 1709, certain libraries are entitled to receive one free copy of every book published in the United Kingdom. These are: the British Library (London); the Bodleian Library (Oxford); the Cambridge University Library (Cambridge); the National Library of Wales (Aberystwyth); the National Library of Scotland (Edinburgh); and Trinity College Library (Dublin).

In all these libraries the researcher can be confident of finding everything he needs that has been published from the 18th century onwards, and also much earlier material (collections that have been bequeathed or titles purchased over the years in the saleroom). A small percentage of stock may have been destroyed during the last war or otherwise mislaid.

Graduates and other *bona fide* researchers and students are able to use the various well-stocked university libraries, of which the University of London Library, the John Rylands University Library of Manchester and the Sydney Jones Library of Liverpool University are excellent examples. Other libraries include those of the major museums, such as (in London) the Imperial War Museum, the National Maritime Museum, the Natural History Museum, the Science Museum and the Royal Botanic Gardens at Kew.

Major reference libraries open to the general public include the Central Reference Library just behind Trafalgar Square, London; Birmingham Central Reference Library; and Newcastle-upon-Tyne Central Library. A visit to the nearest of these and to other reference libraries in the provinces may well fulfil your needs and save you the expense of travelling farther afield.

The British Library is currently preparing to move to new, purpose-built premises – the biggest move in library history, involving some eleven million items. By the end of 1997 all the major London collections, with the exception of the Newspaper Library and the National Sound Archive, will be brought together under one roof at St Pancras, London (between Euston and King's Cross stations). Although for some time to come the hard core of established readers are sure to continue to bemoan the demise of the historic Round Reading Room in Bloomsbury, and the new Library has been so long in the making that it is now said not to be nearly large enough for future needs, conditions in the new building will be an improvement, not only for readers but also for staff and – most importantly – for the preservation of the collections.

Admissions to the British Library, some other copyright libraries and most major libraries is free. The Bodleian Library, Oxford, and Cambridge University Library charge a fee (according to status; details from their Admission offices). Some reading rooms are open to all without formality, but others require a reader's pass. These are issued on personal application only and are for those who need to see material not readily available elsewhere or whose work requires the facilities of a large research library. You will be asked to state the subject of your research and to have your application signed by a university tutor or someone of authority who will vouch for you; a membership card of the Society of Authors or Writers' Guild may be sufficient. Take a couple of passport-size photographs with you (one will be incorporated into the pass).

Holders of public library tickets in their home town may use them to gain admission to the special reference collections of all London public libraries and to borrow books from the lending branches. Tickets may also be used at other libraries by arrangement with the librarian.

Many libraries are open late on certain evenings in the week. At the British Library, the Reading Room does not close until 9 p.m. on Tuesdays, Wednesdays and Thursdays; the Central Reference Library in Westminster is open until 7 p.m. from Monday to Friday. If you have to travel some distance, you would do well to plan your schedule to make the maximum use of the longest possible working day. Books usually have to be handed in half-an-hour before closing time, and photocopying orders will not be accepted after a certain time, so that it is important not only to allow for any necessary last-minute note-taking, but also for ordering, and paying for, photocopies.

For those who can afford it, a subscription to the London Library, 14 St James's Square, London SW1Y 4LG (tel. 0171–930 7705), will prove very worthwhile. Members may take out ten books at a time (fifteen for country members, who may also borrow by post but have to pay the postage in both directions). Subscribers have access to the stacks and the use of a comfortable reading room, equipped with a CD-ROM reader, and may purchase the printed author catalogue and subject index volumes (a boon to those who live in remote areas and wish to order by post or telephone). The annual subscription, currently £120, may be set against a professional writer's tax; short-term subscriptions are available, with or without borrowing facilities (apply to the Librarian for details).

Another London subscription library is the Highgate Literary and Scientific Institution Library, 11 South Grove, Highgate Village, London N6 6BS (tel. 0181–340 3343); the subscription there is £33 for one person, £51 for a family. Among the few surviving provincial subscription libraries are those of Birmingham, Exeter, Leeds, Newcastle-upon-Tyne and Plymouth (see Appendix I, page 184).

Special libraries

The use of libraries in general has been discussed in the previous chapter. The questions that now arise concern location: how to find out about the special libraries that are likely to help you in your particular field, and how to locate in those libraries the particular books you need.

The first place to look is in the *Aslib Directory of Information Sources in the United Kingdom*. This gives a comprehensive listing of practically every library and source of information in this country; it contains a subject index, details such as opening hours and the facilities available; it is brought up to date regularly, and all libraries possess the latest edition – ask for it at the enquiry desk. The Library Association's *Libraries in the United Kingdom and the Republic of Ireland* lists addresses, telephone numbers and names of librarians. Other useful sources are the *Museums Year Book* and a recent publication of the Science and Information Reference Service (SRIS), *Guide to Libraries in London*, which focuses on research collections in all types of library; it has subject and organization indexes and maps enabling the user to locate libraries. The Aslib *Directory of Museum and Special Collections in the United Kingdom* and the *Aslib Directory of Literary and Historical Collections in the United Kingdom* are also excellent, containing details of lesser known as well as the well-known collections. The *Guide to Libraries and Information Units* concentrates on government libraries and those of official and public bodies.

The best guides to libraries and research institutions internationally are *The World of Learning*, the *World Guide to Libraries* and the *World Guide to Special Libraries*. Specifically for Europe there are the *Guide to Libraries in Western Europe*, the *Guide to Libraries in Central and Eastern Europe* and the *Directory of Special Collections in Western Europe*.

Regrettably, space does not permit the mention here of more than a few individual libraries, named in the text under the various subjects of research discussed. A selective list of UK libraries is printed in Appendix I and of foreign libraries under the relevant country in chapter 9, 'Information from and about Foreign Countries'.

Catalogues and guides

Most major libraries now catalogue their collections electronically (online, on CD-ROM or on microfiche, sometimes all three). If, however, you want to look up titles earlier than, say, the mid-1970s, you must use the old card index catalogues, looking first under author or title or, if you do not know precisely what you are looking for, under subject. You can also use the old printed catalogues. For example, the *British Library General Catalogue of Printed Books to 1975* is out of print but is still on many library shelves; it is also on CD-ROM. More recent acquisitions are on microfiche and online.

If, on your first visit, you are unsure how to proceed, ask at the enquiry desk; at the British Library and the larger libraries free booklets are available explaining how to use the catalogues and the online (OPAC) terminals. Be prepared to wait to do an online or CD-ROM search.

Often you may need information at the library on a subject about which you know next to nothing, let alone the name of any author or title; here you must use the subject catalogue or a bibliography (see below). You can also consult *Walford's Guide to Reference Material* or its US equivalent, Sheehy's *Guide to Reference Books*, the latter title being more international in outlook (both have excellent subject indexes). *Printed Reference Material and Related Information Sources*, written for librarians, is a first-class evaluation of reference books for research. Those who use the British Library will appreciate R.C. Alston's *Handlist of Unpublished Finding Aids to the London Collections of the British Library*. The Library's *Subject Catalogue of Printed Books: 1975–1985* is on microfiche. Members of the Institute of Historical Research have a brand-new publication: the *Guide to IHR-Info: Hypertext Internet Server*, part 2 of which is a guide to the library.

At St Pancras readers will use the Online Public Access Catalogue (OPAC) to search under author, title, pressmark, class-mark or keyword for any item they require. This is linked to an automated book request system (ABRS) which will enable the user to request or reserve any catalogued item; the user will be informed almost immediately should the item requested be unavailable. It will save the researcher a lot of working time.

Bibliographies

If a bibliography has been published on the particular subject or person you are interested in, you should find a copy on the reference shelves together with other source books related to that subject. You can check whether a bibliography exists by looking at the *Bibliographic Index*, which is available in most major libraries in printed form and (since November 1984) online. The *World Bibliography of Bibliographies*, compiled by a great 20th-century bibliographer, Theodore Besterman, is comprehensive only up to the mid-1970s. For more recent bibliographies you should check the subject index of the *British National Bibliography* (*BNB*). The bibliographies of other countries are listed in volume 3 of *Walford's Guide to Reference Material* mentioned above, under 'National Bibliographies'. The *World Bibliographical Series* launched in 1977 by Clio Press aims to provide a uniform collection of bibliographies covering every country in the world, at the rate of about fifteen volumes per year.

The Library Association, 7 Ridgmount Street, London WC1E 7AE (tel. 0171–636 7543) has published bibliographies on a variety of subjects over the years; these will be found in most reference libraries or in the Association's own library.

Readers unfamiliar with bibliographic practice should remember that the numbers given in the index are entry numbers, *not* page numbers.

Electronic and other book information services

The use of the computer to access bibliographical data has transformed dramatically the researcher's routine. Most professional researchers are now skilled in online searching, but if you are a beginner and are baffled, even frightened, by the new machines and the new jargon, do not despair. Wherever such a facility exists, whether it is an online open access catalogue or a database search service, help is available. OPAC users receive step-by-step instructions on screen, and for others trained library assistants are on duty to guide the uninitiated through the complexities.

Where a computer search service is on offer, this will be done by a qualified member of staff after consultation with, and preferably in the presence of, the customer. It will be charged according to staff time, the time connected to the computer and the cost of printing out the material retrieved, and may vary from database to database. You have the choice of collecting the print-out a few days later or paying for the references to be printed immediately. There is a minimum charge, and a deposit is usually payable. Ask at the library enquiry desk for details. If the cost seems high, remember that the computer file will be more up to date than the printed equivalent and may contain additional information; the computer search will also be very much quicker than a manual search through many volumes.

Space does not permit a list of all the databases available to UK researchers, as these are now so numerous and vary from library to library, but a few examples of the kind of files available may be of interest. The library enquiry desk will supply a full listing.

The United Kingdom's first bibliographic database, BLAISE-LINE, launched in 1977, now has 21 databases containing some 15 million records in the humanities and social sciences fields. Most useful to the researcher are the British Library General Catalogue of Printed Books to 1975 (BLC); the British Library Catalogue, Humanities and Social Sciences, from 1975 (HSS); the Eighteenth Century Short Title Catalogue (ESTC); *British National Bibliography*, from 1950 (BNBMARC); British Library Information Sciences Service, from 1976 (BLISS); serial publications from the 17th century to the present (ISSN UK Centre); the British Library maps catalogue, from 1974 (MAPS); the British Library printed music catalogue, from 1981 (MUSIC); the British Library Science Reference and Information Service, from 1974 (SRIS); Whitaker's *Books in Print*, from the mid-1960s

(WHI); the Library of Congress catalogue, from 1968 (LC); and European grey literature* (SIGLE).

DIALOG, the world's largest database, which operates from California, offers a variety of files most of which naturally have a strong bias towards US material. There are many others.

Subscribers to the appropriate network provider can also obtain bibliographical data on the Internet.

On a totally different level, the Book Trust (Book House, 45 East Hill, Wandsworth, London SW18 2QZ; tel. 0181–870 9055/ fax 0181–874 4790) operates a Book Information Service for members and non-members (charges on request). It is always worth asking if they have a printed booklist on a particular subject.

Tracing books

Often you want to trace a particular book whose exact title and author you do not remember. Provided you have a vague idea of these, or the approximate date of publication, it is not difficult. In other cases it used to involve a lengthy search, but if you can use the OPAC mentioned on page 39 you will probably be able to trace the item instantly by its keyword.

The earliest listing in this country is the *London Catalogue of Books*, covering the period 1700–1855. *The English Catalogue of Books*, volume 1 of which covers the period 1801–36 and later volumes (variously at three- and five-year intervals), continues until 1968. *Whitaker's Cumulative Book List* (from 1924) used to be published quarterly, with annual and five-year cumulations; in 1984 it was re-titled *Whitaker's Book List*. As mentioned earlier in this chapter, there is now a Whitaker file available for online searching on BLAISE-LINE. All libraries and booksellers subscribe to one or more of the Whitaker bibliographic compilations on CD-ROM or microfiche. The current printed volumes of *Books in Print*, although obviously not quite so up to date, are usually available for quick reference at the library enquiry desk.

So far as American titles are concerned, the *National Union Catalog* is especially useful as it gives authors' dates; from 1968 onwards it may be searched via BLAISE-LINE (LCMARC). You should also look at the *American Book Publishing Record*, the US *Books in Print*, the *Cumulative Book Index* and the *Subject Guide to Books in Print*.

---

* Literature not normally available through bookselling channels and thus difficult for the lay person to find.

International Books in Print and the *Guide to Microforms in Print*, both from Saur, are worldwide in coverage.

It is worth remembering that the weekly trade paper, *The Bookseller*, publishes bumper spring and autumn issues (available as a separate subscription) containing details of forthcoming books for the next six months. Another tip, if you wish to keep fully up to date, is to put yourself on the mailing lists of those firms who publish in your particular field or fields of interest. Use Whitaker's *Publishers in the UK and their Addresses* or the *Cassell Directory of Publishing* to find out where to reach them. And keep an eagle eye open for reviews and advertisements in the national press. It goes without saying that you will be an avid browser in your local bookshop!

Obtaining out-of-print books

If you want to acquire titles that are out of print, either for your own reference collection or for work on a specific project, you should make a point of informing your local antiquarian or second-hand bookseller of your special interest. He will then let you know when suitable books come in and will advertise for them through the trade, probably in *Bookdealer*; there is no charge for this service and no obligation to buy when a quotation is forthcoming, subject to the book or books remaining unsold in the meantime; but the process may take several weeks. *Cole's Register of British Antiquarian and Secondhand Bookdealers* and *Sheppard's Book Dealers in the British Isles* are the handbooks most used by the trade; another recommended title is the *Skoob Directory of Secondhand Bookshops in the British Isles*. You should also look at the *Book and Magazine Collector*.

The best way to obtain an out-of-print title is to use a specialist bookfinding service. Leading UK booksellers who offer customers this service include Blackwell's (Oxford), Hatchard's (Cambridge), and Heywood Hill, Maggs Bros. and Waterstone's (London). Reputable bookfinding specialists include Bookfinders (18 Hawthorndene Road, Bromley, Kent BR2 7DY; tel/fax 0181–462 7331); Len Foulkes (13 Pantbach Road, Birchgrove, Cardiff CF4 1TU; tel. 01222 627703); Melrose Books (35 Dornden Drive, Langton Green, Tunbridge Wells, Kent TN3 0AE; tel. 01892 862078), and Twiggers Books (11 Fairmead Road, Shinfield, Reading RG2 9DL; tel. 01734 882001/fax 01734 885416). The latter firm offers a free service (with stamped addressed envelope) for up to four titles and, at modest cost, an extended, specialist or American search. It must be said, however, that obtaining out-of-print books from abroad is not 100 per cent satisfactory: by the time your dealer has received a quotation and passed it on to you with his commission added on, even before you effect a bank transfer, the books may well have been sold to another customer. (See chapter 9, page 147 for further information on firms importing foreign titles.)

The *Books on Demand* programme of paper facsimile reproductions marketed by University Microfilms International (White Swan House, Godstone, Surrey RH9 8LW; tel. 01883 744123/fax 01883 744024) includes some 132,000 out-of-print titles ranging from the 15th century to the present day.

Newspapers and Periodicals

The major holding in this country of national and foreign papers and periodicals is at the British Library: newspapers and weeklies at the British Library Newspaper Library, Colindale Avenue, London NW9 5HE (tel. 0171–412 7356; fax 0171–412 7379), opposite Colindale Underground Station; all other periodicals at the main Library. The major exceptions to this broad division are the pre-1801 London newspapers, i.e. the Burney and Thomason collections, which are currently at Bloomsbury, and the Oriental collection (formerly at Store Street) and the South Asian collection, both now at Orbit House, 197 Blackfriars Road, London SE1 8NG. All these will be brought to the new St Pancras building by the end of 1997. British Library ticket holders are admitted to the Newspaper Library without formality; for others short-term tickets will be issued on application in person to the Superintendent in the search room, subject to proof of identity.

There is a card-index catalogue at Colindale (with a duplicate at Bloomsbury) listing alphabetically by title all the papers held, with dates. The researcher using this index should remember that where there are several papers or magazines of the same title, the cards are arranged within the title alphabetically under the place of publication. An eight-volume printed *Catalogue of the Newspaper Library, Colindale*, was published in 1975.

For some years now the Newspaper Library has been systematically microfilming its entire collection, so as to preserve the original newsprint from decay through constant handling. Most foreign newspapers are purchased on microfilm and since 1986 all UK newspapers are microfilmed on receipt. This is a great convenience both to the reader and to the library staff, as in many cases up to a year's run of a paper or journal can be housed on one spool, thus eliminating the handling of bulky volumes and conserving storage space. Microfilms of newspapers and journals are currently on sale (prices on application). Photographic or electrostatic enlargements may be obtained from microfilm, and photocopies (a whole page or double spread, according to size, slightly reduced) may be ordered at 75p.–£1.50 an A3/A2 sheet plus VAT, subject to the usual copyright regulations (only one article from any one issue of a paper or periodical at any one time). Copies from microfilm are A2 size. Enhanced photocopies cost from £8 per page. Postal applications are subject to a minimum charge. An express reading room service is available at extra cost. (Full details on application.)

Tracing newspapers and periodicals

The researcher wishing to trace an early English-language newspaper will find all those published in Great Britain and Ireland in the period up to 1900 listed in the *British Library General Catalogue of Printed Books*. *Willing's Press Guide*, first published in 1871 as *Frederick May's London Press Directory*, and now issued annually, is one of the best quick reference guides to modern newspapers and periodicals in the United Kingdom; recent editions also cover publications overseas. A complete set of *Willing's*, together with several earlier newspaper press directories dating from 1846, is on the open shelves at Colindale; it contains an A–Z list, a list of publications under subjects, and (until recently) a list under English counties and towns. *The Newspaper Press in Britain*, an annotated bibliography edited by David Linton and Ray Boston, which contains a useful chronology of British newspaper history 1476–1986 and a location listing of papers and other archives, is highly recommended, together with its more recent companion volume, *The Twentieth-Century Newspaper Press in Britain*. Also very useful is the *Encyclopedia of the British Press 1422–1992*. The British Library's own *Bibliography of British Newspapers* is in progress.

So far as foreign newspapers are concerned, *The Europa World Year Book* gives details of the press of each country; and volume 3 of *Walford's Guide to Reference Material* lists the various national source books under each country in both the 'Newspapers' and 'Periodicals' sections.

Benn's Media (formerly *Benn's Media Directory*) covers the whole world and is the oldest-established media guide: now in three volumes and published annually, it is directly descended from *Mitchell's Newspaper Press Directory*, which was first published in 1846. It covers newspapers, periodicals, house journals and much other related information on embassies and high commissions, news agencies, broadcasting and all aspects of the media including cable and satellite. A handy paperback reference and contacts guide to the media is the paperback *The Media Guide*.

In the general catalogue at the British Library periodicals are entered in a series of volumes filed under 'P' and headed 'Periodical Publications'; the titles are arranged alphabetically under the place of publication. The transactions or proceedings of most learned societies are not here, but catalogued under the name of the society. It is necessary, therefore, first to look in the general catalogue under the title of the periodical, which will give either a finding reference to 'Periodical Publications' (i.e. the place of publication) or to the name of the relevant society, which may be catalogued under a particular country, town or university. This sounds more complicated than it is in practice, and you will very quickly get into the swing of it. Periodicals which are not catalogued may be at the British Library Document Supply Centre; see pages 34–5.

There are two invaluable finding aids for international periodicals: the *ISSN Register*, which lists more than 670,000 periodicals from 180 countries, available on fiche and CD-ROM with quarterly updates, and *Ulrich's International Periodicals Directory*, published in printed, CD-ROM, fiche and magnetic tape editions and also online (through DIALOG).

So far as British newspapers and periodicals are concerned, *Serials in the British Library*, which has replaced the earlier *British Union-Catalogue*, is the standard guide. Cynthia L. White's *Women's Magazines 1693–1968* is a classic in its field; a more recent study is *Women's Magazines: The First Three Hundred Years* by Brian Braithwaite, which has a useful 'births, marriages and deaths' section listing the successes, mergers and failures over the years. Finally, use should be made of the microfiche *Keyword Index to Serial Titles* (*KIST*), which lists all significant words in titles in British Library collections.

Now that *The Times* is on microfilm, you should have no difficulty in finding a library locally where you may have access to the complete run, starting with the first issue of 1 January 1785. Other papers may not be so easy to find in the provinces, but lists of newspapers (worldwide) that are available on film or CD-ROM may be obtained from Research Publications International, P.O. Box 45, Reading RG1 8HF (tel. 01734 583247; fax 01734 591325) and from Chadwyck-Healey Ltd, The Quorum, Barnwell

Road, Cambridge CB5 8SW (tel. 01223 215512; fax 01223 215514). Research Publications International has in progress an ongoing series of Early English Newspapers.

Indexes to newspapers

The most valuable of British newspaper indexes to the researcher is the *The Times Index*. The official index has been published since 1906, and an earlier, slightly less accurate version, known as *Palmer's Index to The Times*, from 1790 to June 1941. The *Index* is now published monthly, with annual cumulations; since 1973 it has included references to the *Sunday Times*, *Times Literary Supplement*, *Educational Supplement* and *Higher Education Supplement*. Other newspapers in the United Kingdom which publish or have at one time published indexes are the *Financial Times* (May 1912–20, and more recently from 1981), the *Glasgow Herald* (annually from 1907) and *The Guardian* (from 1986). All these indexes are on the open shelves at Colindale, together with indexes to several American papers such as the *New York Times*, *Washington Post*, *Chicago Tribune* and *Los Angeles Times*, and indexes to a few Commonwealth and foreign newspapers. Microfilms of indexes to a number of British and continental newspapers are published by Research Publications International of Reading. Since 1991 the same firm has marketed a *British Newspaper Index* on CD-ROM covering all those papers included in *The Times Index* plus the *Financial Times*, *Independent* and *Independent on Sunday*. University Microfilms International offers a number of abstracting and indexing databases including *Newspapers*, which provides access to the *New York Times*, *The Washington Post*, *The Wall Street Journal* and other US newspapers.

Indexes to periodicals

The earliest index to periodicals is *Poole's Index to Periodical Literature*, which covers the period 1802–1906; its comparatively recent author index is extremely useful. The *Reader's Guide to Periodical Literature* is an American publication that dates from 1900; its English equivalent, the *Subject Index to Periodicals*, first published in 1915, changed its name to the *British Humanities Index* in 1962. Some of the more specialised indexes of interest to the researcher are the *Wellesley Index to Victorian Periodicals, 1824–1900*, the *Current Technology Index* (which has replaced the *British Technology Index*), the *British Education Index* and a series published by H.W. Wilson of New York, of which the *Art Index*, the *Biography Index*, the *Business Periodicals Index*, the *Humanities Index*, the *Index to Legal Periodicals* and the *Social Sciences Index* (the last two formerly published as one index 1965–74, and before that date as the *International Index*) are the most likely to be of interest to the UK writer/researcher. *Library and Information Science Abstracts* (*LISA*) is an important database which is international in coverage.

Among the indexes to particular magazines which are of immense value to researchers are those to the *Gentleman's Magazine*: the printed index volumes cover the period 1731–1819, with separate indexes to the biographical and obituary notices. *Notes & Queries* carries indexes to each volume and cumulated indexes for every twelve volumes. Both of these publications are excellent sources of information on a variety of subjects. Among recent indexing projects has been the index compiled by Geraldine Beare to the *Strand Magazine* 1891–1950, also of great value.

The majority of modern periodicals carry volume indexes, which are a great help in tracing material quickly. Where there are no such printed indexes, it is necessary to skim through the contents page of each issue to find a particular paper or feature, or the researcher can apply to the editorial office of the publication concerned, if this is still in existence, where a card index may be held.

Most public libraries keep long runs of local newspapers, county magazines and publications of their local historical and archaeological societies; these will also be found on the shelves of county record offices.

The British Library Science Reference and Information Service houses a vast number of scientific and technical periodicals, including those formerly at the Patent Office Library.

The researcher wishing to trace a medical paper should do so in the *Index Medicus*, to which most medical libraries subscribe.

Press cuttings

Press cuttings have a value, as a starting point, in all research but (in my opinion) should be used with care and never as a substitute for original research. A collection of cuttings is only as reliable and comprehensive as the person or persons assembling the cuttings were (or are) reliable and conscientious.

The major exception to this has to be the admirable press cuttings library of the Royal Institute of International Affairs at Chatham House, 10 St James's Square, London SW1Y 4LE (tel.

0171–957 5700), which contains much material of value to researchers on foreign and Commonwealth matters. The collection prior to 1940 is on microfilm, that of the period 1940–70 has been transferred to the British Library Newspaper Library at Colindale (indexes at Chatham House), and the present library collection runs from 1971.

The Press Association News Library, which has recently moved from Fleet Street to 292 Vauxhall Bridge Road, London SW1V 1AE (tel. 0171–963 7000), has an archive of some 15 million cuttings, as well as a photo bank of five million pictures. It is open seven days a week, fifteen hours a day, to any writer or researcher who can afford to use it: £30 + VAT per hour for use of library, or £43 + VAT per hour if you want a staff researcher to put together the information you require. Photocopies are charged at 33p. + VAT (summer 1995 rates).

Many newspapers, libraries, trade associations and other professional bodies maintain cuttings collections, and it is always worth asking what they have and having a look at them: you may well pick up leads for further research in this way.

Official Publications

Most British official publications are available at the main reference libraries and public libraries. The British Library Official Publications and Social Sciences Service houses government publications of all countries, publications of the European Commission, the United Nations and other international and intergovernmental bodies. British Parliamentary papers, complete sets of *Hansard* and the *London Gazette*, current UK electoral registers and all the main statistical yearbooks are among a large number of reference books on the open shelves.

The definitive source for UK material is *The Catalogue of United Kingdom Official Publications on* CD-ROM *(UKOP)*, which lists both the publications of Her Majesty's Stationery Office and other organizations since 1980. Also useful is the *Catalogue of British Official Publications Not Published by HMSO*. The *Sectional Lists* issued by HMSO, which are available on request free of charge from HMSO bookshops and agents, carry details of departmental publications; they are updated regularly. List no. 60, *History, Museums and Galleries*, is probably the most useful to the researcher.

A vast amount of United Nations bibliographic information will be found on the CD-ROM *UNIBIS Plus*, which is restrospective to 1979 and since 1993 issued quarterly. You can also obtain information on the UN and its specialised agencies from the United Nations Information Centre, Ship House, 20 Buckingham Gate, London SW1E 6LB (tel. 0171–630 1981; fax 0171–976 6478).

On Europe the best source is the bi-monthly *European Access*. *EUROCAT*, published quarterly on CD-ROM, is a complete catalogue of EU publications and documents. Researchers may use the Library and Information Unit at the European Commission, Jean Monnet House, 8 Storey's Gate, London SW1P 3AT (tel. 0171–973 1992; fax 0171–976 6478).

Miscellaneous

The *Essay and General Literature Index*, covering work published since 1900, is the best place to look for miscellaneous articles and reviews. Quotations may be checked in numerous compilations available in every reference library. Use should also be made of concordances to the Bible, to Shakespeare, Tennyson and other major writers; people tend to forget just how time-saving these can be when one is reasonably sure of the author and when one has a major word or phrase to go on. *Granger's Index to Poetry*, with its title, first line, author and subject indexes, is indispensable. The *Song Index* and its supplement are useful sources for songs up to 1934, and there is also the *Song Catalogue* section of the *BBC Music Library Catalogue of Holdings*; the *Popular Song Index* and its supplements bring the catalogues up to the present time. For music bibliographies and catalogues of printed music, see volume 3 of *Walford's Guide to Reference Material*, under 'Music', and the *British Catalogue of Music. The Music Index* on CD-ROM from Chadwyck-Healey is a subject–author guide to music periodical literature from 1981.

If you need to check on any particular kind of literature or printed matter – for example, hymns or nursery rhymes – you should always look in the subject index of the reference library first, to find out the standard work.

Translations

The best source is the *Index Translationum*, which has been published since 1932; it is now issued annually by UNESCO, and most reference libraries subscribe to it.

Street and telephone directories

The Guildhall Library in London has a collection of street directories from the late 18th century, and so has the Westminster History Collection of Westminster City Libraries, at 158–160 Buckingham Palace Road, London SW1W 9UD. Many have been published by the Society of Genealogists on microfiche. There are two useful bibliographies: the *Guide to the National and Provincial Directories of England and Wales, excluding London, published before 1856*, by Jane E. Norton, and P.J. Atkins' *The Directories of London 1677–1977*. For present-day publications consult *Current British Directories* and *Current European Directories*. Most county record offices have sets of their local directories. These are extremely useful for checking addresses and names of neighbours, in biographical and family history research, as are the court guides (for the aristocracy) which also date from the late 18th century. The yellow pages of modern telephone directories may help you to find experts in a particular field.

Maps

The British Library's collection of maps (manuscript and printed) is one of the most important cartographic repositories in the world. There are various catalogues, including, since 1986, an automated 'Cartographic Materials File' on microfiche; information sheets are available to assist the reader in using the catalogues. The Map Library will be transferred to the new British Library at St Pancras by the end of 1997. The Public Record Office, most local record offices and some libraries, such as the Royal Geographical Society Library and Birmingham Central Reference Library, also hold special historical collections. Volume 3 of the *Catalogue of the National Maritime Museum Library* is another good source-guide.

Stanford's, at 12–14 Long Acre, London WC2E 2LP (tel. 0171–836 1321; fax 0171–836 0189), sells antique and modern maps and atlases covering the world. The first edition of the Ordnance Survey has been reprinted, and the historical series is still available; the modern editions, in various scales, may be purchased from HMSO or the main Ordnance Survey agents, the National Map Centre, 22–24 Caxton Street, London SW1H 0QU (tel. 0171–222 2466; fax 0171–222 2619), or ordered from most booksellers.

Unpublished Sources

Manuscripts and private papers

The major source of manuscripts in England is the Department of Manuscripts at the British Library. The collection currently housed at the British Museum will be transferred to St Pancras by the end of 1997. Access to the MSS search room requires a supplementary pass in addition to the normal reader's ticket. There is a ten-volume *Index of Manuscripts in the British Library*, listing in one alphabetical sequence the holdings to 1950; more recent acquisitions, catalogued as Add. MSS, will be found in a series of volumes on open access. A good quick reference guide is M.A.E. Nickson's *The British Library: Guide to the Catalogues and Indexes of the Department of Manuscripts*. This useful booklet also lists the reference books on open access in the MSS search room and the catalogues available there of MSS holdings in other libraries.

If you wish to trace the location of other MSS or to ascertain whether any private papers exist, or to find out if such papers have been deposited or registered, you should first get in touch with the Royal Commission on Historical Manuscripts, Quality House, Quality Court, Chancery Lane, London WC2A 1HP. The Commission maintains a National Register of Archives, consisting of thousands of lists and catalogues of manuscript collections (privately owned records and those held in repositories other than the Public Record Office). Publications of the Commission include a *Guide to Sources for British History* series and an ongoing set of *National Register of Archives Information Sheets* (for titles, see bibliography at end of this chapter). Their *Surveys of Historical Manuscripts in the United Kingdom* is a select bibliography which lists completed surveys (published and unpublished) and those known to be in progress.

The search room at Quality House is open to the public. Only a limited amount of specific enquiries can be handled by post or fax (0171–831 3550). Telephone enquiries are *not* accepted. Search facilities include the use of computerized indexes: Personal, Business and Subject, as well as a Repositories File containing up-to-date details of record offices. A valuable recent title, published jointly by the Commission and the Institute of Historical Research, is R.J. Olney's *Manuscript Sources for British History: their Nature, Location and Use*.

So far as literary manuscripts are concerned, you should look at the *Location Register of English Literary Manuscripts and*

Letters and at the nearly completed *Index of English Literary Manuscripts*, covering the period 1450–1900. There is a new project under way jointly by Reading University and the University of Texas which goes by the name of WATCH (*Writers and their Copyright Holders*) and is available on the Internet/World Wide Web.

An excellent finding aid to unpublished material is the Chadwyck-Healey *National Inventory of Documentary Sources in the United Kingdom and Ireland* (*NIDS*), on microfiche, updated eight times a year and also on CD-ROM. Most major libraries subscribe, and there are useful leaflets explaining how to use the inventory. *British Archives: A Guide to Archive Resources in the United Kingdom and Ireland*, by Janet Foster and Julia Sheppard, is another indispensable reference tool, listing archive collections by town, by county and alphabetically; the introduction contains useful advice to the first-time user of archival material. David Iredale's *Enjoying Archives* is both practical and entertaining.

Public records

The Public Record Office holds archives going back to the 11th century; nowadays all official records are automatically deposited within thirty years and (with certain exceptions) are open to the public thirty years after their creation. The bulk of the records were moved in 1976 from the old building in Chancery Lane to a modern one in Kew, a few classes of records being retained in central London. A new building is scheduled to open there in 1996, and the existing one is to be extended, so that eventually all records will be housed at Kew, with the possible exception of census records; these, or copies of them, will remain in the basement of the old PRO building in Chancery Lane. During the transition period intending researchers should telephone in advance of their visit to check on availability of the records they wish to search (tel. 0181–876 3444). Readers' passes are valid in both places; short-term or day tickets are available.

At the PRO documents requests are made on computer terminals and readers are issued with bleepers keyed to their seat number which let them know when they can collect from the issue desk. There is a large typing room and an efficient photocopy and microfilm ordering service. As documents are classified by department or ministry rather than by subject, you must first ascertain to which class the files you need belong. In the class lists you can then look chronologically to find the piece number(s) you need to order. It is not as complicated as it sounds. There are several free information leaflets available, and qualified staff are on hand to deal with enquiries and to help first-time users to operate the computer terminals. The current *Guide to the Contents of the Public Record Office* is available online and on microfiche (at the PRO and most university libraries).

Parliamentary records from 1497 are at the House of Lords Record Office, and records of British rule in India to 1947 at the British Library Oriental and India Office Collections, 197 Blackfriars Road, London SE1 8NG but will move to St Pancras by the end of 1997. The Imperial War Museum, Lambeth Road, London SE1 6HZ, houses documentary and illustrative material on the two World Wars, and the Churchill Archives Centre at Churchill College, Cambridge CB3 0DS, is collecting papers of 20th-century politicians, scientists and both military and naval commanders; however not all of these are yet open to the public.

At the Guildhall Library in London you will find records relating to the City from medieval times, including those of many of the City livery companies (although some of these perished in the Great Fire of 1666). Consult the *Guide to Archives and Manuscripts at Guildhall Library*.

The National Library of Scotland possesses a priceless collection of manuscripts, ranging from early monastic writings to modern political papers; there are printed and manuscript indexes. Also in Edinburgh are the Scottish Record Office and the National Register of Archives (Scotland).

The National Library of Ireland and Trinity College Library, both in Dublin, house many Irish records. You should also contact the Public Record Office of Northern Ireland in Belfast. When the old Public Record Office in Dublin was destroyed in 1922 most, but not all, of the records perished.

The addresses, telephone and fax numbers of all national and provincial record offices will be found in the Royal Commission on Historical Manuscripts booklet, *Record Repositories in Great Britain*. See also Appendix I of this book (pages 172–81).

Theses

It is always worthwhile checking on dissertations, as these can be a most valuable source of information. Aslib has since 1950 published an *Index to Theses accepted for Higher Degrees in the Universities of Great Britain and Ireland*; it is now published quarterly under the title *Index to Theses with Abstracts*; also annually on CD-ROM and, from 1996, on the Internet (WWW). The universities of Oxford, Cambridge and London publish separate annual lists. There are *Abstracts of Dissertations* for Oxford and Cambridge going back to 1925, and lists for London in the University Calendar 1930–40, as well as *Subjects of Dissertations, Theses etc. for Higher Degrees* covering 1937–51. The Institute of Historical Research has published annual lists since 1901. Issued in May each year, *History Theses* consists of two parts: 'Theses completed' and 'Theses in progress'. You can also check on work in progress in *Current Research in Britain*; there are separate volumes for the Humanities, Social Sciences, Biological Sciences and Physical Sciences.

For North American doctoral dissertations and master theses consult the UMI *Dissertation Abstracts*, available in printed form or on CD-ROM. UMI also offers a Datrix Direct customized title search for a nominal fee. A wide range of reproductions is available on paper and microform. Ask for details: UMI, White Swan House, Godstone, Surrey RH9 8LW (tel. 01883 744123; fax 01883 744024).

Broadcast and televised material

There have been many changes in the worlds of radio and television in the wake of the Broadcasting Act 1990. While these changes do not much affect the researcher into historical material, if you are seeking current information you should contact the relevant radio or television company direct. Barrie Macdonald's *Broadcasting in the United Kingdom: A Guide to Information Sources* is an essential reference tool. *The Media Guide* contains addresses and telephone/fax numbers of the various companies and also a list of independent producers (with telephone numbers).

Most sizeable reference libraries possess the Chadwyck-Healey microfiche editions of *BBC Radio: Author and Title Catalogues of Transmitted Drama, Poetry and Features, 1929-1975* and *BBC Television: Author and Title Catalogues of Transmitted Drama and Features, 1936–1975 (with Chronological List of Transmitted Plays)*. Also available on microfiche are the *Radio Times*, from 1923, *The Listener*, from 1929, and the *BBC Home Service: Nine O'Clock News 1939–1945* (60,000 pages of newsreaders' typescripts).

The BBC Written Archives Centre, Caversham Park, Reading RG4 8TZ (tel. 01734 472742, ext. 281/282; fax 01734 461145) is open to *bona fide* researchers by appointment only. The BBC Sound Archives are not open to the public but may be accessed through the British Library National Sound Archive (NSA).

One of the largest and most diverse sound archives in the world, the National Sound Archive contains broadcasts and published recordings, and also a unique collection of unpublished recordings, dating from 1890 to the present day. The Library and Information Service of the NSA is on open access, but if you wish to use the Listening and Viewing Service you must make an appointment in advance. There is a Northern Listening Service at Boston Spa, near Wetherby, West Yorkshire, and there will be a similar facility at the new British Library in St Pancras. The Archive itself will *not* be moving to St Pancras, but will remain at 29 Exhibition Road, South Kensington, London SW7 2AS (tel. 0171–589 6603; fax 0171–823 8970).

Under the terms of the new Broadcasting Act the National Film Archive is to maintain a national television archive. Its new name is therefore the National Film and Television Archive (NFTA).

Filmed and recorded material

The researcher interested in filmed material and the history of the cinema should contact the British Film Institute at 21 Stephen Street, London W1P 1PL (tel. 0171–255 1444). The library is open to non-members as a separate subscription or daily rate (for details see Appendix I, page 188). The National Film and Television Archive, a division of the BFI, is administered from the same address, but the films themselves are stored at Berkhamsted. A viewing service is available for *bona fide* researchers.

So far as newsreels are concerned, the British Universities Film and Video Council (BUFVC) has recently taken over the Slade Film History Register (newsreels 1896–1979) and is currently working on a four-year project to create an electronic database. In the meantime the Register is accessible to *bona fide* researchers on payment of a small viewing fee. Contact the Head of Information, BUFVC, 55 Greek Street (First Floor), London W1V 5LR (tel. 0171–734 3687).

There are two recently published indispensable guides for the researcher: *Film and Television Collections in Europe: The Map-TV Guide* ('Map' meaning the Mercury Archive Programme, Strasbourg), which contains detailed information on 1,900 film and television collections in 40 different countries, and *The Film Researcher's Handbook*, which is a guide to sources in Africa, Asia, Australasia, North America and South America.

Halliwell's Film Guide is a standard reference tool. Among a wealth of other titles I recommend the *International Dictionary of Film and Filmmakers* and *International Film Index*. For the early period of cinema, there is the mammoth *History of the Cinema 1895–1940*, a collection of 3,574 microfiches plus printed guide and index from Chadwyck-Healey. The same firm publishes the *Film Index International*, which is updated annually.

Oral history collections

Although the term 'oral history' is a fairly recent one, in fact this was the very first kind of history, as Paul Thompson has pointed out in *The Voice of the Past*. The growth of oral history study groups today reflects an interest in and awareness of the value of this field of research, which demands quite different skills from those of the historian who handles only documentation.

Researchers interested in the subject should consider joining the Oral History Society; membership includes a subscription to the Society's journal, *Oral History*. Contact the Society at the Department of Sociology, University of Essex, Colchester, Essex CO4 3SQ (tel. 01206 873333; fax 01206 873410). The best introduction to the subject, apart from the Thompson title above-mentioned, is *Oral History: Talking about the Past*, by Robert Perks; the same author has compiled *Oral History: An Annotated Bibliography 1945–1989*. In the United States, where there is also much activity and interest in this field, there are a number of guides and also the *Oral History Association Newsletter*.

The *National Life Story Collection*, a National Sound Archive project currently in progress, is bringing together recordings of 20th-century people from all walks of life; this is bound to prove a valuable source for researchers.

It is a sobering thought that by the year 2000 less than 50 per cent of all records may be on paper, as opposed to film, tape and computer storage systems. Future researchers will therefore spend an increasingly greater proportion of their working time looking and listening instead of poring over the printed or handwritten page in library and record office. Whether we like it or not, the revolution is under way, and we are going to have to get used to it, so the sensible thing to do is to prepare ourselves by acquiring the necessary new skills.

Abstracts of Dissertations approved for the PhD, MSc and MLitt Degrees 1925/6–1956/7, Cambridge University Press, 1927–59
Abstracts of Dissertations for the Degree of Doctor of Philosophy 1925–40, Oxford University Press, 12 vols, 1928–47 (BLitt and BSc theses are included in vols 10 and 12)

American Book Publishing Record, published weekly and monthly, with annual and 5-year cumulative volumes, by Bowker, New Providence, N.J. There are sets of cumulative volumes covering the period 1950–84 and an earlier volume for the years 1876–1949.

Art Index, published quarterly since 1929 by H.W. Wilson, New York

Aslib Directory of Information Sources in the UK, published by Aslib, London and regularly updated, 2 vols, 8th edn, ed. K.W. Reynard, 1994; also on CD-ROM

Aslib Directory of Literary and Historical Collections in the United Kingdom, ed. K.W. Reynard, Aslib, London, 1993

BBC Home Service: Nine O'Clock News, 1939–1945, microfiche, Chadwyck-Healey, Cambridge

BBC Radio: Author and Title Catalogues of Transmitted Drama, Poetry and Features, 1929–1975, microfiche, Chadwyck-Healey, Cambridge

BBC Television: Author and Title Catalogues of Transmitted Drama and Features, 1936–1975, with Chronological List of Transmitted Plays, microfiche, Chadwyck-Healey, Cambridge

Benn's Media (formerly *Benn's Media Directory*), 3 vols, published annually by Miller Freeman Information Services Ltd, Tonbridge

Bibliographic Index, published since 1938 by H.W. Wilson, New York; now twice a year in paperback with annual cumulation volumes; online from November 1984

Bibliography of British Newspapers, British Library, London, in progress, 1982–

Biography Index, published since 1946 by H.W. Wilson, New York; now quarterly with annual cumulations, also online and CD-ROM from July 1984

Book and Magazine Collector, published monthly since March 1984, London

Bookbank, published monthly and bi-monthly on CD-ROM by Whitaker, London; also *Bookbank OP*, annually on CD-ROM since 1995

Bookdealer, published weekly since 1971 by Werner Shaw, London

Books in Print, monthly on microfiche by Whitaker, London; also in printed form, 5 vols, annually

Books in Print (US), published annually by Bowker, New Providence, N.J., 10 vols; also on fiche, CD-ROM and online; also *Books in Print Plus, Books in Print with Book Reviews Plus, Books Out-of-Print with Book Reviews Plus*

Books now OP, on microfiche, 1976–95, Whitaker, London, 1995; now annually

The Bookseller, published weekly by Whitaker, London; special spring and autumn issues

British Archives: A Guide to Archive Resources in the United Kingdom and Ireland, by Janet Foster and Julia Sheppard, Macmillan, London, 3rd edn, 1995

British Catalogue of Music, published three times a year by Bowker-Saur, East Grinstead

British Education Index, first issued 1954, now published by Leeds University Press, Leeds; 4 part issues plus one annual cumulation

British Humanities Index, published quarterly since 1963, with annual cumulations, by the Library Association, London; since January 1990 by Bowker-Saur, East Grinstead; also quarterly as *BHI Plus*, on CD-ROM

British Library General Catalogue of Printed Books: original edition to 1975 out of print; reprinted, with supplements, to 1989, by Saur, Munich, 1980–88; CD-ROM by Saztec Europe, distributed in UK by Chadwyck-Healey, Cambridge; microfiche edition, updated regularly, British Library, London, 1986–; also online via BLAISE-LINE

The British Library: Guide to the Catalogues and Indexes of the Department of Manuscripts, by M.A.E. Nickson, British Library, London, 2nd edn, 1982

British National Bibliography (BNB), weekly since 1950, with cumulative monthly, annual and some 5-yearly volumes; now published by British Library, London; also available on microfiche, CD-ROM and online via BLAISE-LINE

British Newspaper Index (BNI), updated quarterly on CD-ROM, Research Publications International, Reading

British Union-Catalogue of Periodicals, originally published in 4 vols by Butterworth, London, 1955–58; some supplementary vols; replaced in 1981 by *Serials in the British Library*, *q.v.*

Broadcasting in the United Kingdom: A Guide to Information Sources, by Barrie Macdonald, Mansell, London, 2nd rev. edn, 1994

Business Periodicals Index, published since 1958 by H.W. Wilson, New York, now monthly; online and CD-ROM from July 1982

Cassell Directory of Publishing, 2 vols, published annually by Cassell, The Publishers Association and the Federation of European Publishers

Catalogue of British Official Publications Not Published by HMSO, published bi-monthly, updated every two months, and annual cumulation, with separate *Keyword Index*, Chadwyck-Healey, Cambridge

Catalogue of the National Maritime Museum Library, vol. 3, *Atlases and Cartography*, HMSO, London, 1971

Catalogue of the Newspaper Library, Colindale, compiled by P.E. Allen, 8 vols, British Library, London, 1975

The Catalogue of United Kingdom Official Publications (UKOP), on CD-ROM, retrospective to 1980, updated and cumulated quarterly, Chadwyck-Healey, Cambridge

Cole's Register of British Antiquarian and Secondhand Bookdealers, published annually by Michael Cole, 7 Pulleyn Drive, York YO22 2DY

Cumulative Book Index, published annually since 1928 by H.W. Wilson, New York; now monthly, with quarterly cumulations and annual volumes; also online and CD-ROM from 1982

Current British Directories, CBD Research, Beckenham, 12th edn, 1993

Current European Directories, CBD Research, Beckenham, 3rd edn, 1994

Current Research in Britain, 4 vols, published annually by British Library Document Supply Centre, Boston Spa

Current Technology Index (CTI), (formerly *British Technology Index*), published since 1962; previously by Library Association, London, now bi-monthly by Bowker-Saur, East Grinstead; also *CTI Plus*, quarterly on CD-ROM

The Directories of London 1677–1977, by P.J. Atkins, Cassell, London, 1990

Directory of Museum and Special Collections in the United Kingdom, ed. Peter Dale, Aslib, London, 1993

Directory of Special Collections in Western Europe, ed. Alison Gallico, Bowker-Saur, East Grinstead, 1993

Dissertation Abstracts, from 1861, printed and on CD-ROM, UMI, Godstone

Encyclopedia of the British Press 1422–1992, ed. Dennis Griffiths, Macmillan, London, 1990

The English Catalogue of Books: first vol. 1801–36 and subsequent 3- and 5-year cumulations; discontinued (last vol. published 1969)

Enjoying Archives, by David Iredale, Phillimore, Chichester, 1985

Essay and General Literature Index, published since 1934 by H.W. Wilson, New York; now twice a year with annual cumulation, online and CD-ROM since January 1985

EUROCAT: The Complete Catalogue of EU Publications and Documents, quarterly on CD-ROM, Chadwyck-Healey, Cambridge

The Europa World Year Book, 2 vols, published annually by Europa Publications, London

European Access, ed. Ian Thomson, published bi-monthly, by the European Documentation Centre, University of Wales College of Cardiff

Film and Television Collections in Europe: The Map-TV Guide, Blueprint, London, 1995; CD-ROM in preparation

Film Index International, on CD-ROM, updated annually, Chadwyck-Healey, Cambridge

The Film Researcher's Handbook, compiled by Jenny Morgan, Blueprint, London, 1995

Financial Times Index, from 1981, monthly with annual cumulations, Research Publications International, Reading

Gentleman's Magazine: General Index to the first 56 volumes (1731–86), 2 vols; *General Index . . . 1787–1819, Index to the Biographical and Obituary Notices, 1731–1780* and *1781–1819*, 2 vols: 1st vol, British Record Society, London, 2nd vol, Garland, New York and London

Glasgow Herald Index, published annually since 1907 by Outram, Glasgow

Global Bookbank, published monthly on CD-ROM using Whitaker, Bowker and D.W. Thorpe databases, by Whitaker, London

Granger's Index to Poetry, first published 1904; 8th edn, ed. W.E. Bernhardt, Columbia University Press, New York, 1986

The Guardian Index, from 1986, microform, monthly with annual cumulations, UMI, Godstone

Guide to Archives and Manuscripts at Guildhall Library, Guildhall Library, London, 1989

Guide to the Contents of the Public Record Office, current edition on microfiche and online, available at PRO and university libraries

Guide to IHR-Info: Hypertext Internet Server, ed. Glen Segell, Institute of Historical Research, London, 1995

Guide to Libraries and Information Units, ed. Peter Dale, British Library SRIS, London, 31st edn, 1993

Guide to Libraries in Central and Eastern Europe, compiled by Maria Hughes, British Library SRIS, London, 1992

Guide to Libraries in London, compiled by Valerie McBurney, British Library SRIS, London, 1995

Guide to Libraries in Western Europe, ed. Peter Dale, British Library SRIS, London, 2nd edn, 1994

Guide to Microforms in Print, published annually by Saur, Munich; also *Subject Guide to Microforms in Print*

Guide to the National and Provincial Directories of England and Wales, excluding London, published before 1856, by Jane E. Norton, Royal Historical Society, London, 1950; reprinted with corrections, 1984

Guide to Reference Books, ed. Eugene P. Sheehy, American Library Association, Chicago, 10th edn, 1986

Guide to Reference Material, ed. A.J. Walford; see below under *Walford's Guide* . . .

Guide to Sources for British History: 1, *Papers of British cabinet ministers 1782–1900*; 2, *The manuscript papers of British scientists 1600–1940*; 3, *Guide to the location of collections described in the Reports and Calendars series 1870–1980*; 4, *Private papers of British diplomats 1782–1900*; 5, *Private papers of British colonial governors 1782–1900*; 6, *Papers of British churchmen 1780–1940*; 7, *Papers of British politicians 1782–1900*; 8, *Records of British business and industry 1760–1914: textiles and leather*; 9, *Records of British business and industry 1760–1914: metal processing and engineering*; 10, *Principal family and estate collections, Part I*, Royal Commission on Historical Manuscripts, London, 1982–1995, continuing

Halliwell's Film Guide, HarperCollins, 10th edn, 1995

Handlist of Unpublished Finding Aids to the London Collections of the British Library, by R.C. Alston, British Library, London, 1991

Hansard: Parliamentary Debates, 1803 onwards; now published daily during sessions by HMSO, London. Chadwyck-Healey, Cambridge, publishes various series of Parliamentary Papers from 1715, in microform

History, Museums and Galleries, Sectional List no. 60, HMSO, London, updated regularly (gratis)

History of the Cinema 1895–1940, 3,574 microfiches plus printed guide and index, Chadwyck-Healey, Cambridge

History Theses, 3 vols, covering the period 1901–1990, Institute of Historical Research, London, 1976, 1984, 1994

Humanities Index, published since 1974 by H.W. Wilson, New York; now quarterly with annual cumulative volumes, also online and CD-ROM since February 1984

Index of English Literary Manuscripts, covering the period 1450–1900, 4 vols to date, Mansell, London, in progress, 1980–

Index to Legal Periodicals, published since 1952 by H.W. Wilson, New York, now monthly; online and CD-ROM from August 1981

Index of Manuscripts in the British Library, 10 vols, Chadwyck-Healey, Cambridge, 1985

Index Medicus, published monthly since 1960 by National Library of Medicine, Washington

Index to Theses with Abstracts (continuing series *Index to Theses* published since 1950), now published by Expert Information Ltd, for Aslib, London, quarterly; on CD-ROM since 1970, on Internet (WWW) from 1996

Index Translationum, published quarterly 1932–40, and annually since 1949 by UNESCO, Paris

International Books in Print, 2 vols, published annually by Saur, Munich; also on CD-ROM

International Dictionary of Film and Filmmakers, ed. Christopher Lyon, 3 vols, Macmillan, London, 1987–91

International Film Index 1895–1990, ed. Alan Goble, 2 vols, Saur, Munich, 1991

ISBN Listing, published on microfiche twice a year since January 1995 by Whitaker, London

ISSN Register (formerly *ISDS Register*), published by the ISSN International Centre, Paris; also *ISSN Compact* quarterly on CD-ROM, Chadwyck-Healey France

Keyword Index to Serial Titles (*KIST*), microfiche, British Library, London; updated regularly

Libraries in the United Kingdom and the Republic of Ireland, published annually by the Library Association, London; 21st edn, ed. Ann Harrold, 1994

Library and Information Science Abstracts (*LISA*), published monthly by Bowker-Saur, East Grinstead; also *LISA Plus*, quarterly, on CD-ROM and *LISA Online*, updated monthly

The Listener, weekly, 1929–91, BBC, London; microform edition, Chadwyck-Healey, Cambridge

Location Register of English Literary Manuscripts and Letters, ed. David Sutton, 4 vols, British Library, London, 1988–95: *18th and 19th Centuries*, 2 vols, 1995; *20th Century*, 2 vols, 1988

London Catalogue of Books, series of overlapping catalogues covering the years 1700–1855 (first vol., Bent, 1773)

London Gazette, published since 1665; now daily, Monday to Friday, HMSO, London

Manuscript Sources for British History: their Nature, Location and Use, by R.J. Olney, Institute of Historical Research/Royal Commission on Historical Manuscripts, London, 1995

The Media Guide, ed. Steve Peak, published annually by Fourth Estate, London, 3rd edn, 1995 (a *Guardian Book*)

Mitchell's Newspaper Press Directory, first published 1846; now *Benn's Media*, *q.v.*

Museums Year Book, published annually by the Museums Association, London

The Music Index, CD-ROM edition published by Chadwyck-Healey, Cambridge annually since 1981, with cumulated entries

National Inventory of Documentary Sources in the United Kingdom and Ireland (NIDS), by subscription (8 units per year) from Chadwyck-Healey, Cambridge; also on CD-ROM

National Life Story Collection, in progress at the British Library National Sound Archive, London

National Register of Archives Information Sheets: Sources for 1, *Labour History*; 2, *Colonial History*; 3, *History of Women*; 4, *History of Education*; 5, *Business History*; 6, *Family History*; 7, *History of Film, Theatre and Television*; 8, *History of the Armed Forces*; 9, *Criminal and Legal History*; 10, *Newspaper History*; further titles in preparation

National Union Catalog (US), Library of Congress, Washington: printed vols to 1982; on microfiche from 1983; may be accessed via BLAISE-LINE (LCMARC)

New and Forthcoming Books, published weekly on microfiche by Whitaker, London

The Newspaper Press in Britain: An Annotated Bibliography, eds David Linton and Ray Boston, Mansell, London, 1987

Notes & Queries, published since 1849 by Oxford University Press, Oxford, with various index vols and cumulated indexes; now quarterly

Oral History, journal of the Oral History Society, 1969–; published twice a year

Oral History Association Newsletter (formerly *Oral History Review*), quarterly journal of the Oral History Association, Los Angeles, Calif., 1967–

Oral History: An Annotated Bibliography 1945–1989, compiled by Robert Perks, British Library, London, 1990

Oral History: Talking about the Past, by Robert Perks, Historical Association, London, 1992

Outlets for Specialist New Books in the UK (formerly *Directory of Specialist Bookdealers in the UK Handling Mainly New Books*), Peter Marcan, London, 6th edn, 1995

Palmer's Index to The Times, 1791–1941; see under *The Times Index*

Poole's Index to Periodical Literature, 1802–1906, Boston, Mass., reprinted 1938, 1969; *Cumulative Author Index*, Pierian Press, Ann Arbor, Michigan, 1971

Popular Song Index, by Patricia P. Havlice, Scarecrow Press, Metuchen, N.J., 1975; supplements, 1978, 1984, 1989

Printed Reference Material and Related Information Sources, eds P.W. Lea and A. Day, Library Association, London, 3rd edn, 1990

Publishers in the UK and their Addresses, published annually by Whitaker, London

Radio Times, weekly, BBC Worldwide Publishing, London; on microfilm 1923–79 and microfiche from 1980, both Chadwyck-Healey, Cambridge

Reader's Guide to Periodical Literature, published since 1900 by H.W. Wilson, New York; now monthly, with quarterly and annual cumulations; online and CD-ROM since January 1983

Record Repositories in Great Britain, Royal Commission on Historical Manuscripts, HMSO, London; updated regularly (latest, 9th edn revised 1994)

Serials in the British Library, microfiche, quarterly with annual cumulations, British Library, London, since 1981; *Serials in the British Library 1976–86*, microfiche cumulation, British Library, London, 1988

Sheppard's Book Dealers in the British Isles, published annually by Richard Joseph Publishers, Farnham

Skoob Directory of Secondhand Bookshops in the British Isles, Skoob, London, 5th edn, 1994; 6th edn due April 1996

Social Sciences Index, published since 1974 by H.W. Wilson, New York, quarterly with annual cumulations; online and CD-ROM from February 1983

Song Catalogue, in *BBC Music Library Catalogue of Holdings*, 4 vols, BBC, London, 1966

Song Index, by M.E. Sears and P. Crawford, H.W. Wilson, New York, 1926; supplement, 1934

Strand Magazine: Index 1891–1950, by Geraldine Beare, Greenwood, Westport, Conn./London, 1982

Subject Catalogue of Printed Books: 1975–1985, on microfiche, British Library, London, 1985

Subject Guide to Books in Print, published annually since 1957 by Bowker, New Providence, N.J.; now also on microfiche, CD-ROM and online

Subject Index to Periodicals, published annually 1915–53, then quarterly with annual cumulations, 1954–61; now the *British Humanities Index*, *q.v.*

Subjects of Dissertations, Theses and Published Work presented by Successful Candidates at Examinations for Higher Degrees, covering the period 1937–51, University of London Library, London

Surveys of Historical Manuscripts in the United Kingdom: A Select

Bibliography, Royal Commission on Historical Manuscripts, London, 2nd edn, 1994

The Times, microfilm edition 1785 to present day, Research Publications International, Reading

The Times Index, 1785 to present day, currently by subscription monthly with annual cumulative volume, Research Publications International, Reading; on microfilm for years 1906–76. Also *Palmer's Index to The Times, 1790–June 1941* (out of print) but on CD-ROM 1790–1905, Chadwyck-Healey, Cambridge

The Twentieth-Century Newspaper Press in Britain: An Annotated Bibliography, compiled by David Linton, Mansell, London, 1994

Ulrich's International Periodicals Directory (includes *Irregular Serials and Annuals*), published annually with free quarterly supplement to subscribers, 5 vols, Bowker, New Providence, N.J.; also *Ulrich's on Microfiche*, quarterly, *Ulrich's Plus*, quarterly on CD-ROM, and *Ulrich's Online*, updated monthly, Bowker-Reed Reference Electronic Publishing

UNIBIS Plus, databases of the United Nations Bibliographic Information System, on CD-ROM quarterly (one retrospective file 1979–1992), Chadwyck-Healey, Cambridge

The Voice of the Past, by Paul Thompson, Oxford University Press, Oxford, 2nd edn, 1988; reprinted 1989

Walford's Guide to Reference Material, 3 vols: 1, *Science and Technology*, eds M. Mullay and P. Schlicke, 7th edn, 1996; 2, *Social and Historical Sciences, Philosophy and Religion*, eds A. Day and J. Harvey, 6th edn, 1994; 3, *Generalia, Language and Literature, The Arts*, eds A. Chalcraft, R. Prytherch and S. Willis, 5th edn, 1991. Each volume updated every few years

Wellesley Index to Victorian Periodicals, 1824–1900, ed. W.E. Houghton, 3 vols, University of Toronto Press/Routledge, London, 1966–79

Whitaker's bibliographic services, see under *Bookbank, Books in Print, Books now OP, The Bookseller, Global Bookbank, ISBN Listing, New and Forthcoming Books, Publishers in the UK and their Addresses*

Whitaker's Book List (entitled *Whitaker's Cumulative Book List 1924–83*), now annually on microfiche, Whitaker, London

Willing's Press Guide (first published 1871 as *Frederick May's London Press Directory*), now annually by Reed Information Services, East Grinstead, 2 vols

Women's Magazines 1693–1968, by Cynthia L. White, Michael Joseph, London, 1970

Women's Magazines: The First Three Hundred Years, by Brian Braithwaite, Peter Owen, London, 1995

World Bibliographical Series, Clio Press, Oxford, in progress, 1977–

World Bibliography of Bibliographies, compiled by T. Besterman, 4th edn, 4 vols + index, Societas Bibliographica, Lausanne, 1965, 1966; *Supplement 1964–1974*, ed. Alice Toomey, 2 vols, Bowker, New York, 1977

World Guide to Libraries, Saur, Munich, 11th edn, 1993

World Guide to Special Libraries, Saur, Munich, 3rd edn, 1994

The World of Learning, published annually by Europa Publications, London

Writers and their Copyright Holders (WATCH), joint project of University of Reading and University of Texas; on Internet/ World Wide Web

Note: Bowker-Saur are part of Reed Reference Publishing. Their titles are distributed in the UK by Bowker-Saur Ltd, Maypole House, Maypole Road, East Grinstead, West Sussex RH19 1HH (tel. 01342 330100; fax 01342 330191). Scarecrow Press titles are distributed in the UK by Shelwing Ltd, 127 Sandgate Road, Folkestone, Kent CT20 2BL (tel. 01303 850501; fax 01303 850162), and H.W. Wilson titles by Thompson Henry Ltd, London Road, Sunningdale, Berks SL5 0EP (tel. 01344 24615; fax 01344 26120).

4

Factual and Historical Research

The more research you undertake, the more you learn about sources. If you keep a careful note of every reliable source used (a card index filed under subjects is the best for easy reference), you can build up for yourself not only a unique and valuable research tool, but one that will save you hours of searching whenever a similar problem crops up in your work. It will prove its worth time and time again.

So much is in print these days that there can be scarcely any subject from, say, animated cartoons to Zimbabwe, on which you are not going to find some 'standard' work or encyclopedia; nor any trade, profession, ethnic or religious group for which there is no recognised association, biographical dictionary or 'Who's Who' – all essential sources for the researcher. Obviously it is impossible in one short chapter to deal exhaustively with particular sources. Some starting points only are suggested here, therefore, under the two headings 'Factual' and 'Historical' research, together with a warning of some of the pitfalls that lie in the path of the unwary. In all research you have to begin by consulting first one authoritative source, which leads you to the next, and that in turn to another, and so on, until you have satisfied yourself that you have found out all that you need to know. Patience and persistence are the essential qualities. Remember, too, that a negative result in research may have value.

Factual Research

The major difficulty here has always been that topical facts and figures are usually out of date by the time they are published. The same applies to all writing on modern society, for nothing stands still in the world, which is developing and changing with every day that passes. To some extent, from the researcher's viewpoint, online cataloguing and access to the various databases that are updated at frequent intervals has made it easier to get at more up-to-date information than was previously the case. Even so, a book, once it has gone to the typesetter, may be only lightly corrected at proof stage. That said, it is sometimes possible, if you are expecting some vital new facts or statistics to be released between delivery of your typescript and the day it actually goes to press, to indicate to your editor at the outset that you may wish to update specific points at the very last moment, either in the text or (which may be easier) by way of an explanatory footnote. If the editor is willing, then you will have the opportunity of accessing the relevant database or telephoning the source from which your original information came and asking for the most recent facts and figures. All such updatings to your text must be kept to the absolute minimum, however, as anything above an agreed percentage will be charged to the author and will eat into your royalties.

Another problem is that the bases used for the calculation of statistics vary from one subject to another, and from one organization to another, so that comparison can be, at worst, highly dangerous, and at best, misleading; often, also, you may find it impossible to obtain the precise breakdown you seek. Without expert help and knowledge it is unwise to meddle with statistics: where these do not exactly fit the context, the best solution is to quote them as they are presented and to add a footnote to this effect.

Sources of factual information

Use of the computer search services on offer at major libraries is becoming widespread, and many writers have purchased the necessary software and subscribe to one or more databases, which they can access from home. Subscribers to the Internet can locate a vast amount of information on the World Wide Web (WWW). However, by no means all writers or researchers enjoy or wish to use these facilities. In any case, much factual research must still be done from printed sources and by personal contact with experts in the field. Ideally, a combination of both will produce the best results.

So far as printed sources are concerned, encyclopedias provide an excellent starting point, but should always be supplemented by reference to the latest yearbook. You can find out what yearbooks exist on a given subject by consulting *Current British Directories* or *Current European Directories*, both of which have detailed subject indexes, or *Ulrich's International Periodicals Directory* (which includes the former *Irregular Serials and Annuals*). Other publications most useful to the English writer for quick reference are *Whitaker's Almanack*, *The Statesman's Year-Book*, *The Annual Register of World Events*, *The Europa World Year Book* and *Britain: An Official Handbook*.

The Times newspaper is the best source for recent events; its *Index* is now published monthly, with annual cumulations. *Keesing's Record of World Events*, which started in July 1931 as a weekly publication, *Keesing's Contemporary Archives*, is now published ten times a year, with interim supplements (subject and name indexes and an annual bound volume; it has an excellent reputation, and most reference libraries subscribe to it. You can also rely on its US equivalent, *The Facts on File Weekly World News Digest*.

So far as UK statistics are concerned, there are two free booklets published annually by the Central Statistical Office (CSO) which are invaluable: *Government Statistics: A Brief Guide to Sources* and *The UK in Figures*. The CSO also publishes a *Monthly Digest of Statistics* and an *Annual Abstract of Statistics*. There is a great deal more information available, both in printed and in electronic form, and researchers are recommended to contact the CSO Library and Enquiry Point at Government Buildings, Cardiff Road, Newport, Gwent NP9 1XG (tel. 01633 812973; fax 01633 812599) for further information. For Europe a useful publication, regularly updated, is *Statistics Europe*. The historical aspect is well covered by *British Historical Statistics* and by *European Historical Statistics 1750–1975*. The statistical masterfiles of the Congressional Information Service of the United States are held on CD-ROM in the Official Publications and Social Sciences Collection at the British Library.

On facts in general the most up-to-date compilations at the time of writing (summer 1995) include the *Chambers Book of Facts*, *The Cambridge Factfinder*, *Hutchinson Info*, the *Larousse Desk Reference Encyclopedia* and the *Larousse Pocket Factfinder*. Depending on your subject, it is also well worth looking at the various titles in the *Larousse Pocket Guides* and the *Chambers Compact Reference* series. *The Guinness Book of Records* is a classic, and *The New Shell Book of Firsts* is a goldmine of information. No one writing about Britain should be without a copy of Bamber Gascoigne's recent *Encyclopedia of Britain*.

The use of bibliographies, concordances, books of quotations and other reference tools has been discussed in the previous chapter. The researcher keen on tracking down factual information should be able to get at what he needs without any problem. Sometimes, however, professional help may be necessary, especially if time is an important factor.

The Information Bureau (51 The Business Centre, 103 Lavender Hill, London SW11 5QL; tel. 0171–924 4414), formerly the *Daily Telegraph* Information Bureau, offers a general research and information service on a subscription basis, using printed and online resources, a vast press cuttings collection, and business and media contacts built up over many years. For non-account subscribers requiring quick checking of dates, facts and figures, or names to contact in associations, there is a minimum charge (valid summer 1995) of £5 + VAT (hourly rate £65 + VAT).

The Science Reference and Information Service of the British Library (SRIS), offers an unrivalled service to those who seek information on science and technology, business and industry, and patents. Basic services, including use of three reading rooms (at Holborn, Aldwych and Chancery House), are free, but enquiries which require much staff time and use of resources, including the many databases available, are priced. A detailed information pack will be sent on demand; write to Marketing and Public Relations, The British Library, Science Reference and Information Service, 25 Southampton Buildings, London WC2A 1LA. A quick information telephone enquiry point for business information is operated free of charge, sponsored by Lloyds Bank; the numbers to ring are 0171–412 7454 and 0171–412 7977. Again, in-depth research projects will be charged. SRIS current rates (summer 1995) are £70 per hour staff time, divided into 15-minute periods, plus expenses such as the cost of an online search and VAT when appropriate. If you are experienced in online searching you can hire a terminal at £2.50 per minute. The SRIS will be moving to St Pancras by 1997, but in the meanwhile the following addresses and telephone/fax numbers apply: the Holborn reading room (physical and applied sciences, business and patents), 25 Southampton Buildings, London WC2A 1AW (general enquiries tel. 0171–412 7494/7496; fax 0171–412 7495); the Chancery House reading room, opposite Southampton Buildings (foreign patents), tel. 0171–412 7902; and the Aldwych reading room (life and earth sciences and mathematics), 9 Kean Street, London WC2B 4AT (enquiries tel. 0171–412 7288; fax 0171–412 7217). The Business Information Service number is 0171–412 7457 (fax 0171–412 7453).

This may sound rather complicated to the new researcher seeking information in the field of business or science, but you will find the SRIS staff very helpful. There are also a number of reference tools: a *Guide to Directories at the Science Reference and Information Service*, *Scientific Abstracting and Indexing Periodicals in the British Library: a guide to SRIS holdings and their use*, and the SRIS *Key Resource* series of library reference guides, some of which are mentioned in this chapter by title. The current catalogue of the SRIS is held on microfiche and is known as the SCICAT.

For suggestions on how to obtain the services of a professional freelance researcher, see chapter 8 (pages 141–2).

Getting hold of experts

You may sometimes find yourself at a loss as to how to contact experts on particular subjects when there is no one in your immediate circle who can help. Here the best advice to be given is, 'Do not be shy. Go straight to the horse's mouth' – in other words, look up the professional or trade association concerned (or it may be an international company, a bank, or almost any other kind of group), and either write or telephone to the general secretary, press or public relations officer. Remember that all these people have a vested interest in being portrayed correctly, and also that the expert is always flattered to be consulted. If the person you approach is too busy or unable for some other reason to give you what you want, he will usually be able to put you in touch with someone else.

The best way to find out if there is a relevant association is to look in an up-to-date *Directory of British Associations & Associations in Ireland* or the equivalent volumes for Europe, the *Directory of European Industrial & Trade Associations* and the *Directory of European Professional & Learned Societies*. Another goldmine of information of this nature, and fully up to date, is the *Hollis Press & Public Relations Annual*, which lists an enormous number of press contacts (with addresses and telephone numbers) in virtually every field of professional, industrial and commercial life, as well as official and public information sources, PR consultancies and much other invaluable data. The same firm now publishes a similar directory for Europe, *Hollis Europe*. There is also a list of societies and institutions in *Whitaker's Almanack*, but this is not so informative, nor is it as comprehensive as the two publications mentioned above. The researcher concerned with making contacts in the arts or the media will find *The Media Guide* and *The Marcan Handbook of Arts Organisations* indispensable. Information and press officers in government departments are listed in the *IPO Directory*. Lastly, do not overlook your local 'yellow pages' directory, in case there is some contact on your own doorstep.

The *NUJ Freelance Directory* is a computerized catalogue of freelance journalists in Britain and Ireland (and some overseas), listed alphabetically, geographically and by subject speciality. It is available at modest cost to non-members and has a useful role to play in the finding of local contacts.

Historical Research

History itself does not change, but the interpretation of history changes constantly as new material comes to light. There will always therefore be a demand for writing that offers a new slant – a reappraisal of events and of people – based on the latest research. This applies almost as much to the history of, say, the 'Dark Ages' as to that of the present day. There are also 'fashions' in historical writing: recently the medieval period has been much explored, especially by social historians of the European countries. Insofar as the twentieth century is concerned, in the United Kingdom official papers are released for public examination after thirty years. Every January the Public Record Office braces itself for an onslaught of historians, journalists and researchers who descend sleuth-like upon Kew from all over the world, intent on scrutinising every memo or minute or other scrap of paper emanating from the Cabinet Office, the Foreign and Commonwealth Office and the various ministerial departments. Nearly every year something is pounced upon that makes a headline in the national press. But the bulk of the raw material gathered filters only very gradually into print.

When you go to the reference library to look up an historical fact, you will find that the titles are usually grouped in the following manner: history generally, then world history, British history, European history, and (if the collection is large enough) history country by country. In the general section there are all the great standard works published by the Cambridge and Oxford university presses, cheek by jowl with less weightier more modern volumes. It is advisable to go first to the modern works, to get the benefit of recent research; the 'standard histories' *are* updated but, being rather learned tomes, not very frequently. Use them for corroborative, in-depth research.

One of the best ways of keeping abreast of the latest research is to read the journals and other publications of the major historical societies. If you have time, join one and attend its lectures and conferences. You may like to know that a subscription to the Historical Association's *The Historian* includes membership of a local branch. Contact the Secretary at 59a Kennington Park Road, London SE11 4JH (tel. 0171–735 3901; fax 0171–582 4989) and ask for details, including a catalogue of the Association's current publications. You should also look at the *Transactions* and other serial publications of the Royal Historical Society. The *Writings on British History* series, now called the *Annual Bibliography of British and Irish History* is a useful tool, and the Society also publishes a number of handbooks and guides for students and scholars. If you are a graduate you will be able to join and use the Institute of Historical Research library at Senate House, London.

It is impossible in one short chapter to do more than touch on a few of the problems that confront the novice setting out to find historical information. There is one point I should like to stress: in this current age of obsession with access to information by electronic means, we should not lose sight of the value of the original document. A database is only as good as the information fed into it and is subject to human error of transcription. The original document must always be the primary source.

So far as titles are concerned, obviously every writer will purchase to keep at his elbow as many of the major works on his subject as he can afford. For general reference on British history I recommend *The Cambridge Historical Encyclopedia of Great Britain and Ireland*. The *English Historical Documents* series covers the period from *c.* 500 to 1914. There is also the Macmillan *Historical and Political Facts* series. Winston S. Churchill's *A History of the English-Speaking Peoples* is a classic, and as a quick reminder of the dates of our kings and queens, and the salient points of their reigns, you cannot better an old favourite, Ronald Hamilton's *Now I Remember*. There are many others.

Some recent social histories of Europe are mentioned in chapter 5 (page 85). *International Historical Statistics Europe 1750–1988* and *European Political Facts 1918–1990* are very useful. You should also look at the work of Eric Hobsbawm, especially his four-volume work, *The Age of Revolution 1789–1848*, *The Age of Capital 1848–1875*, *The Age of Empire 1875–1914* and *Age of Extremes: The Short Twentieth Century 1914–1991*.

For quick reference on world history, a recommended work is the *Chambers Dictionary of World History*. Space does not permit here the inclusion of sources for the history of individual countries, but some titles are recommended in chapter 9 (pages 146–61). Look also at *Walford's Guide to Reference Material*, volume 2, under 'Ancient', 'Medieval' or 'Modern' history and the area of the world (or country), as appropriate.

Researchers dedicated to the computer will welcome two recent titles: *Database Systems and Historical Research*, by Charles

Harvey and Jon Press, and *Historical Computing: An Introduction*, by Peter Denley and Deian Hopkin.

Conflicting authorities

One of the main problems that you must be prepared to encounter in historical research is that of conflicting authorities. Inevitably at some stage in your work you will come across two, if not three, or more, different dates or interpretations of the same event. How do you know which one to trust?

Wherever possible, you should yourself go back to the original, contemporary source. If this is not feasible, you have the choice of either weighing up the theories advanced by the various historians and coming down firmly on one side – and sticking to it – or, if you have the space and the inclination, of giving an account of the conflicting views and your reasons for preferring one to all others.

Dates

The different reckonings of dates in historical documents often confuse the beginner. Under the Julian calendar, which was in universal use throughout the Middle Ages and in some countries, such as England and Russia, until as late as the 18th and early 20th centuries respectively, the year began on 25 March. The Gregorian calendar, in which 1 January was reckoned as the beginning of each year, was introduced on the Continent in 1582, when ten days were cut out of that year in order to take care of accumulated errors of reckoning. This new calendar was not adopted in England until 1752, although for some years prior to that date a double indication was normally given in official documents (and in some private papers) for dates falling between 1 January and 24 March, as, for example, '24 February 1655/6'. The trap is that during the period 1582–1752 a traveller could leave, say, Italy, on one date and arrive in England several days earlier, because of the discrepancy in the calendar. From the end of the 16th century most English official correspondence with foreign powers carries either both dates, i.e. '12/22 December 1635', or an indication of the reckoning used, i.e. 'O.S.' (Old Style) or 'N.S.' (New Style).

The practice followed by most modern historians is to take the beginning of the historical year as 1 January. All dates between 1 January and 24 March are thus written as, for example, '22 February 1559' rather than '22 February 1558/9', except in quoted matter, where the date should always be copied faithfully as in the original text and an explanatory 'O.S.' or 'N.S.' added in square brackets if necessary. For a full discussion of this whole question, see C.R. Cheney's *Handbook of Dates for Students of English History*. This useful book contains, among other information, tables of regnal years, Easter days and calendars for all possible dates of Easter from AD 500 to the year 2000, which will enable the researcher to avoid the most common errors of dating in historical work. (A new edition is in preparation for use after the year 2000.) Another standard reference work on the subject is the *Handbook of British Chronology. Whitaker's Almanack* contains a 'Calendar for Any Year' from 1770 to 2030.

Dates in private papers sometimes cause the researcher a headache. Letter-writers not infrequently give an incomplete date or omit it altogether, and another trap to watch out for is that at the new year people through the ages have tended to forget, writing, for example, '5 January 1888' when they meant '5 January 1889'. Where neither contents nor letterheading provide the answer, and the date does not become clear as research progresses, you will have to choose between doing without that particular document and hazarding an intelligent guess – in which case you should make it clear that the original is undated. The Society of Genealogists has published a useful booklet on dating systems of the past, to aid family historians in the interpretation of references: *Dates and calendars for the genealogist*. It will be of use to all who do historical research.

The use of periodicals in historical research

Periodicals of interest to the historical researcher include *Historical Research*, formerly the *Bulletin of the Institute of Historical Research*, the *English Historical Review*, the Historical Association's two publications, *History* and *The Historian*, and also *History Today*. Check them – not forgetting back numbers – for articles on your subject. Women's magazines and newspapers are an excellent source for fashion, prices and entertainments at a particular date, while *The Tatler* and *Illustrated London News* contain useful background information on the social scene. Cartoons, from the national press, *Punch* and other sources, may also be of value to the researcher. Advertisements sometimes yield as much information as textual material.

The Age of Revolution 1789–1848, The Age of Capital 1848–1875, The Age of Empire 1875–1914, by Eric Hobsbawm,

Cardinal Books, 1988–89; *Age of Extremes: The Short Twentieth Century 1914–1991,* by same author, Michael Joseph, London, 1994; reprinted 1995

Annual Abstract of Statistics, Central Statistical Office, HMSO, London

Annual Bibliography of British and Irish History (previously *Writings on British History*), published by Oxford University Press for the Royal Historical Society

The Annual Register of World Events, published 1758–1994 by Longman, London; since 1995 by Pearson Professional, Southport

Britain: An Official Handbook, HMSO, London, annually

British Historical Statistics, by B.R. Mitchell, Cambridge University Press, Cambridge, 1988

British Political Facts 1900–94, eds David Butler and Gareth Butler, *Historical and Political Facts* series, Macmillan, London, 7th edn, 1994

The Cambridge Factfinder, ed. David Crystal, Cambridge University Press, Cambridge, rev. edn, 1995

The Cambridge Historical Encyclopedia of Great Britain and Ireland, ed. Christopher Haigh, Cambridge University Press, Cambridge, 1985; paperback edn, 1990

Chambers Book of Facts, Chambers (Larousse PLC), London, 1993

Chambers Compact Reference series, Chambers (Larousse PLC), London, in progress

Chambers Dictionary of World History, Chambers (Larousse PLC), London, 1993; rev. edn, 1994

Current British Directories, published by CBD Research, Beckenham, 12th edn, 1993

Current European Directories, published by CBD Research, Beckenham, 3rd edn, 1994

Database Systems and Historical Research, by Charles Harvey and Jon Press, Macmillan, London, 1995

Dates and calendars for the genealogist, by Clifford Webb, Society of Genealogists, London, 1994

Directory of British Associations & Associations in Ireland, published by CBD Research, Beckenham, 12th edn, 1994

Directory of European Industrial & Trade Associations, published by CBD Research, Beckenham, 5th edn, 1991

Directory of European Professional & Learned Societies, published by CBD Research, Beckenham, 5th edn, 1995

Encyclopedia of Britain: The A-Z of Britain's Past and Present, by Bamber Gascoigne, rev. edn, Macmillan, London, 1994

English Historical Documents, ed. D.C. Douglas, 12 vols, Eyre & Spottiswoode, London, 1953–75

English Historical Review, published quarterly since 1886 by Longman, Harlow.

The Europa World Year Book, 2 vols, published annually by Europa Publications, London

European Historical Statistics 1750–1975, ed. B.R. Mitchell, Macmillan, London, 2nd rev. edn, 1981

European Political Facts 1918–1990, eds Chris Cook and John Paxton, *Historical and Political Facts* series, Macmillan, London, 1994

The Facts on File Weekly World News Digest, published by Facts on File, New York; available in UK from Steeple Services Ltd, 7 The Ride, Tubney Wood, Oxon OX13 5QF (tel. 01865 390613; fax 01865 390428)

Government Statistics: A Brief Guide to Sources, published annually by HMSO, London (gratis)

Guide to Directories at the Science Reference and Information Service, SRIS, British Library, London, 1991

The Guinness Book of Records, published by Guinness, Enfield; regularly updated

Handbook of British Chronology, eds E.B. Fryde *et al.*, Royal Historical Society, London, 3rd edn, 1985

Handbook of Dates for Students of English History, by C.R. Cheney, Royal Historical Society, London, 1978; latest reprint 1995; new edition in preparation

Historical Computing: An Introduction, by Peter Denley and Deian Hopkin, Macmillan, London, 1995

Historical Facts series, published by Macmillan, London: 6 vols covering period 1485–1985 (first 2 vols entitled *English Historical Facts*, subsequent vols *British Historical Facts*), 1975–88

Historical and Political Facts series, Macmillan, London, updated regularly

Historical Research (formerly the *Bulletin of the Institute of Historical Research*), since 1987 published three times a year by Blackwell, Oxford, for the IHR

The Historian, quarterly magazine of the Historical Association, London

History, published three times a year by the Historical Association, London

A History of the English-Speaking Peoples, by W.S. Churchill, 4 vols, Cassell, London, 1956–58

History Today, published monthly since 1951, London

Hollis Press & Public Relations Annual, published by Hollis Directories, Sunbury-on-Thames, Middx

Hollis Europe, published annually by Hollis Directories, Sunbury-on-Thames, Middx

Hutchinson Info, published annually by Helicon, Oxford; on floppy disks, 1995; *Info '96*, published October 1995 in hardback, paperback and CD-ROM simultaneously

Illustrated London News, weekly from May 1842; now six issues per year, London

International Historical Statistics Europe 1750–1988, ed. Brian R. Mitchell, Macmillan, London, 3rd edn, 1992

IPO Directory, published bi-annually by the Central Office of Information, London

Keesing's Record of World Events (formerly *Keesing's Contemporary Archives*), published since 1931; now 11 issues per year (July–August = double issue), with one interim and one full index, annual reference supplement (published in spring, review of previous year); annual bound volume available as alternative. Now published by Cartermill Publishing, London. Available on microfiche 1931–80, from Research Publications International, Reading

Larousse Desk Reference Encyclopedia, Larousse, London, 1995

Larousse Pocket Factfinder, Larousse, London, 1995

Larousse Pocket Guides, ongoing series, Larousse, London

The Marcan Handbook of Arts Organisations, Peter Marcan, London, 4th edn, 1995

The Media Guide, ed. Steve Peak, published annually by Fourth Estate, London, 3rd edn, 1995 (a *Guardian Book*)

Monthly Digest of Statistics, Central Statistical Office, HMSO, London

The New Shell Book of Firsts, ed. Patrick Robertson, Headline, London, 1994 (formerly entitled *Shell Book of Firsts*, 2nd rev. edn, Michael Joseph, London, 1984)

Now I Remember, by Ronald Hamilton, Chatto & Windus, London, rev. edn, 1983; paperback edition, Hogarth Press, 1984

NUJ Freelance Directory, National Union of Journalists, London, updated regularly

Punch, published weekly 1841–1992, London

Royal Historical Society Transactions, published annually, now by Cambridge University Press, Cambridge, for the RHS

SCICAT, current catalogue of SRIS, on microfiche; by annual subscription, SRIS, British Library, London

Scientific Abstracting and Indexing Periodicals in the British Library: a guide to SRIS holdings and their use, compiled by Rodney Burton, SRIS, British Library, London, 4th edn, 1991

The Statesman's Year-Book, published annually by Macmillan, London

Statistics Europe, published by CBD Research, Beckenham, 6th edn, 1995

The Tatler, first published in 1709, now monthly, London

The Times Index, 1785 to present day, currently by subscription monthly plus annual cumulation, Research Publications International, Reading; available on microfilm for years 1906–76, and on CD-ROM (included in *British Newspaper Index*) from 1990. Also *Palmer's Index to The Times, 1790–1905* on CD-ROM, Chadwyck-Healey, Cambridge

Ulrich's International Periodicals Directory 1994–95 (including *Irregular Serials and Annuals*), 5 vols with *Ulrich's Update* three times a year, Bowker, New Providence, N.J., 1994; also *Ulrich's on Microfiche 1994–95*. *Ulrich's Plus*, quarterly on CD-ROM, and *Ulrich's Online*, updated monthly, Bowker-Reed Reference Electronic Publishing, East Grinstead

The UK in Figures, booklet published annually by the Central Statistical Office, HMSO, London (gratis)

Walford's Guide to Reference Material, vol. 2, *Social and Historical Sciences*, Library Association, London, 6th edn, 1994

Whitaker's Almanack, published annually by Whitaker, London

Writings on British History, now *Annual Bibliography of British and Irish History*, *q.v.*

Note: From 1995 serial publications of the Royal Historical Society are published by Cambridge University Press. Back titles to 1990 are available from CUP; titles published before 1990 from Oxbow Books Ltd, Park End Place, Oxford OX1 1HN. Reprints of the first 15 volumes of *Writings on British History* are available from Dawson Book Service, Cannon House, Folkestone, Kent CT19 5EE: 12 volumes covering the period 1946–74, published by the Institute of Historical Research, are available from the IHR. The *Annual Bibliography of British and Irish History*, covering the years since 1975, is published and distributed by Oxford University Press for the RHS.

5

Research for Fiction Writers and Dramatists

The depth of research to be undertaken by the writer of fiction will depend upon his choice for the story's setting and his own knowledge of that setting, and upon his acquaintance with the kind of people he is writing about. Basically, the research will be concerned with the creation of an authentic background to the plot and with writing dialogue in the correct idiom. As the problems which face the writer of modern fiction and drama differ from those of the writer of historical fiction and drama, they are here examined separately. All that is said about the novel applies equally to the short story and to drama.

The Modern Novel

Background

There is no substitute for a personal visit to every place in which your story, or scene of a story, is to be set. Only through first-hand experience will you absorb the atmosphere of a place, find out exactly how long it will take your character to get from A to B and what buildings or other landmarks he will pass on the way; by using your eyes and ears and nose, by travelling on the local bus, and by spending a few evenings at the pub, you can learn pretty well everything you need to know about the way the locals live, behave and talk. Make a point of attending at least once each kind of event that is going to crop up in your story or play – whether it is a boxing match, a race meeting, a sale at Sotheby's, a ballet performance, a court hearing, or anything else.

Inevitably, sometimes, a personal visit is out of the question, and then you have no choice but to rely on secondary sources. If this is the case, equip yourself with a good, large-scale map or two – preferably a street map of each town in which the action of your story is to take place, as well as a map of the whole district. You can obtain much free information of this nature from town halls or tourist offices.

Travel brochures are always a helpful source, and there are any number of excellent general topographical guides to various regions of the United Kingdom. The *Blue Guides* (separate volumes for *England* and *London*) are detailed and up to date. Look also at the publications of the motoring organisations. (How to obtain information on places abroad is dealt with in chapter 9, 'Information from and about Foreign Countries', pages 146–61). The researcher wishing to find out more about the origin and meaning of place-names should consult *The Concise Oxford Dictionary of English Place-Names*, *The Concise Dictionary of Modern Place-Names in Great Britain and Ireland*, and a recent compilation, the *Hutchinson Pocket Dictionary of Place Names*, as well as the volumes (by county) published by the English Place-Name Society.

If you need to describe particular buildings you will find Nikolaus Pevsner's *Buildings of England* series, also one per county, enormously helpful; also the *Guide to Country Houses* series. In addition, all stately homes and castles open to the public produce their own guidebooks, some more comprehensive and informative than others. Two annual publications, *Historic Houses, Castles and Gardens in Great Britain and Ireland* and the AA's *Historic Houses in Britain*, carry brief details of all such properties. The curators of these historic houses are well informed, but may be too busy to talk to you on days when the public is admitted; a telephone call or preliminary letter beforehand may lead to a special appointment and personally guided tour, with much additional information.

Other essential reference tools are railway and bus time-tables of the area you are describing and, if appropriate, an air time-table: these should save you from making an elementary mistake such as putting a character on a train or plane at the wrong rail or air terminus or misjudging the time taken for a particular journey. A writer setting his tale on board a cruise ship or private yacht will find the *World Cruising Handbook* a mine of information on harbour regulations, ports of call, and much else.

An excellent way to get the 'feel' of a place, when it is not possible for you to visit it, is to take out a subscription to the local newspaper and county magazine; you will find lists of these, under towns, in both *Benn's Media* and *Willing's Press Guide* (see chapter 3, 'Basic Sources of Information', pages 44–5).

People

Often the background to a story or play will concern a particular profession or industry, and here too the best method of research is to mix as much as possible with people in the field. The secretary of the relevant professional or trade association (check names and addresses in the current *Directory of British Associations & Associations in Ireland,* in the *Hollis Press & Public Relations Annual,* or in *Whitaker's Almanack* – see chapter 4, page 71) will usually be very helpful if you do not have any personal contacts, and most large corporations or companies have a press and public relations department or member of staff who will assist you. You should not feel diffident about approaching such people; it is rare for a genuine request for information to be refused point blank, and very often the enquirer will be invited to visit a factory or training establishment or to attend as an observer one or two meetings of the relevant society – all this is grist to the mill. Nevertheless, it is unfair to impinge too much on someone else's time or expertise – even if this is being paid for by his company – and so a luncheon or dinner invitation is a nice gesture. An incredible amount can be learned from an hour's conversation face to face.

Much of what has been said about background research also applies to finding out about people, for there is nothing better than to spend time with whatever age, regional, or occupational group the writer wishes to bring into his story. It is essential to observe at first hand how people behave, talk and dress. Every writer should try, therefore, to cultivate a wide circle of friends in all walks of life, and the fiction writer especially will do well to get to know a psychologist with whom he can discuss the actions and reactions of his characters, as well as a doctor with whom he can verify medical symptoms and treatments. The crime writer ought to be on friendly terms with at least one member of the police force who is willing to put him right on procedures and jargon; only as a last resort should he telephone or write to New Scotland Yard (where, however, if he has a genuine problem an information officer will usually help). He will find *Moriarty's Police Law, Butterworth's Police Law* and Keith Simpson's *Forensic Medicine* indispensable.

Careers pamphlets and training manuals for the relevant trade or profession yield a good deal of information. The memoirs and diaries of eminent people in that trade or profession should be looked at, and also the relevant in-house or trade journals, for these will all provide up-to-date material and jargon, and sometimes also historical detail.

So far as the behaviour of your characters is concerned, personal observation may be supplemented by a simple textbook on psychology or behavioural study. Recommended titles are Desmond Morris's *Bodytalk: A World Guide to Gestures*, Peter Collett's *Foreign Bodies: A Guide to European Mannerisms* and Roger Axtell's *Gestures: The Dos and Taboos of Body Language Around the World*.

Useful sources of information on nicknames (both modern and historical) are the *Handbook of Pseudonyms and Personal Nicknames* compiled by H. Sharp, the *Pseudonyms and Nicknames Dictionary* published by Gale Research of Detroit, USA, and Carl Sifakis's *The Dictionary of Historic Nicknames*.

On names in general, the best up-to-date source is Adrian Room's *Brewer's Dictionary of Names*, which has 8,000 entries and a guide to nearly 100 languages; it covers not only the origins of personal and place names, but brand names, literary characters, rock groups, and almost every other category. For recommendations on literary pseudonyms and names of characters in published fiction, see the penultimate paragraph of this chapter, pages 92–3. More academic genealogical studies are mentioned in chapter 7, 'Family and Local History', pages 122–40.

Language

It is highly dangerous for the writer who is unfamiliar with a foreign language, local dialect or occupational slang to dabble in these fields, but if he must do so he should always try to get what he has written verified by an expert. So far as English is concerned, your first step should be to consult the National Sound Archive (29 Exhibition Road, London SW7 2AS; tel. 0171–589 6603); an appointment will be arranged for you to listen to relevant recordings. (This can be in London or Yorkshire, see page 55.) Among printed works Peter Trudgill's *The Dialects of England* is first class. Most reference libraries will also have the four-volume *Survey of English Dialects* by H. Orton and E. Dieth, and the *English Dialect Dictionary* by J. Wright.

There are a number of so-called 'slang dictionaries', and these have their uses. However, since it is necessary first to know the word or expression whose meaning you wish to look up in them, their value must be limited. Happily there is now *The Thesaurus of Slang*, a splendid compilation containing an alphabetical list of 12,000 standard English words for which you can look up some 150,000 slang terms, common idioms and colloquialisms. The late Eric Partridge's *Slang Today and Yesterday*, with its separate sections dealing with slang spoken in chronological periods and in various occupational groups, is still valid historically. Mr Partridge also compiled *A Dictionary of the Underworld, British and American*, which will serve the crime writer well (although this too is arranged as a dictionary), and also a fascinating *A Dictionary of Catch Phrases* (British and American) from the 16th century to the present day. Up-to-date compilations include *Newspeak: A Dictionary of Jargon*, *Slang Down the Ages* and *The Slang Thesaurus*, all three by Jonathon Green, and *The Macmillan Dictionary of American Slang*.

Quite often a writer is at a loss to know how one of his characters would address another, perhaps someone in an elevated position. Here either *Debrett's Correct Form* or *Titles and Forms of Address* will provide the answer, supplying as a bonus a guide to practically every situation likely to arise, socially and professionally, including American usage. These books will also be invaluable for the researcher wishing to know how to write or talk to titled or official persons whom he needs to contact for information.

The Historical Novel

The writer of an historical novel must be thoroughly familiar with the period in which his story is set, and especially knowledgeable about the manners, customs and daily life of the people concerned. He must also be accurate about major events and prominent people. This will not present any great difficulty so long as he keeps at his elbow as he works a general bibliography and authoritative history of the period, as well as a good biographical dictionary (suggested titles are mentioned in chapter 4, 'Historical Research' (pages 72–4) and chapter 6, 'Biography and Autobiography' (pages 101–21)). A trap that inexperienced writers sometimes fall into is one of anachronisms: that is, the mention of, say, ice cream or zip fasteners at a period before these came on the scene. You can avoid such errors by checking in an encyclopedic dictionary or *The New Shell Book of Firsts*.

In recent years a number of gifted historians, notably the French writers Fernand Braudel, Georges Duby and Roy Ladurie (all now translated into English) have added a new dimension to social history, for which we humble researchers, seeking ever more detail on the private lives of people through the ages, must be enormously grateful. For reasons of space I have had to be ruthlessly selective in considering which titles to recommend here in order to introduce some newer studies that are European in scope and written with the benefit of contemporary research. Readers who have read and absorbed my chapters 3 and 4 should be more than adequately equipped to ferret out other titles on more specific subjects.

It is of the utmost importance to use contemporary sources wherever possible, and you should make good use of the *English Historical Documents* series. Also recommended are the *They Saw It Happen* and the *Human Documents* series; some of these are now out of print, but they will be found in most reference libraries. G.M. Trevelyan's *English Social History* remains one of the best general accounts of life in this country through the ages, while a more recent study is Asa Briggs' *A Social History of England*. Two admirable multi-volume works are Fernand Braudel's *Civilization and Capitalism 1400–1800* and *A History of Private Life*, edited by P. Ariès and G. Duby. The lifestyle of the upper classes is admirably portrayed in Mark Girouard's *Life in the English Country House*. R. Graves and A. Hodge's *The Long Week-End* is very evocative of the years between the two world wars. Among numerous social histories relating to particular periods, I mention a few, to give readers an idea of what to look out for: E.N. Williams' *Life in Georgian England*, Dorothy Marshall's *English People in the 18th Century*, J.H. Plumb's *Georgian Delights*, John Fisher's *The World of the Forsytes*, the *How We Used to Live* series from A & C Black (early Victorian times to the present), and Norman Longmate's *How We Lived Then: A History of Everyday Life during the Second World War*. G.D.H. Cole and R. Postgate's *The Common People 1746–1938* has become a standard work; see also *The Common People: A History from the Norman Conquest to the Present*, by J.F.C. Harrison, two studies by E.P. Thompson, *Customs in Common* and *The Making of the English Working Class*, and *The Labourer 1760–1832* by J.L. and Barbara Hammond. J.M. Brereton's *The British Soldier: A Social History* provides a reliable background to army life from the 17th century. *British Trials 1660–1900* contains first-hand accounts of thousands of trials. In lighter vein, but very informative, are C.L. Graves' *Mr Punch's History of Modern England*, covering the years from 1841 to 1914, and Leslie Baily's *BBC Scrapbooks 1896–1939*. Rona Randall's *The Model Wife* is a well-illustrated mine of information about marriage and the role of a wife in the 19th-century household. For the present century it is worth looking at the recent *Portrait of a Decade* series.

Autobiographies and diaries are extremely useful as source-material for the historical novelist in that they provide absolutely authentic accounts of day-to-day life and thought of the period, written in the contemporary idiom. *British Autobiographies*, compiled by William Matthews, is an annotated bibliography of material printed or published before 1951. John Burnett has made two useful studies of working-class material, the three-volume *Autobiography of the Working Class*, covering the period 1790–1945, and a paperback, *Useful Toil: Autobiographies of Working People from the 1820s to the 1970s*.

William Matthews' *British Diaries 1442–1942* and John Stuart Batts' *British Manuscript Diaries of the 19th Century* are standard works, both listing the diaries under the year in which they commence, which enables the researcher to ascertain what material exists for a particular period. Matthews also compiled an annotated bibliography of *American Diaries* written prior to 1861 and *American Diaries in Manuscript 1580–1954*. His work has been updated, expanded and continued by another American bibliographer, Patricia Pate Havlice, in an invaluable volume, *And So To Bed: A Bibliography of Diaries published in English*; this contains an index to Matthews' listings and also a general index of authors, editors, titles and subjects. Also worth consulting are *English Family Life 1576–1716: An Anthology of Diaries*, edited by Ralph Houlbrooke, and *Women's Diaries, Journals and Letters: An Annotated Bibliography*, compiled by Cheryl Cline.

Most public libraries have a local collection, and you should always ask if there is a book dealing with a particular region, town, industry or local family, in the period about which you are writing. (For further suggestions, see chapter 7, 'Family and Local History' pages 122–40.)

One good method of keeping the story of an historical novel or play in line with world or national events is to refer constantly to a published chronology. I recommend the *Chronology of World History*, available either in four volumes (you can buy only the one you need) or in a compact edition or on CD-ROM. There is also *The People's Chronology*, which contains much information on human events, inventions, etc. not listed elsewhere. There is a wide choice of dictionaries of dates from various publishers. In these volumes the major events of each year are listed month by month, while also included are annual listings of the developments in the arts, sciences, politics, etc., together with the births and deaths of famous people.

Problems likely to be encountered by the writer of historical fiction and some suggestions as to how they may be solved are discussed below.

Places

Many of the places and buildings you may want to mention in your novel or play still exist today, but have changed out of all recognition in the last few hundred years, and it is not easy to find out exactly how they looked at a particular date. You should always ask at the local library or record office if they have maps of approximately the right date, and where these exist you will find it valuable to keep a photocopy of the map in front of you as you write. There is an historical series of the Ordnance Survey, which may be useful, and you can buy reprints of the first (one-inch) edition. A good historical atlas such as *The Times Atlas of World History* or the *Penguin Atlas of World History* is essential. There is also a comparatively inexpensive series published by Penguin with separate volumes for *Ancient*, *Medieval* or *Recent History*.

Like the writer of modern fiction, the historical novelist should try to visit every place or building that comes into his story. If this is quite impossible, the best course is to enquire at your local library or county record office for a reliable parish history and for any books about life in the district during the period in which you are interested. If your story is set in the 18th century or later, you will be able to study the local newspaper. Where buildings have to be described, Nikolaus Pevsner's *Buildings of England* series, already mentioned, will be most useful. For buildings in London, there is the very detailed *Survey of London*. Other useful sources include the *Britain in Old Photographs* series, as well as current guidebooks to the historic castles and stately homes open to the public.

Dates

The problems that arise over dating have been discussed in the previous chapter. In historical fiction work the writer will most often need to find out on what day of the week a certain anniversary or religious festival fell. This can be done very easily by first looking up the date of Easter in the chronological table at the back of the *Handbook of Dates for Students of English History* and then by turning to the appropriate calendar section, in which there is a double-page spread for all the years from AD 500 to 2000 in which Easter fell (or is going to fall) on that particular day. In the same *Handbook* you will find a list of saints' days and religious festivals, but if you need more detail on festivals you should consult the *British Calendar Customs* series published by the Folklore Society. *Whitaker's Almanack* contains an 'Any Year' calendar from 1770 to 2030.

Weather

What the weather was like on a certain day, or if a particular winter was severe, or when there was a heatwave and how long it lasted, can be vital to an historical novel. *Whitaker's Almanack* (from 1868) is a good source, and so are local and regional newspapers. *The Times* has employed a regular weather correspondent since the early 1870s, but earlier reports – from 1731 – appeared in *Gentleman's Magazine*, where you will find not only monthly tables giving temperatures and rainfall, but a calendar with brief descriptions against each day, such as 'cloudy morning, but bright later'; 'windy and wet all day'; 'heavy rain in the south, snow in the north'.

Two excellent works which are rare books and to be found nowadays only at the major libraries are T.H. Baker's *Records of the Seasons, etc. . . . observed in the British Isles* and E.J. Lowe's *Natural Phenomena and Chronology of the Seasons* (of which Part I only was ever published, containing records from AD 220 to 1753). Among other useful reference books are Ingrid Holford's *The Guinness Book of Weather Facts and Feats*; D. Bowen's *Britain's Weather*, which has an appendix listing notable gales, blizzards, floods and frosts; J.H. Brazell's *London Weather*, with its useful chronology from AD 4 to 1964; and W. Andrews' *Famous Frosts and Frost Fairs in Great Britain*. For information about the weather in different regions of the globe, the best source is *The World Weather Guide*. The *World Climate Disc*, on CD-ROM, contains data from 1854 to 1990.

In England, the Meteorological Office has published records since the 1860s. Its Library and Archives Department contains many earlier records, covering the entire world; researchers are allowed to use the Library, and in special cases books are loaned by post for the cost of postage only. The Librarian will usually recommend titles or will pass a specific query on to the relevant department, who may charge a fee if extensive research has to be undertaken by staff. Enquiries should be addressed in the first instance to the Meteorological Office Library, London Road, Bracknell, Berks RG12 2SZ (tel. 01344 420242, ext. 4843).

Language

Getting the idiom right in historical fiction is often a big worry to the writer. The best advice that can be given is that he should read extensively the best novels and plays of the relevant age; by so doing, he will gradually acquire the 'feel' of the spoken English of the time. Eric Partridge's *Slang Today and Yesterday*, as mentioned earlier in this chapter, has useful sections on the slang spoken at different periods (16th to mid-20th century). *Slang Down the Ages* is arranged by subject, with a word index. If you are setting your story in the last war, you should look at *The Language of World War II*, which covers not only spoken expressions but also the slogans and abbreviations then current, as well as the popular songs of the time.

Cost of living, currencies and wages

How much people earned and what they paid for their food and clothing are queries that frequently crop up in historical writing. J. Burnett's *A History of the Cost of Living* will answer most needs: it has chapters dating from the Middle Ages to the present day, and also a good bibliography. Unfortunately it has been allowed to go out of print, but most libraries will have it; should you ever see it on offer secondhand, be sure to snap it up! A more recent paperback, written primarily for family and local historians, is Lionel Munby's *How Much is that Worth?* Another exceptionally informative source is the *What It Cost the Day Before Yesterday Book* by Harold Priestley, which is divided into three periods: 1851–1914, 1915–70 and (to take account of inflation) 1971–78. *Prices and Wages in England from the 12th to the 19th Century* by Lord Beveridge and others is a standard work, and Peter Wilsher's *The Pound in your Pocket 1870–1970* is a very readable and well-researched study of the pound and its purchasing power over the last hundred years. Newspapers and women's magazines are valuable sources from the early 19th century onwards – Alison Adburgham's *Shops and Shopping* covers the period 1800–1914, whereas a new publication, Bill Lancaster's *The Department Store: A Social History*, deals with the subject from the mid-19th century to the present day, on both sides of the Atlantic.

Currency Conversion Tables: A Hundred Years of Change* by R.L. Bidwell is a most useful guide to the fluctuations in rates of exchange of most countries of the world since 1870; it also has a table of London gold prices. For money values in earlier times I recommend John McCusker's *Money and Exchange in Europe and America 1600–1775*, Peter Spufford's *Handbook of Medieval Exchange* and Pierre Vilar's *A History of Gold and Money 1450–1920*. For more historical or monetary information, write or telephone to the Bank of England Library and Information Services, Threadneedle Street, London EC2R 8AH (tel. 0171–601 4715).

Fashion, etiquette and food

The standard work on English costume is the series by C.W. and P.E. Cunnington, which consists of *Handbooks* covering the medieval period and the 16th, 17th, 18th, 19th and 20th centuries in separate volumes. For quick reference there is the *Dictionary of English Costume 900–1900* by C.W. and P.E. Cunnington and Charles Beard. Also useful is *The Evolution of Fashion: Pattern and Cut from 1066 to 1930* by M. Hamilton Hill and Peter Bucknell, while Alison Lurie's study *The Language of Clothes* is both a thoroughly researched and witty comment on dress and manners that will help both the modern and the historical novelist. The new *Fashions of a Decade* series, published by Batsford, is useful for the 20th century. Other titles are listed in the booklet *Costume: A General Bibliography*, published by the Costume Society. There is now a Costume and Fashion Research Centre at 4 Circus Road, Bath, Avon BA1 2EW (tel. 01225 477752), which may be able to help further. Enquiries should be addressed in writing to the Keeper of Costume in the first instance. On hairdressing there is R. Corson's *Fashions in Hair: The First 5000 Years*, R. Turner Wilcox's *Modes in Hats and Headdress* (from ancient Egyptian to the present day) and G. de Courtais' *Women's Headdress and Hairstyles in England from* AD *600 to the Present Day*.

The best guides to English manners and etiquette are J. Wildeblood and P. Brinson's *The Polite World* (covering the 13th to the 19th centuries) and *A Punch History of Manners 1841–1940*, by A. Adburgham. On eating habits and diet there are Arnold Palmer's *Movable Feasts*, J.C. Drummond and A. Wilbraham's *The Englishman's Food: A History of Five Centuries of English Diet*, J. Burnett's *Plenty and Want: A Social History of Diet in England from 1815 to the Present Day*, Reay Tannahill's *Food in History* and Margaret Visser's *The Rituals of Dinner*.

Transport and travel

One of the best general studies is E.A. Pratt's *History of Inland Transport and Communications*. David & Charles and Alan Sutton are publishers who specialise in transport history; send for their catalogues. Finding out exactly how long a particular journey would have taken at a particular date is not easy. So far as train journeys are concerned, try to find an early Bradshaw (first published in 1839) – you may have to settle for the one nearest in date to your story. Stage-coach time-tables will be found in the early London directories. ABC International, now part of the Reed Travel Group, have a collection of old rail and air time-tables; telephone them on 01582 695242.

Children's Fiction

Research done by the children's writer is not much different from that carried out by the writer of stories for adults. Children of all ages being highly critical and quick to spot mistakes, it is very important that background and language are absolutely right.

The correct idiom is vital. It is a good idea, if you are embarking on a modern story, to study a selection of juvenile magazines for a time. You will also want to find out about published children's books. The Young Book Trust, which is part of the Book Trust (Book House, 45 East Hill, London SW18 2QZ; tel. 0181–870 9055), maintains an excellent library and information service; it holds a copy of every children's book published in the past two years. You can also consult the *Children's Fiction Index*, which will be found at the children's librarian's desk in most libraries.

On sources generally, there is the recent *Children's Fiction Sourcebook*. As well as the standard work, *The Oxford Companion to Children's Literature*, you will find Arthur Mortimore's *Index to Characters in Children's Literature* very useful. If you write for young children, you may want to have works such as *The Classic Fairy Tales*, *The Fairies in Tradition and Literature* or the *Oxford Dictionary of Nursery Rhymes* on your reference bookshelf.

So far as school stories are concerned, you cannot do better than delve into Peter Opie's *The Lore and Language of School Children*. Isabel Quigly's *The Heirs of Tom Brown*, with its excellent bibliography, will help with a public school setting. Another very useful book is *Children's Games in Street and Playground*, by Iona and Peter Opie.

Various slang dictionaries have been mentioned on pages 83–4. However, it cannot be stressed too strongly that language is changing all the time – and especially the language of the young – so that there can be no substitute for the writer mixing with, and talking and listening to, the younger generation, in order to get the idiom exactly right.

Background too must be up to date: remember single-parent families and the mixed nationalities encountered by children today in playgroup and school!

Science Fiction

The best source in this country is the Science Fiction Foundation Research Library, now at Liverpool University Library, P.O. Box 123, Liverpool L69 3DA (tel 0151–794 2733/2696). The collection includes the library of the British Science Fiction Association. Intending researchers should telephone in advance for an appointment. A new reference tool is *The Ultimate Guide to Science Fiction: An A–Z of Science Fiction Books by Title* by D. Pringle.

Finding out about Published Fiction

In addition to the specific research problems connected with his own work, the fiction writer or playwright frequently wants to know what other novels or plays or short stories have been published with similar themes or backgrounds. He may also wish to check on whether any other writer has used the title which he has in mind. (There is no copyright in titles, but for the exact legal position, see the Society of Authors' *Quick Guide* on the 'Protection of Titles'.)

Most public libraries possess copies of the *Fiction Index*, the *Play Index* and the *Short Story Index*; you should ask for them at the readers' enquiry desk. There are cumulated volumes of the *Fiction Index* for 1945–60 and 1960–69; since 1970 every five years. Titles are listed under some 3,000 subject headings. A recent compilation is the *Reference Guide to Short Fiction*, which covers the 19th and 20th centuries and includes foreign language writers and translations.

The researcher wishing to find out about published historical fiction should look at the *World Historical Fiction Guide* and at Irene Collins' *Recent Historical Novels*. J. Nield's *Guide to the Best Historical Novels and Tales* deals with titles published before 1929; it is out of print, but available in most reference libraries.

Literary pseudonyms may be traced in Frank Atkinson's *Dictionary of Literary Pseudonyms*. There are three useful sources for finding out about characters in published fiction: the

Dictionary of Characters in British Novels, the *Dictionary of Fictional Characters* and the *Dictionary of Real People and Places in Fiction*.

Finally, but by no means least, for the advice of a successful novelist (as opposed to that of a humble researcher, albeit one who has worked for many novelists), read Jean Saunders' *How to Research your Novel*.

American Diaries: An Annotated Bibliography of American Diaries written prior to Year 1861, by William Matthews, University of California Press, Berkeley and Los Angeles, 1945, 1959

American Diaries in Manuscript, 1580–1954, by William Matthews, University of Georgia Press, Athens, 1974

And So To Bed: A Bibliography of Diaries published in English, by Patricia Pate Havlice, Scarecrow, Metuchen, 1987

Autobiography of the Working Class, by John Burnett, 3 vols, Harvester, Hemel Hempstead, 1984–89

BBC Scrapbooks, by Leslie Baily, 2 vols: 1, *1896–1914*; 2, *1918–1939*, Allen & Unwin, London, 1966–68

Benn's Media, 3 vols, published annually by Miller Freeman Information Services, Tonbridge (formerly Benn Business Information Services)

Blue Guide England, by Ian Ousby, A & C Black, London, 11th edn, 1995

Blue Guide London, by Ylva French, A & C Black, London, 15th edn, 1994

Bodytalk: A World Guide to Gestures, by Desmond Morris, Jonathan Cape, London, 1994

Brewer's Dictionary of Names, compiled by Adrian Room, Helicon, Oxford, 1995

Britain in Old Photographs series, published by Alan Sutton, Far Thrupp, Stroud

Britain's Weather, by David Bowen, David & Charles, Newton Abbot, 1969

British Autobiographies: An Annotated Bibliography of British Autobiographies published or written before 1951, by William Matthews, University of California Press, Berkeley and Los Angeles, 1955

British Calendar Customs: England, 3 vols; *Scotland*, 3 vols; *Orkneys and Shetland*, 1 vol, published by The Folklore Society, London, 1936–46

British Diaries 1442–1942: An Annotated Bibliography of British Diaries written between 1442 and 1942, by William Matthews, University of California Press, Berkeley and Los Angeles, 1950

British Manuscript Diaries of the 19th Century: An Annotated Listing, by John Stuart Batts, Centaur Press, Fontwell and London, 1976

The British Soldier: A Social History, by J.M. Brereton, Bodley Head, London, 1986

British Trials 1660–1900, microfiche series, Chadwyck-Healey, Cambridge, in progress, 1990–

Buildings of England series, originally ed. by Nikolaus Pevsner, 46 vols, 1951 onwards, Penguin Books, Harmondsworth; revised editions in progress

Butterworth's Police Law, Butterworth, London, updated regularly

Children's Fiction Index, published by Association of Assistant Librarians, London, 7th edn, 1995

Children's Fiction Sourcebook, compiled by J. Madden and M. Hobson, Scolar Press, London, 1995

Children's Games in Street and Playground, by Iona and Peter Opie, Oxford University Press, Oxford, 1969; paperback edn, 1984

Chronology of World History, 4 vols: *Ancient World, Medieval World, Expanding World, Modern World*; originally published by Barrie & Rockcliff, London, 1969–76; reprinted editions, Helicon, Oxford; compact edition and CD-ROM, Helicon, Oxford, 1995

Civilization and Capitalism 1400–1800, by Fernand Braudel, 3 vols: 1, The Structures of Everyday Life; 2, The Wheels of Commerce; 3, The Perspective of the World, Collins, London, 1981–85

The Classic Fairy Tales, by Iona and Peter Opie, Oxford University Press, Oxford, 1974; reprinted 1992

The Common People 1746–1938, by G.D.H. Cole and R. Postgate, Methuen, London, 1938; reprinted 1965

The Common People: A History from the Norman Conquest to the Present, by J.F.C. Harrison, Fontana, London, 1984

The Concise Dictionary of Modern Place-Names in Great Britain and Ireland, compiled by Adrian Room, Oxford University Press, Oxford, 1985

The Concise Oxford Dictionary of English Place-Names, compiled by E. Ekwall, Oxford University Press, Oxford, 4th edn, 1960; reprinted 1974

Costume: A General Bibliography, by P. Anthony and J. Arnold, published by The Costume Society, London, 1974

Currency Conversion Tables: A Hundred Years of Change, by R.L. Bidwell, Rex Collings, London, 1970

Customs in Common, by E.P. Thompson, Merlin, London, 1991

Debrett's Correct Form, rev. paperback edn, Headline, London, 1992

The Department Store: A Social History, by Bill Lancaster, Pinter (Mansell), London, 1995

The Dialects of England, by Peter Trudgill, Blackwell, Oxford, 1990

A Dictionary of Catch Phrases British and American, from the Sixteenth Century to the Present Day, by Eric Partridge, Routledge & Kegan Paul, London, 2nd edn ed. Paul Beale, 1985

Dictionary of Characters in British Novels, by John Greenfield, 2 vols, Facts on File, Oxford, 1994

Dictionary of English Costume 900–1900, by C.W. and P.E. Cunnington and Charles Beard, A & C Black, London, 1960; reprinted 1976

Dictionary of Fictional Characters, by William Freeman, Everyman Reference series, Dent, London, 3rd edn revised, 1973

The Dictionary of Historic Nicknames, compiled by Carl Sifakis, Facts on File, Oxford, 1984; paperback edn, 1986

Dictionary of Literary Pseudonyms, compiled by Frank Atkinson, Library Association, London, 4th edn, 1987

Dictionary of Real People and Places in Fiction, compiled by M.C. Rintoul, Routledge, London, 1991

A Dictionary of the Underworld, British and American, compiled by Eric Partridge, Routledge, London, 3rd edn revised, 1968

Dictionary of British Associations & Associations in Ireland, published by CBD Research, Beckenham, 12th edn, 1994

English Dialect Dictionary, compiled by J. Wright, 6 vols, Frowde, London, 1896–1905; new edn, Oxford University Press, Oxford, 1981

English Family Life 1576–1716: An Anthology of Diaries, ed. R. Houlbrooke, Blackwell, Oxford, 1989

English Historical Documents, ed. D.C. Douglas, 12 vols, Eyre & Spottiswoode, London, 1953–75

English People in the Eighteenth Century, by Dorothy Marshall, Longman, London, 1956

English Place-Name Society, volumes by county, in progress since 1923, published by the Society, c/o University of Nottingham

English Social History, by G.M. Trevelyan, Longman, London, new edn, 1978; paperback edn, Penguin Books, Harmondsworth, 1986

The Englishman's Food: A History of Five Centuries of English Diet, by J.C. Drummond and A. Wilbraham, Cape, London, 1958; reprinted, Pimlico, London, 1991

The Evolution of Fashion: Pattern and Cut from 1066 to 1930,
by M. Hamilton Hill and P. Bucknell, Batsford, London, 1967;
reprinted 1987

The Fairies in Tradition and Literature, by K.M. Briggs,
Routledge, London, 1977; reprinted Bellew, London, 1989

Famous Frosts and Frost Fairs in Great Britain, by W. Andrews,
Redway, London, 1887

Fashions in Hair: The First 5000 Years, by R. Corson, Peter Owen,
London, 1965

Fashions of a Decade series, published by Batsford, London, in
progress, 1991–

Fiction Index, published annually by the Association of Assistant
Librarians, London, since 1970; cumulated vols covering the
period 1945–1989, now every 5 years. Latest editions, compiled
by Marilyn E. Hicken: *Fiction Index 1993* and *Cumulated
Fiction 1990–1994*, both published 1995

Food in History, by Reay Tannahill, Eyre Methuen, London, 1973

Foreign Bodies: A Guide to European Mannerisms, by Peter
Collett, Simon & Schuster, London, 1993

Forensic Medicine, by Keith Simpson, E. Arnold, 9th edn, 1985

Gentleman's Magazine, 1731–1922; weather reports

Georgian Delights, by J.H. Plumb, Weidenfeld & Nicolson,
London, 1980

*Gestures: The Dos and Taboos of Body Language Around the
World*, by Roger E. Axtell, John Wiley, London, 1991

Guide to the Best Historical Novels and Tales, by J. Nield,
Matthews, London, 5th edn, 1929

Guide to Country Houses series, Burkes' Peerage/Savill, London,
in progress, 3 vols to date

The Guinness Book of Weather Facts and Feats, by Ingrid
Holford, Guinness Superlatives, Enfield, 1977

Handbook of Dates for Students of English History, ed. C.R.
Cheney, Royal Historical Society, London, 1978; latest reprint
1995; new edition in preparation

Handbook of English Costume series, by C.W. and P.E.
Cunnington, Faber, London, 1952–73

Handbook of Medieval Exchange, by Peter Spufford, Royal
Historical Society, London, 1986

Handbook of Pseudonyms and Personal Nicknames, compiled by
Harold S. Sharp, 2 vols, Scarecrow, Metuchen, N.J., 1972;
supplements, 1975, 1982

The Heirs of Tom Brown, by Isabel Quigly, Chatto & Windus,
London, 1982; paperback edn, Oxford University Press,
Oxford, 1984

Historic Houses, Castles and Gardens in Great Britain and Ireland, published annually by Reed Information Services, East Grinstead

Historic Houses in Britain, AA Publishing, Basingstoke, 1994

A History of the Cost of Living, by John Burnett, Penguin Books, Harmondsworth, 1969

A History of Gold and Money 1450–1920, by Pierre Vilar, Verso, USA, 1991 (distributed in UK by Marston Book Services, Oxford)

History of Inland Transport and Communication, by E.A. Pratt, 1912; reprinted, David & Charles, Newton Abbot, 1970

A History of Private Life, eds P. Ariès and G. Duby, translated from French, 5 vols, Belknap, Harvard University Press, Cambridge, Mass. and London, 1987–91

Hollis Press & Public Relations Annual, published by Hollis Directories, Sunbury-on-Thames, Middx

How Much is that Worth?, by Leslie Munby, Phillimore, Chichester, 1989

How to Research your Novel, by Jean Saunders, Allison & Busby, London, 1993

How We Lived Then: A History of Everyday Life during the Second World War, by Norman Longmate, Hutchinson, London, 1971; paperback edn, Arrow, London, 1977

How We Used to Live: Victorians Early and Late, by David Evans, A & C Black, London, 1990

Human Documents series, ed. R.E. Pike, Allen & Unwin, London (out of print)

Hutchinson Pocket Dictionary of Place Names, by Adrian Room, Helicon, Oxford, 1995

Index to Characters in Children's Literature, compiled and published by Arthur D. Mortimore, Bristol, 1977

The Labourer 1760–1832, by J.L. and Barbara Hammond, 1-vol paperback edn, Alan Sutton, Far Thrupp, Stroud, 1995

The Language of Clothes, by Alison Lurie, Heinemann, London, 1981; paperback edn, Hamlyn, London, 1983

The Language of World War II, compiled by A.M. Taylor, H.W. Wilson, New York, 1948

Life in the English Country House, by Mark Girouard, Yale University Press, New York and London, 1978; paperback edn, Penguin Books, Harmondsworth, 1980

Life in Georgian England, by E.N. Williams, Batsford, London, 1962

London Weather, by J.H. Brazell, HMSO, London, 1968

The Long Week-End: A Social History of Great Britain 1918–1939, by Robert Graves and Alan Hodge, Hutchinson, London, 1985

The Lore and Language of School Children, by Iona and Peter Opie, Oxford University Press, Oxford, 1959; reprinted 1987

The Macmillan Dictionary of American Slang, compiled by R.L. Chapman, Macmillan, 1995

The Making of the English Working Class, by E.P. Thompson, Gollancz, London, 1980

Mr Punch's History of Modern England, by C.L. Graves, 4 vols, Cassell, London, 1921–22

The Model Wife, by Rona Randall, Herbert Press, London, 1989

Modes in Hats and Headdress, by R. Turner Wilcox, Scribner's, New York, rev. edn, 1959

Money and Exchange in Europe and America 1600–1775, by John McCusker, Macmillan, London, 1978

Moriarty's Police Law, Butterworth, London, updated regularly

Movable Feasts: Changes in English Eating-Habits, by Arnold Palmer, Oxford University Press, Oxford, 1984

Natural Phenomena and Chronology of the Seasons, by E.J. Lowe, Part I only, London, 1870

The New Shell Book of Firsts, ed. Patrick Robertson, Headline, London, 1994; previously entitled *The Shell Book of Firsts*

Newspeak: A Dictionary of Jargon, by Jonathon Green, Routledge, London, 1984; paperback edn, 1985

Ordnance Survey: first edition reprinted by David & Charles, Newton Abbot; modern editions, HMSO/Ordnance Survey, London and Southampton

The Oxford Companion to Children's Literature, by H. Carpenter and M. Prichard, Oxford University Press, Oxford, 1984

Oxford Dictionary of Nursery Rhymes, eds Iona and Peter Opie, Oxford University Press, Oxford, 1951

Partridge's Dictionary of Catch Phrases, ed. P. Beale, Routledge, London, 2nd edn, 1986; paperback edn, 1990

Penguin Atlas of Ancient History, by C. McEvedy, Penguin Books, Harmondsworth, 1970

Penguin Atlas of Medieval History, by C. McEvedy, Penguin Books, Harmondsworth, 1979

Penguin Atlas of Recent History: Europe since 1815, by C. McEvedy, Penguin Books, Harmondsworth, 1982

Penguin Atlas of World History, 2 vols, Penguin Books, Harmondsworth, 1974; reprinted 1984

The People's Chronology, compiled by James Trager, Heinemann, London, 1980; 3rd rev. edn, Henry Holt, New York, 1992 (distributed in UK by Gazelle Book Services, Lancaster)

Play Index, published by H.W. Wilson, New York, since 1949 (8 vols to date, covering 1949–92)

Plenty and Want: A Social History of Diet in England from 1815 to the Present Day, by John Burnett, Routledge, London, 3rd edn, 1989

The Polite World: A Guide to English Manners and Deportment from the 13th to the 19th Century, rev. edn by J. Wildeblood and P. Brinson, Oxford University Press, Oxford, 1974

Portrait of a Decade series, published by Batsford, London, 9 vols covering the period 1900–1980s

The Pound in Your Pocket 1870–1970, by Peter Wilsher, Cassell, London, 1970

Prices and Wages in England from the 12th to the 19th Century, by Lord Beveridge and others, Frank Cass, London, 1965

'Protection of Titles', Society of Authors *Quick Guide*, (free to members or available from Publications Department of the Society, 84 Drayton Gardens, London SW10 9SD, £1.50 post free)

Pseudonyms and Nicknames Dictionary, ed. Jennifer Mossman, Gale Research, Detroit, 2nd edn, 1982

A Punch History of Manners 1841–1940, by Alison Adburgham, Hutchinson, London, 1961

Recent Historical Novels, ed. Irene Collins, Historical Association, London, 1990

Records of the Seasons and Prices of Agricultural Produce & Phenomena observed in the British Isles, by T.H. Baker, Simpkin Marshall, London, 1883

Reference Guide to Short Fiction, ed. Noelle Watson, St James Press, Detroit, 1994

The Rituals of Dinner, by Margaret Visser, Penguin Books, Harmondsworth, 1991

Shops and Shopping, by Alison Adburgham, Allen & Unwin, London, 2nd edn, 1981

Short Story Index, published annually with 5-year cumulations by H.W. Wilson, New York; 9 permanent retrospective volumes covering 1900–88; a single volume *Collections Indexed 1900–1978*

Slang Down the Ages, by Jonathon Green, Kyle Cathie, London, 1993

The Slang Thesaurus, by Jonathon Green, Penguin Books, Harmondsworth, 1988

Slang Today and Yesterday, by Eric Partridge, Routledge, London, 4th edn, 1970

A Social History of England, by Asa Briggs, Weidenfeld &

Nicolson, London, 1983; paperback edn, Penguin Books, Harmondsworth, 1987

Survey of English Dialects, by H. Orton and E. Dieth, introductory vol. and 4 regional vols, E.J. Arnold, Leeds, 1962–70

Survey of London, 41 vols to date, originally published by the LCC, subsequently by Athlone Press, London, 1900–

The Thesaurus of Slang, compiled by E. and A. Lewin, Facts on File, Oxford, 1988

They Saw It Happen series, published by Blackwell, Oxford; 4 vols covering 55BC–1940 (out of print)

The Times Atlas of World History, 4th edn, 1993; *Concise Times Atlas of World History*, 5th edn, 1994; HarperCollins, London, updated regularly

Titles and Forms of Address: A Guide to Correct Use, A & C Black, London, 19th edn, 1990

The Ultimate Guide to Science Fiction: An A–Z of Science Fiction Books by Title, by D. Pringle, Scolar Press, London, 1995

Useful Toil: Autobiographies of Working People from the 1820s to the 1970s, by John Burnett, Penguin Books, Harmondsworth, 1984

What It Cost the Day Before Yesterday Book, by H. Priestley, Kenneth Mason, Emsworth, 1979

Whitaker's Almanack, published annually by Whitaker, London

Willing's Press Guide, 2 vols, published annually by Reed Information Services, East Grinstead

Women's Diaries, Journals and Letters: An Annotated Bibliography, compiled by Cheryl Cline, Garland, New York and London, 1989

Women's Headdress and Hairstyles in England from AD600 to the Present Day, by G. de Courtais, Batsford, London, rev. edn, 1986

World Climate Disc, CD-ROM, Chadwyck-Healey, Cambridge, 1995

World Cruising Handbook, by Jimmy Cornell, A & C Black, London, 1991

World Historical Fiction Guide, compiled by D.D. McGarry and S. Harriman White, Scarecrow, Metuchen, N.J., 2nd edn, 1973

The World of the Forsytes, by John Fisher, Secker & Warburg, London, 1976

The World Weather Guide, by E.A. Pearce and C.G. Smith, Helicon, Oxford, 3rd edn, 1993

6

Biography and Autobiography

Biographical writing may consist of a short article on a celebrity, past or present, to be published perhaps in commemoration of a centenary or an eightieth birthday, or it may be a full-length study. It sometimes happens that a book grows out of the research undertaken for a newspaper or magazine article. Occasionally biographies are written of people who during their lifetime were neither renowned nor eminent, but whose papers (usually diaries or letters) make a unique contribution to the social history of their time. Autobiographies, whether of celebrities or of lesser mortals, are also of value, provided that they are well researched and well written and not mere exercises in self-promotion or name-dropping.

There is a growing trend for biographies to be written while their subjects are still alive, or very soon after their death; this may have something to do with the fear of the modern biographer that once the biographee and his contemporaries have gone, there may be little material to work on, seeing that letter-writing is a dying art and telephoning an increasing convenience. The academic view of such work, however, is that it constitutes a 'study' or 'profile' of the person concerned rather than a true biography, and that while the study or profile as such may prove to be of inestimable value to a future biographer, it is essential for a certain number of years to have elapsed before any life can be properly evaluated and seen in perspective to its time.

The autobiography of a well-known personality is often published at the peak of that person's career rather than towards the end of his or her life; subsequent volumes may follow. There is much to be said for starting to write your memoirs early on – or at least assembling the material – while the people you need to mention are alive and events fresh in your mind. You may not know at that stage whether you will achieve the status that merits a published autobiography, but if in the event you do not, then at least you will have written a piece of family history that can be handed down to the grandchildren. And if you deposit a copy with your local record office or at the Society of Genealogists in London, you will have made a worthwhile contribution towards the social history of the period for which future researchers and historians will be immensely grateful. Such documentation may be rather thin on the ground for researchers of the 21st century!

The author who embarks on a biographical project normally has some good reason for wanting to write it – kinship to the subject, or an intimate working relationship with him or her, and/or the possession of – and access to – original papers. Or, if a number of 'lives' have already been published on the person concerned, the writer may simply have a burning desire to write from a fresh angle, to 'set the record straight' or to throw new light on some controversial aspects as a result of recent research. It is generally accepted that the famous characters of history will stand new biographies every ten years.

Whatever the motive, it is advisable to try to get the work commissioned and – especially where a full-length book is envisaged – to secure a cash advance, for there will be a considerable amount of research to be undertaken and expenses to be met. In calculating the likely total costs, you should not forget to take into account your own working time. Out-of-pocket expenditure will include travel, meals away from home, postal and telephone charges, photocopying, photographs and stationery, at the very least; there may well be 'extras' such as library search fees, fees payable to a genealogist or research assistant, the cost of professional typing and indexing, reproduction fees for illustrations, and so on.

Before a publisher signs a contract, or parts with any money to a writer who is unknown to him, he will normally ask to see a synopsis, or maybe even a chapter or two, of the proposed work. The research that has to be done for the purposes of writing this synopsis is roughly the same as that required for a short biographical article: both must include the salient points of the life and mention the existence of any hitherto unpublished material and/or recent research that provide a new angle. It must be done in sufficient depth so as to convince the potential publisher that the book will be a good investment.

The writer who has reached this stage is bound to be familiar with the outline life of his subject. However, it may not be out of place to record here, as an *aide-mémoire*, the main sources open to biographers and to researchers seeking biographical information for use in other work.

The importance of researching 'in the round' has been stressed in an earlier chapter. In biographical research this is particularly important. It is essential to uncover the whole person, 'warts and all', so that at the research stage nothing should be avoided or glossed over or left unexplored. Motives for a person's actions may be discussed in the final work, and whether the biographer writes from a more or a less sympathetic angle is a matter of interpretation rather than one of research: this is a decision each individual writer must make once he has satisfied himself as to the true facts.

Private Papers

One good reason for allowing a certain amount of time to elapse before writing a biography is that there may not be access to private papers for a given number of years after a person's death; although the writer may have possession of his subject's own papers and the blessing of the family concerned to make use of them, it is very probable that some relevant material will be contained in the papers of others and that this may be subject to restrictions. Papers deposited in record offices and other archives are normally subject to the thirty-year closure rule or, in special cases, to an even longer period. Permission may be needed from the family or the estate before the documents may be seen. Although the copyright of correspondence belongs to the writer, the actual letters belong to the recipient or to his heirs or executors, or to anyone else who has acquired them; in practice, unless there is some good reason to the contrary, permission is usually forthcoming – but it may be stipulated that the text of the biography must be submitted before going to press. It is important always to make due acknowledgment to the source of such material and to comply with any request for prior submission of the text.

It is true that modern biographies *are* often written without the permission of the subject's family and thus without access to the private papers, but a writer who decides to embark on such a work should be fully aware beforehand of the difficulties that can arise. Quite apart from missing out on material and close family recollections and anecdotes, it may be less easy to obtain other people's help (there is no doubt that when seeking interviews or writing for information, magic phrases such as 'the official biography', 'sanctioned by the family', and so on, *do* carry weight and often swing the balance in the biographer's favour where someone is hesitant about supplying information). More serious can be the reaction of relatives to an 'unauthorised' biography, with the possibility that if they are seriously displeased they may seek an injunction through the courts.

The location of unpublished source material in general has been discussed in an earlier chapter (see pages 51–6). For the biographer needing to find out whether any private papers exist and, if so, their whereabouts, the first point of call must be the National Register of Archives, maintained by the Royal Commission on Historical Manuscripts at Quality House, Quality Court, Chancery Lane, London WC2A 1HP; enquiries should be made in person or in writing, or by fax (0171–831 3550) but not by telephone. The highly efficient catalogue and cross-referenced indexing system will enable the researcher to find out the precise location of correspondence and other papers on his subject. He should also consult the valuable *Guide to Sources for British History* series which the Commission has in progress, based on private papers and other unpublished information held in the National Register of Archives; the ten volumes published to date include guides to the papers of cabinet ministers, churchmen, colonial governors, diplomats, politicians and scientists (as listed on page 61).

The Department of Manuscripts in the British Library and the Public Record Office are both major sources. Many universities have important holdings. The National Maritime Museum at Greenwich has a comparatively recent manuscript collection of interest to the naval biographer. The Churchill Archives Centre at Churchill College, Cambridge is collecting papers of 20th-century politicians, scientists and both military and naval commanders. Use should also be made of the 'General Index to Collections' at the back of *British Archives: A Guide to Archive Resources in the United Kingdom.*

The papers of lesser-known persons are more difficult to track down. If you are not in touch with the family or cannot trace any relatives, and the local record office has no deposited papers, you may be able to trace executors or other persons likely to be in possession of a deceased person's papers through a will at Somerset House (see chapter 7, 'Family and Local History'). If you are writing a biography of someone who lived in the last fifty years, even if you do have access to family and private papers, an advertisement in the national or local press is recommended: many unexpected and valuable 'fish' are netted in this way, in the shape of replies from friends, teachers, colleagues, employees and others who have known or met the subject at some period of his life, and may well produce fascinating and very usable factual or anecdotal material of which you would otherwise remain unaware.

It is important to remember that the papers of even the most eminent public personages contain a certain amount of correspondence from people in lesser walks of life, and if you have reason to believe that the subject of your biography had dealings with someone whose papers have been catalogued and/or deposited, do not overlook this source. When researching for biographical information on professional people, it is always worth contacting the librarian or archivist of the relevant society or institution; some of these bodies hold collections of important private papers and most have biographical information that you may not find easily elsewhere, going back to the date of their foundation.

'Private papers' in this context are not limited to correspondence, but may consist of almost any kind of documentary material, such as account books, scrapbooks and photograph albums, visitors' books, personal diaries, and so on.

Printed and Other Sources

Biographical dictionaries

The major source of biographical information on nationals of this country is the *Dictionary of National Biography*, known to scholars, librarians and researchers as 'the *DNB*'. In the current edition there are twenty-two volumes containing entries in alphabetical sequence for the period up to 1900, and for the 20th century one volume per decade up to 1980 and one volume for 1981–85. There is also a *Missing Persons* volume containing entries for all those worthy persons 'omitted' from the main *DNB* from its beginning up to 1985. Also very useful is the *Chronological and Occupational Index to the DNB*. Few individuals can afford the money or the shelf space for the complete set, but the *Concise DNB*, in three volumes, should be in every writer's study: it contains entries for every person in the main *DNB*, with finding references to the relevant volume and page number, which you can then look up at the library. A CD-ROM of the complete *DNB* is now available (1995). Many foreign countries publish their own equivalent to the *DNB*: these are listed under 'Biography' in *Walford's Guide to Reference Material*, vol. 2, under each country.

An important and ongoing modern reference tool is the *Biographical Archive* series, which has a wide international, regional and occupational coverage and spans many centuries; it is marketed on microfiche with printed index volumes. The *British Biographical Archive (BBA)*, the first to be produced, in 1986, is now in its second series. There are similar *Archives* for America, Australia, Latin America, Africa and several European countries; also a *Jewish Biographical Archive*. More will follow. Indexes to the British, German, Spanish, Portuguese and Latin American *Archives* are contained in the first edition of the *World Biographical Database on CD-ROM*, which lists some 650,000 people.

The *Biography Index*, published by H.W. Wilson of New York, claims to be international, but has a definite American bias. More useful is the *Biography and Genealogy Master Index*, produced by Gale Research International of Detroit, USA, which, in its microfiche cumulative version, is available at most major libraries in the United Kingdom and is known as the 'Bio-Base'. Information is extracted from more than 600 English language biographical dictionaries and is regularly updated. Birth and death dates are stated, together with the source (in abbreviated form), which may be verified in an accompanying booklet.

With such massive modern tools at the researcher's disposal (see also the subheading 'Bibliographies' below), it seems unnecessary to list the many biographical dictionaries on offer. However, every writer needs at least one for quick reference. Outstanding among such compilations are *Chambers' Biographical Dictionary*, *The Cambridge Biographical Encyclopaedia*, and the *St James Guide to Biography*. The best quick reference for contemporary biography is *Who's Who*. There are also eight *Who Was Who* volumes containing entries for those who died during the years 1897–1990, and a *Cumulated Index* volume (1897–1990). The two Debrett volumes, *Distinguished People of Today* and *People of Today*, carry entries for a number of people who have not qualified for inclusion in *Who's Who*.

International reference works of contemporary biography include the *International Who's Who*, the *Dictionary of International Biography* and *Who's Who in International Affairs*. Many foreign countries publish their own *Who's Who* volumes; a selection of these are listed under individual countries in chapter 9 (see pages 146–61).

There are now biographical dictionaries and *Who's Who* volumes relating to almost every trade or profession from acting to zoology, some of which are published annually and others at irregular intervals. Readers will find some recommended titles listed by subject in Appendix I (see pages 185–97). These should be easily located in the reference library, or ask at the enquiry desk for them. The *Oxford Companion* series is another useful source of biographical information.

Encyclopedias are invaluable for quick reference, both for contemporary and historical lives; the articles are often followed by a brief bibliography which will lead the researcher on to other sources. The *Who's Who in British History* series covers the British Isles from Roman to Victorian times.

Bibliographies

If you want to find out whether a biography has been published about a particular individual, your best source is the British Library *Bibliography of Biography*, known for short as '*BoB*'; since 1992 this has been available on CD-ROM and is regularly updated. If you do not have access to this tool, try the *International Bibliography of Biography 1970–1987*, the *British National Bibliography* (*BNB*), and your own library's subject catalogue.

In Germany a massive international research tool, the *Index Bio-Bibliographicus Notorum Hominum*, is in progress. Of the 200 volumes planned, 61 have been published to date and will be found in most major reference libraries.

Most scholarly non-fiction works contain up-to-date bibliographies, and if you find there is a recently published study of your subject or of any of his close friends or contemporaries, it will probably be a good investment to buy rather than borrow such a book, so that you can keep it at your elbow and make notes and underlinings in it of special sources, people and places. If you cannot buy the book, then be sure to photocopy the bibliography – it will make an excellent starting point for your research. With luck, it will include references to newspaper and periodical articles. If it does not, you should make a search in the *British Humanities Index* or, if appropriate, one of the earlier subject indexes to periodicals mentioned in chapter 3 (see pages 46–7).

Obituaries

Obituaries are an excellent source and often the starting point for biographical research, since the more recent notices usually provide both an outline of a person's life and an evaluation of his career.

To find notices of people who died earlier than the mid-19th century, the six-volume *Musgrave's Obituary* is the first place to look; you should also use the *Indexes to the Biographical and*

Obituary Notices in the *Gentleman's Magazine* (the two volumes cover the years 1731–1819) and, if you know the approximate year of death, *The Annual Register*. For obituaries of prominent persons who have died since the early 1800s, *The Times* is the best source; in recent years as many as six hundred obituary notices have been printed annually in that paper. Provided you have an approximate date of death, a search in *The Times Index* should not take long, while for recent obituary notices there are now three published volumes, *Obituaries from The Times*, for the years 1951–60, 1961–70 and 1971–75. A more recent compilation, *Annual Obituary*, covers the years from 1980, one volume per year.

Not everyone you may expect to find in *The Times* has achieved an obituary there (much depends on how many other eminent people died the same day), and so the *Daily Telegraph*, the *Guardian* and the relevant local newspapers should be checked. The local paper of the area in which a person was resident often prints a notice that did not 'make' the nationals or one that goes into greater detail. Professional and trade journals, where appropriate, are especially useful for the evaluation of a person's career.

International notices, but with an American bias, are best checked in the *New York Times Obituaries Index*, from 1858, or in the *New York Times Personal Name Index*, from 1851. For notices relating to persons of other countries, look also at the relevant national paper.

Diaries, letters and memoirs

A great deal of information will be obtained about a person from the published diaries, letters or memoirs of his friends and contemporaries. As research progresses, therefore, it is an excellent plan to keep an ongoing list of all names that crop up and systematically to check these out at the library. Use the indexes to these books to locate the relevant passages. If you think there may be unpublished journals or correspondence, consult the National Register of Archives, as explained earlier in this chapter under the heading 'Private Papers'.

School and university records

School and university records provide excellent source-material, not only for details of a person's scholastic and academic achievement, but also for information concerning his extra-curricular activities (sports, drama, public-speaking, etc.) and – especially important – the names of his contemporaries and friends, school-masters and tutors. Should any of these people still be alive, they may have useful contributions to make and can usually be traced through the school or university, or – if they themselves have achieved eminence – in the current *Who's Who*.

The registers of many universities, schools and colleges in the United Kingdom have been printed. If the particular one you seek is not listed in the library catalogue, get in touch with the college or school secretary. Research of this nature may involve you in a visit to the educational establishment concerned, or you may be put in touch with the secretary of the relevant 'Old Boys' or 'Old Girls' association. Don't overlook the college or school magazines, as these will yield important information on your subject's contemporaries as well as (possibly) on his or her own classroom or sporting achievements. Addresses, with names of current headmasters and headmistresses, will be found in the *Independent Schools Yearbook* and the *Education Authorities Directory and Annual*. Universities and colleges are listed in *The World of Learning*. The registers of Oxford and Cambridge, *Alumni Oxonienses* and *Alumni Cantabrigienses*, and A.B. Emden's *Biographical Registers* of both these universities to 1500 are of special value to the historian, while the *Historical Registers* series for Oxford and Cambridge brings the records up to the present day.

Service records

You should encounter no great problem in obtaining details of a person's Service career. Records more than one hundred years old are held at the Public Record Office, where there are also complete runs of the *Army*, *Navy* and *Air Force Lists*; current volumes of these are usually available in all reference libraries.

Regimental histories are another good source and may be traced in the Society for Army Historical Research's *Bibliography of Regimental Histories*. J.M. Brereton's *Guide to the Regiments and Corps of the British Army* includes, along with other information, addresses of regimental headquarters to whom to write for further details. Another highly recommended book is G. Hamilton-Edwards' *In Search of Army Ancestry*. The Public Record Office leaflet no. 9, 'British Military Records as Sources for Biography and Genealogy', is obtainable on request from the PRO, Ruskin Avenue, Kew, Richmond, Surrey TW9 4DU.

So far as naval records are concerned, ask at the Public Record Office for handbook no. H22, 'Naval Records for Genealogists'.

The National Maritime Museum has published a useful list, *The Commissioned Sea Officers of the Royal Navy 1660–1815*; another informative source-book is the *Dictionary of British Ships and Seamen*.

The first port of call for research into Air Force records should be the Royal Air Force Museum (Department of Aviation Records, Grahame Park Way, Hendon, London NW9 5LL; tel. 0181–205 2266; fax 0181–200 1751).

The whereabouts of the records of all three Services can be ascertained from R. Higham's admirable *Guide to the Sources of British Military History*.

Business records

Details of a person's business career can often be obtained from the organization or company by whom he was employed. Naturally there are often restrictions on the amount of information that will be divulged to an outsider, but in special circumstances the researcher may be allowed access to the relevant files. Check first in the *Dictionary of Business Biography*, which contains entries for business people active in Britain in the period 1860–1980.

There may be a company history, either published or printed for private circulation, which will provide extremely useful background material. You can check this in the *International Directory of Company Histories* or the *International Bibliography of Business History*. Annual returns and other statutory documents, including lists of all directors and company secretaries, of public, private limited and guarantee companies may be inspected (on microfiche) at Companies House (Department of Trade and Industry), 55 City Road, London EC1Y 1BB (tel. 0171–253 9393) or at the Companies Registration Office, Crown Way, Maindy, Cardiff CF4 3UZ (tel. 01222 388588); a modest search fee is payable per file, and there are full photocopying facilities. The Business Archives Council, The Clove Building, 4 Maguire Street, London SE1 2NQ (tel. 0171–407 6110; fax 0171–234 0300), maintains a library and will advise researchers about records available; its Scottish counterpart, the Business Archives Council of Scotland, is at Glasgow University Archives and Business Records Centre, 13 Thurso Street, Glasgow GL11 6PE (tel. 0141–339 8855, ext. 6079; fax 0141–330 4158). Researchers may also make use of the British Library Business Information Service, which is currently at 25 Southampton Buildings, London WC2A 1AW (tel. 0171–412 7457; fax 0171–412 7453), but will move to St Pancras by 1997 (see page 70).

Members of Parliament and government officials

Dod's Parliamentary Companion, first published in 1832, is the indispensable British biographical source-book for the modern period. Earlier information will be found in the Institute of Historical Research series (nine volumes published to date), *Office Holders in Modern Britain*. There is one volume per ministry, some of the lists beginning in 1660 and covering the entire period up to 1870; in preparation are volumes on officials of Royal Commissions of Inquiry 1870–1939 and on officers of the Royal Household. Another good source is the four-volume *Members of Parliament*, in which you will find the names of all MPs in England from 1213 and in Scotland and Ireland from 1357 and 1559 respectively; the lists continue up to 1874, for the United Kingdom, and there is an index volume. For further information, or if you fail to find what you are seeking in printed sources, write to the Clerk of the Records at the House of Lords Record Office, House of Lords, London SW1A 0PW. For the location of private papers of Members of Parliament and selected public servants, consult *Sources in British Political History 1900–1951*, the Royal Commission on Historic Manuscripts' *Guide to Sources for British History*, volumes 1 and 7, and the *Guide to the Papers of British Cabinet Ministers 1900–1951*, published by the Royal Historical Society.

Public speeches and broadcasts

Speeches of significance are usually reported in the national press and may be traced in *The Times Index* either under the speaker's name or under the name of the society or conference addressed. The texts of Members' speeches in Parliament are printed in *Hansard: Parliamentary Debates* (separate series for the House of Commons and the House of Lords). Lectures or papers read before learned or professional bodies will normally be found in the transactions or proceedings of such institutions at a later date.

To check on broadcast or televised speeches and interviews, your best plan is first to contact the National Sound Archive, 29 Exhibition Road, London SW7 2AS (tel. 0171–412 7440; fax 0171–412 7441); an appointment will be made for you to listen to or view the relevant transmission, provided it is in their collections. (Note that the NSA includes a collection of Parliamentary sound recordings.) Once you have ascertained the date, it may be possible to obtain a transcript from the BBC Written Archives Centre at Caversham Park, Reading RG4 8TZ (tel. 01734

472742; fax 01734 461145) or the independent radio or television company. (The availability of transcripts is subject to certain copyright restrictions.)

Travel

Obtaining information about a person's travel may be unexpectedly complicated, where no diary or travelogue was kept. Hotel registers and shipping company records are not always retained for more than a few years, although it is always worth asking. (For example, the P. & O. Group's archives were deposited at the National Maritime Museum in Greenwich in the autumn of 1977.)

British Transport historical records are now at the Public Record Office in Kew, and so are the records of the former Board of Trade (now the Department of Trade and Industry) from *c.* 1890; the latter contain lists of all arrivals in, and departures from, the United Kingdom, but only a sample (roughly one-tenth) of passengers' lists and ships' logs, so that it is very much a matter of luck whether the information you seek will be obtainable. For more recent information you should write to the Department of Transport, Anchor House, Cheviot Close, Parc-ty-Glas, Llanishen, Cardiff CF4 5FU. Factual details such as dates of departure, ports of call, tonnage, and which company owns a particular vessel may be quite easily verified in *Lloyd's Shipping Index* or *Lloyd's Voyage Record*.

Further Research

Having cast your net, and hauled in your initial catch of material, your next task will be to sort the documentation into periods, or other natural chapters, of the life and, as you proceed, to make a note of any supplementary research to be undertaken. For a short biographical feature or the synopsis of a book, you can fairly safely rely on the standard or most recent work, plus your own special knowledge; but if you are embarking on a full-length biography you must go through and evaluate for yourself all the published material. It is a good idea to make index cards or slips for each book or article read, and to keep these in alphabetical sequence; this will take only a few minutes at the time and will be of immense value both for quick reference as you write and at the end of the day, when it comes to compiling the bibliography (see chapter 10, 'Preparation for the Press', pages 162–70).

Some professional help may be required for your chapter on family ancestry (see chapter 8, 'Specialist Research', pages 141–5) and if so, this should be arranged at the earliest possible moment, as good genealogists are frequently booked up for several months ahead. At the same time the question of employing outside researchers should also be carefully considered: where the source material is located at some distance from your home, or if it is essential to go through several years of a particular paper that is available only at the British Library Newspaper Library at Colindale, for instance, it may pay you to off-load part of the routine research and leave yourself free to tackle the more complicated aspects of the work.

Inevitably some travelling will be involved, and it makes sense to plan this so that several sources and/or interviews can be combined on each trip. A visit to the family home, if it still exists, is essential, and on such a visit time must be allowed for conversations with local inhabitants and – particularly important – with anyone close to the family who is still alive, such as a gardener, nanny or cook, where appropriate, or perhaps the vicar or local schoolmaster or publican. It goes without saying that this applies only when you are researching for biographies of people who are either still alive or recently deceased; in the case of subjects who were born earlier than the turn of the century, you have no choice but to rely on documentary sources such as the local newspaper or church magazine, or the records of any local societies with which the family is known to have been connected. The local librarian or secretary of the local historical society will usually be helpful in this respect, and you could strike lucky in that the descendants of an old family retainer may have cherished stories handed down verbally from one generation to the next, along with old photographs or other mementoes, so that any opportunity of visiting such people should always be taken up.

Corroboration of family births, marriages and deaths since 1837 can be obtained at the General Register Office, and of divorces (since 1852) and wills (since 1858) from the Principal Registry of the Family Division at Somerset House (for details and how to trace earlier records, see chapter 7, 'Family and Local History', pages 122–40). To verify the date of an engagement you may need to search the appropriate pages of *The Times*, *Daily Telegraph* or local paper; these papers will also carry reports of christenings, weddings, funerals and memorial services in the case of prominent members of society.

If the subject of your biography was involved in any major legal proceedings, you will be able to check this in the *All England*

Law Reports, which begin in 1558 and are indexed; or use *The Times Index* and look up the law report in that paper (these have been published since January 1788). Once you have the date of the court proceedings you can, if you require a more popular account or a 'sensational' headline to quote, then go to other newspapers of the same date.

Special Problems

The problems most likely to crop up during research for an autobiography or a biography are the following:

Names

In private correspondence and diaries people are often mentioned by nickname or given name only, and their identity may not be clear to you at the outset of research. It is an excellent idea to keep an alphabetical list or card index of everyone who crops up in the course of your work on a biography; apart from its value to you personally as a private 'who's who' of identification, it will come in very useful should any editorial note be required and also later on for the index. Among pitfalls to avoid are the danger of confusing titles (always check on which duke or earl you are referring to at any one time) and the various names by which a woman may be known during her life, due to a series of marriages and/or divorces and the possibility that she may have reverted to her maiden name for professional or other reasons. To add to the confusion, titled persons are sometimes referred to by title and sometimes by surname, which may not be the same.

Dating letters

Letters all too frequently present the biographer with unforeseen problems. Far too many people had (and still have) the habit of dating their correspondence 'Thursday', 'Sunday, 12th' or 'Amsterdam, Monday', or – which is worse from the researcher's point of view – of not dating them at all. You should also be aware that some individuals are prone to stuff free hotel or club stationery into their briefcases and to use it weeks or even months later, so that although such correspondence may be dated, you cannot be absolutely certain that the writer was actually resident at the hotel or club at the time: if there is any doubt at all in your mind on this score, try to verify the date and/or place in another source.

Some expert detective work will sometimes be needed before you can establish the correct chronological sequence of a bundle of correspondence. The most obvious clues are: the address from which the letter is, or is alleged to be, written; the person to whom it is written; the subject-matter. Look also at the hand-writing; the ink; the paper: should there be a watermark, this will not give you the precise date of the letter, but it will provide firm evidence that the document cannot have been written earlier than the date of the watermark.

If, on first reading, a letter does not appear to offer any clue of this kind, do not despair. Re-examine it closely for mention of any family, national or world event – perhaps the death of a well-known person, an exhibition or play seen, a new novel read, and so on, the dates of which can then be checked out in the national press, *Whitaker's Almanack* and other sources. Letters that you cannot even guess at dating should be kept apart from the rest; sooner or later, as work progresses, you are more than likely to stumble on some information (nearly always when you are not looking for it) that will enable you to slot such letters into their right sequence. The use of the *Handbook of Dates for Students of English History* for checking the day of the week of given dates has been explained on page 87.

Handwriting is a great revealer of character, and in recent years more and more biographers have sought the help of trained graphologists (a trend which has spread from France). However, you should not be tempted to try to do it yourself with the aid of any one of a number of books on the subject, entertaining as many of them are (on doodles, for example), as you could go very wrong. It takes up to twenty years to qualify as a profes-sional graphologist; there are currently only fifty in the United Kingdom with an internationally recognised diploma. Mary Nicholson, at The Graphology Business, 97 Claxton Grove, London W6 8HB (tel. 0171–385 3940; fax 0171–610 2558) heads a team of qualified graphologists whose fees range from £40 to £300, depending upon the depth of study required. Read her article, 'Graphology and the Biographer' in *The Author*, winter 1994. If you decide to ask for an analysis, be sure to send a selec-tion of letters or other documents of varying dates.

Verbal information

It is beyond the scope of this chapter to examine in detail all the possibilities open to the biographical researcher, but if the basic principle is followed of taking each natural phase of the life in turn, verifying dates and events in printed and other records and supplementing the documentary material with the recollections of contemporaries wherever obtainable, you will not go far wrong. A word of warning about the use of verbal information, however: human nature being what it is, people do frequently tend to try to enhance their own status (either in the researcher's eyes or their own or with a view to their name appearing in print) by exaggerating their intimacy or acquaintance with a well-known person, and memories in general are, sadly, far from infallible. Similarly with autobiography. How many of us can rely on being able to recall with 100 per cent accuracy the exact sequence of events in a particular week or how passionately we felt about something or someone, say, twenty or more years ago? We *think* we remember. But *do* we – *truthfully*? Imagining how it was is a poor substitute for the comment recorded at the time. The human memory plays strange tricks. Try always, therefore, to make a point of double-checking any story that is told to you or any event you think you remember. If you cannot verify it from a reliable printed source, try to get corroboration from a second person. Confidences must, of course, be respected at all times, and care must be taken to avoid giving offence to relatives or other persons who are still alive. Where private individuals have been especially helpful or informative, it is good manners to let them see the draft text before going to press, and to acknowledge their assistance in the book.

There is considerable concern among British biographers as to the implication of the Lord Chancellor's consultation paper, 'The Infringement of Privacy' (1993), which, should it become law as it stands, will curtail drastically the writer's freedom to make, and the publisher's to publish, any statement that might be construed as causing 'substantial distress' to relatives or descendants. No one will shed a tear over the passing of the offensive unauthorised type of biography or the intrusive antics of certain 'investigative' journalists. But there is bound to be much heated debate before responsible biographers relinquish their traditional liberty to portray their subjects 'warts and all'. We must await developments.

Air Force List, published annually since 1949 by HMSO, London
All England Law Reports: reprint 1558–1935, 36 vols + index, published 1966–68; since 1936 weekly, with 4 bound vols and cumulative index annually, Butterworth Publishers, London
Alumni Cantabrigienses: A Biographical List of all known

Students, Graduates and Holders of Office to 1900, by J. and J.A. Venn, 10 vols, Cambridge University Press, 1940–54; Kraus reprint, 1974

Alumni Oxonienses: The Members of the University of Oxford 1500–1886, by J. Foster, 8 vols, Parker, Oxford, 1888–92; Kraus reprint, 1968

Annual Obituary, published since 1981 by St James Press, previously London, now Detroit

The Annual Register of World Events, published 1758–1994 by Longman, London, since 1995 by Pearson Professional, Southport; 'Obituary' chapter

Army List, now published bi-annually by HMSO, London (first published 1814; an earlier series from 1754 may be seen at the PRO, Kew)

Bibliography of Biography (*BoB*), British Library CD-ROM, 1992; updated regularly

Bibliography of Regimental Histories, compiled by A.S. White, Society for Army Historical Research with The Army Museums Ogilby Trust, London, 1965 (now out of print, but the library of the National Army Museum, Royal Hospital Road, London SW3 4HT (tel. 0171–730 0717) maintains a regularly updated interleaved version)

Biographical Archive, ongoing international series published on microfiche by Saur, Munich; printed index volumes

Biographical Register of the University of Cambridge to 1500, by A.B. Emden, Cambridge University Press, Cambridge, 1963

Biographical Register of the University of Oxford to 1500, by A.B. Emden, 3 vols, Oxford University Press, Oxford, 1957–59; reissued 1989. *Supplement 1501–1540*, 1974

Biography and Genealogy Master Index ('Bio-Base'), 8 vols, Gale Research International, Detroit, 1980; updated regularly on microfiche

Biography Index, published by H.W. Wilson, New York, since 1946; now quarterly, with annual and 2-year cumulative volumes; available online and CD-ROM since July 1984

British Archives: A Guide to Archive Resources in the United Kingdom, by Janet Foster and Julia Sheppard, Macmillan, London, 3rd edn, 1995

British Biographical Archive (*BBA*), on microfiche, with 4 vols printed index, Saur, Munich, 1984–88; Series II, 1991–94

British Humanities Index (*BHI*), published quarterly 1963–89, with annual cumulations, by the Library Association, London, and from January 1990 by Bowker-Saur, East Grinstead; since 1985 available on CD-ROM as *BHI Plus*

'British Military Records as Sources for Biography and Genealogy', Public Record Office leaflet no. 9, PRO, London

British National Bibliography (*BNB*), weekly since 1950, with cumulative monthly, annual and some 5-yearly volumes; now published by the British Library, London; also available on microfiche, CD-ROM and online (BLAISE-LINE)

The Cambridge Biographical Encyclopedia, ed. David Crystal, Cambridge University Press, Cambridge, 1994

Chambers' Biographical Dictionary, first published 1897; 5th edn (ed. M. Magnusson), Chambers Harrap, Edinburgh, 1990; reprinted 1993, and now available in revised paperback

The Commissioned Sea Officers of the Royal Navy 1660–1815, National Maritime Museum, London, 1954

Debrett's Distinguished People of Today, Debrett's Peerage, London, 1988

Debrett's People of Today, published by Debrett's Peerage, London, annually from 1990

Dictionary of British Ships and Seamen, by G. Uden and R. Cooper, Allen Lane, Harmondsworth, 1980

Dictionary of Business Biography, ed. David J. Jeremy, 5 vols, Butterworth, London, 1984–86

Dictionary of International Biography, published since 1963; 23rd edn, Melrose Press, Cambridge, 1994

Dictionary of National Biography (*DNB*): to 1900, 22 vols, Oxford University Press, London, 1885–1900; 8 later vols, each covering 10 years, for the period 1901–1980, published 1912–86; *DNB 1981–1985*, published 1990. *The Concise DNB*, to 1985, 3 vols, 1992. *A Chronological and Occupational Index to the DNB*, 1985. *Missing Persons*, 1993. CD-ROM edition of complete *DNB*, 1995

Dod's Parliamentary Companion, published annually since 1832 by Dod's Parliamentary Companion Ltd, Hurst Green, East Sussex

Education Authorities Directory and Annual, published by the School Government Publishing Company, Redhill

Gentleman's Magazine: Index to the Biographical and Obituary Notices, 2 vols: *1731–1780*, British Record Society, London, 1891; *1781–1819*, by B. Nangle, Garland Publishing, New York and London, 1980

'Graphology and the Biographer', by Mary Nicholson, *The Author*, winter 1994

Guide to the Papers of British Cabinet Ministers 1900–1951, compiled by C. Hazelhurst and C. Woodland, Royal Historical Society, London, 1974

Guide to the Regiments and Corps of the British Army, by J.M. Brereton, Bodley Head, London, 1985

Guide to the Sources of British Military History, ed. R. Higham, Routledge, London, 1972; supplement, ed. G. Jordan, Garland, New York and London, 1988

Guide to Sources for British History, Royal Commission on Historical Manuscripts, HMSO, London, in progress since 1982, 10 vols to date (listed in full on page 61)

Handbook of Dates for Students of English History, ed. C.R. Cheney, Royal Historical Society, London, 1978; latest reprint published by Cambridge University Press for the Society, 1995; new edition in preparation

Hansard: Parliamentary Debates, 1803 onwards; now published daily during sessions by HMSO, London. Chadwyck-Healey, Cambridge, publishes various series of Parliamentary Papers from 1715 on microfilm, microfiche and CD-ROM; also on CD-ROM *Hansard Indexes 1803–1941* and a quarterly *Index to Current Parliamentary Papers* (House of Commons)

Historical Register series (Universities of Cambridge and Oxford): Cambridge University Press and Oxford University Press respectively

In Search of Army Ancestry, by G. Hamilton-Edwards, Phillimore, Chichester, 1977

Independent Schools Yearbook (Boys' Schools, Girls' Schools, Coeducational Schools and Preparatory Schools), published annually by A & C Black, London

Index Bio-Bibliographicus Notorum Hominum, Biblio Verlag, Osnabrück, in progress, 1972– (61 vols to date)

International Bibliography of Biography 1970–1987, published by Bowker, New Providence, N.J., 12 vols, 1988

International Bibliography of Business History, Routledge, London, 1995

International Directory of Company Histories, St James Press, formerly London, now Detroit, in progress, 1988– (12 vols to date)

International Who's Who, published annually by Europa Publications, London

Jewish Biographical Archive, on microfiche, Saur, Munich, 1994–96

Lloyd's Shipping Index, first published in 1880, now weekly by Lloyd's of London Press, Colchester, Essex

Lloyd's Voyage Record, published weekly since 1946 by Lloyd's of London Press, Colchester, Essex

Members of Parliament, 4 vols: I–II, *England 1213–1702*; III, *Great Britain 1705–1796*, *United Kingdom 1801–1874*,

> *Scotland 1357–1707, Ireland 1559–1800*; IV, *Index*, HMSO, London, 1878–91
>
> *Musgrave's Obituary prior to 1800*, ed. Sir G.J. Armytage, 6 vols, Harleian Society, London, 1899–1901
>
> 'Naval Records for Genealogists', Public Record Office Handbook H22, PRO, London, 1988
>
> *Navy List*, published annually since 1814 by HMSO, London (earlier listings at PRO, Kew)
>
> *New York Times Obituaries Index*, from 1858; cumulative volumes 1858–1968 and 1969–79, Glen Rock, N.J., now annually by Mecklen Corporation, N.Y.
>
> *New York Times Personal Name Index 1851–1974*; supplement *1975–1984*, compiled by B.A. and V.R. Falk, Roxbury Data, Succasunna, N.J.
>
> *Obituaries from The Times*, 3 vols covering the period 1951–75, Research Publications International, Reading, 1975–79; no later vols
>
> *Office Holders in Modern Britain*, Institute of Historical Research, London, 9 vols, 1972–84; 2 further vols in preparation
>
> *Oxford Companion* series (over 40 titles), Oxford University Press, Oxford, regularly revised; some paperback editions
>
> *St James Guide to Biography*, St James Press, Detroit, 1991
>
> *Sources in British Political History, 1900–1951*, ed. Chris Cook, Macmillan, London, 6 vols, 1985
>
> *The Times Index*, first published 1790; now monthly with annual cumulations, Research Publications International, Reading; *Palmer's Index to The Times, 1790–1905*, on CD-ROM, Chadwyck-Healey, Cambridge
>
> *Walford's Guide to Reference Material*, vol. 2, Library Association, London, 6th edn, 1994
>
> *Whitaker's Almanack*, published annually by Whitaker, London
>
> *Who Was Who*, published by A & C Black, London, 8 vols to date, covering the period 1897–1990; *Cumulated Index 1897–1990*, 1991
>
> *Who's Who*, published annually by A & C Black, London
>
> *Who's Who in British History*, ed. Geoffrey Treasure, Shepheard Walwyn, London, 6 vols to date, 2 more scheduled for 1996; some paperback editions
>
> *Who's Who in International Affairs*, Europa Publications, London, 1990
>
> *World Biographical Database on CD-ROM*, Saur, Munich, 1st edn, 1994
>
> *The World of Learning*, published annually by Europa Publications, London

Note: Space does not permit a full listing of the *Who's Who* volumes for the various professions and foreign countries, of which there are now over 70 titles published by different firms; the researcher should have no difficulty in tracing these in the major library cataloguing systems. Selected titles are listed in chapter 9 under country and by subject in Appendix I.

7

Family and Local History

In recent years people have become increasingly interested in tracing their own family ancestry. Largely as a result of teaching in schools and evening classes, many students embark on a local or family history project which they later wish to develop into a full-length study. Biographers and authors of historical novels also need to do some research in this field, and some of the problems they are likely to encounter have been outlined in chapters 4 and 6, 'Factual and Historical Research' and 'Biography and Autobiography'.

The first thing to be said is that research for family or local history can be exceedingly complex. For those who look on it as a hobby and for whom time is no object, it will be a lengthy and often frustrating, but always in the end rewarding, task. Writers with publishers' press deadlines to meet, and who need only certain facts to fill out their work – for example, ancestral research for the first chapter of a biography, or the tracing of a particular will, or the detail of some event in a certain parish needed for an historical novel – should consider using the services of a professional genealogist or record agent (see 'Specialist Research', pages 141–5). Those who wish to undertake their own research in this field should be prepared to do a considerable amount of preliminary study so as to familiarise themselves with the classes of records available and the kind of information to be derived from them.

Space does not permit to do more here than suggest the major sources of information, as well as some of the standard textbooks on genealogy and local archives. Most adult education centres run courses on local history and genealogy, but very few on palaeography (the study of old handwriting). For details of a comprehensive course, leading to a diploma, that may be followed on a full- or part-time basis, or as a correspondence course, write to the Registrar, the Institute of Heraldic and Genealogical Studies, 79–82 Northgate, Canterbury, Kent CT1 1BA (tel. 01227 768664; fax 01227 765617).

The Society of Genealogists, 14 Charterhouse Buildings, Goswell Road, London EC1M 7BA (tel. 0171–251 8799) periodically organizes day conferences and lectures for beginners (members only). Members of the Society have free use of the library, with its unique collection of printed, manuscript, microfiche and microfilmed material, free attendance at lectures and the benefit of a reduced rate for research carried out by members of the staff; they also receive a quarterly journal, *Genealogists' Magazine*. The society's other quarterly periodical, *Computers in Genealogy*, is offered to members at a reduced subscription. A leaflet, 'Using the Library of the Society of Genealogists', is available. The writer who intends to do any extensive genealogical research, and who lives in or with good access to London, will find membership very worthwhile. Non-members may use the library on payment of a small fee, currently £3.00 for one hour, £7.50 for four hours, £10.00 for a day, or a day and evening, and may subscribe to both publications.

There are family history societies and local history groups in most counties of the United Kingdom. Subscriptions are modest, and members benefit from advice on their researches as well as the exchange of information with fellow genealogists and historians. An up-to-date list of these societies, giving the secretaries' names and addresses, is available on receipt of a first-class stamped addressed envelope or two international reply coupons from the Administrator, Federation of Family History Societies (FFHS), c/o Benson Room, Birmingham & Midland Institute, Margaret Street, Birmingham B3 3BS.

A subscription to the Guild of One-Name Studies, which is closely associated with the Society of Genealogists and the FFHS, would be worthwhile in the long term, but probably not if you are engaged on a 'one-off' search for the ancestry chapter of one book. Members receive a quarterly journal, *One-Name Studies*, and also a Register listing the names that are currently being researched worldwide, with the name and address of a 'registered member' to contact for information on each name. A select bibliography is in preparation. Members may register a name for a small fee, provided it has not already been registered; but when you do this, you give an undertaking to deal with all reply-paid enquiries about that name – so consider carefully before you commit yourself (it could be a drain on your writing time!). The Hon. Secretary of the Guild may be contacted at Box 6, 14 Charterhouse Buildings, Goswell Road, London EC1M 7BA.

The leading publishers of family and local history in this country are Phillimore & Co. Ltd, Shopwyke Manor Barn,

Chichester, W. Sussex PO20 6BG (tel. 01243 787636; fax 01243 787639). The Phillimore bookshop, at the same address, also stocks titles from other publishers and will supply books by post. Ask to be put on the catalogue mailing list. Both the Society of Genealogists and the FFHS publish handbooks and leaflets to assist the amateur family and local historian (the FFHS list includes the popular 'Gibson' and 'McLaughlin' guides).

Among a number of journals of interest are *Family History News and Digest*, published twice a year (spring and autumn) by the FFHS; *Family Tree Magazine*; and *The Local Historian* (formerly *The Amateur Historian*). A subscription to the annual *Genealogical Research Directory* entitles you to register up to fifteen names in which you are interested; the book is circulated throughout the world and may eventually bring you the bonus of an exchange of information with other subscribers.

Using County Record Offices, Archaeological Societies and Other Collections

The writer embarking on a family or local history should first of all visit his local record office, where the archivist or an assistant archivist will usually be glad to discuss the project and to explain what records are available. Some county record offices publish useful pamphlets for students on how to trace the history of a parish or of a family, and most have a printed or microfiche guide to their collections, as well as regularly updated lists of parish registers and other documents that have been deposited.

A short list of record offices will be found in Appendix I, but more detailed information is given in the pamphlet *Record Repositories in Great Britain*. An excellent guide is J.S.W. Gibson and P. Peskett's *Record Offices: How to Find Them*. The Federation of Family History Societies' *Never Been Here Before?* is a most helpful guide for researchers unfamiliar with the PRO. Another useful tool is Stella Colwell's *Dictionary of Genealogical Sources in the Public Record Office*.

The principal public libraries have local history collections, and those of local archaeological societies are usually open to *bona fide* researchers (non-members may be asked to pay a modest search fee). Where information is needed from outside your own district, it is always worth sending a preliminary letter (with self-addressed stamped envelope) to the local archivist or chief reference librarian. Most county archivists are happy to answer simple enquiries, such as the verification of not more than one or two entries in a parish register (a baptism, marriage or burial), but especially nowadays, owing to the severe cutback in local government expenditure, staff are not available to undertake extensive searches. However, advice will always be given on the records to consult, as well as practical help over any problems encountered in the search room; and most county record offices will, on request, also supply the names and addresses of local record agents. Occasionally a record office or public library will offer to do research for you, on a fee-paying basis; however, it has to be said that you will almost certainly obtain results faster by employing a freelance record agent direct. You should nevertheless always enquire on your first visit whether there is any member of staff who happens to have a special knowledge of, or interest in, your subject. Photocopies and photographs of most documents are usually obtainable.

A list of local archaeological societies, with names and addresses of secretaries, will be found in *Whitaker's Almanack*.

Family History

A family history may have as its starting point a rough tree drawn up by a relative or ancestor, or – if you are lucky – a more professional pedigree and possibly also a collection of papers handed down from one generation to another or recently discovered in an attic of the ancestral home. The first thing to do is to make reasonably sure that a history has not already been written or a tree drawn up. This can be checked in one of several ways: in the catalogue or subject index of one of the copyright libraries; at the library of the Society of Genealogists; at the College of Arms; at the local record office nearest to the family home. Remember that many family histories are privately printed or may have been deposited at the record office, or donated to the local library, in typescript.

If the family is likely to have been recorded in any of Burke's publications, the place to look is *Burke's Family Index*. This useful volume has references to some twenty thousand different family histories.

The next step is to verify, one by one, the dates of all births, marriages and deaths, and – other people's memories being what they are – also to check the names, allowing for variations in spelling. The usual procedure is to work methodically backwards in time, either from yourself or from the person you are writing about, first to the parents, then the grandparents, and so on, generation by generation. If you are fortunate enough to own a personal computer, you could invest in some specially designed software to help you store and sort the fruits of your research. Alternatively, set up a card index system, with a separate card for each individual, on which you enter each piece of information as it is verified; or there are specially printed genealogical record cards or 'research work-books' on the market (available from the Society of Genealogists, among others).

You can draw up your own draft family tree as you proceed; but if the tree is to be published, it is best to have it professionally drawn.

Terrick Fitzhugh's *How to Write a Family History* is highly recommended reading.

Verifying births, marriages and deaths

Since 1 July 1837 all births, marriages and deaths in England and Wales, together with some overseas (consular) and service returns, births and deaths at sea, etc. have been centrally recorded at the General Register Office in London. Formerly at Somerset House, these records are now permanently at St Catherine's House, 10 Kingsway, London WC2B 6JP. In Scotland registration began in 1855, the records being housed at the office of the Registrar General, New Register House, Edinburgh EH1 3YT. In Ireland, the records from 1864 to 1921 are at the office of the Registrar General, Joyce House, 8–11 Lombard Street East, Dublin 2, for the whole of the country and for the Republic since 1922; Northern Ireland records dating from partition are in the care of the Registrar General, Oxford House, 49–55 Chichester Street, Belfast BT1 4HL.

Searches may be made in person at St Catherine's House but access is only to the indexes, not to the actual registers. The index volumes are arranged according to the quarter of the year in which the event (birth, marriage or death) was registered, and alphabetically under surnames. Unless you have an approximate date to go on, you must be prepared for a long haul – and an exhausting one, as pulling out one heavy volume after another is exceedingly tiring. The information printed in the indexes is minimal, so that sometimes you may not be certain that you have found the correct entry; but if you request a copy of the relevant certificate and the parentage and/or spouse does not match with the information you have to give on the application form, a refund will be made. As full certificates now cost £6.00 apiece, this is an important consideration. (There is a shorter form of certificate

– available for births only – but this is not normally sufficient for genealogical research purposes as it contains only the name, sex, date and place, but *not* the parentage.)

It is always worth getting copies of birth, marriage and death certificates, as the detail given on them, such as the occupation of a child's father, the witnesses to a marriage, the cause of death and the address at which it occurred, will be invaluable and may lead you on to other channels of enquiry. For those who live a long way from London (or Edinburgh, Dublin or Belfast), copies of certificates may be obtained by post, in which case a higher fee is charged (currently £12 if you supply references or £15 without references; this includes a search carried out by staff over a five-year period). Certificates ordered in person are available for collection after four working days; those requested by post will take three to six weeks. There may be slight variations between the different registries. It all sounds very involved to the uninitiated, but Eve McLaughlin's booklet *St Catherine's House* will give you confidence.

A useful starting point for family history research is the Hyde Park Family History Center of the Church of Jesus Christ of Latter-Day Saints (known more familiarly as the Mormon Church), at 64–68 Exhibition Road, London SW7 2PA (tel. 0171–589 8561). The Library of the London Mission is open to all, but you should make an appointment in advance to use one of their computers. You will then be able to use the Family History Library Catalog, searching under both locality and surname to ascertain which records in the library contain the information likely to help you. Among other research tools at the Center are the Ancestral File and the mammoth International Genealogical Index (IGI) of some 187 million names, mostly birth and baptismal (but also some marriage) entries dating from the early 1500s. The complete world listing of the IGI has been updated on computer to 1993 and may be searched at the Center, where, if you feed in a family name and a county, you can obtain a print-out for 5p (this has to be the best value in London!). The microfiche edition (1992) of the IGI is also available at the Library of the Society of Genealogists; most record offices and some public libraries hold sections relating to their own localities. Entries are arranged alphabetically by surname within each county. Time-saving as this great research tool is, users of the IGI should note that it is neither comprehensive nor, sadly, 100 per cent accurate: coverage and accuracy do vary from county to county, and the information should always be double-checked in original sources.

Nonconformist registers were required by law to be surrendered to the Registrar General in 1840, and these are now at the Public Record Office. (Some registers were exempt – where they were kept in the same books as other records, such as members' lists, minutes of meetings, etc. – and you may be lucky enough to find them at local record offices.) The Religious Society of Friends, before surrendering their records, prepared 'Digest Registers' which, together with other valuable Quaker material, may be seen at Friends' House, Euston Road, London NW1 2BJ (tel. 0171–387 3601). Records of Huguenots in England since the mid-16th century have been published by the Huguenot Society, University College, Gower Street, London WC1E 6BT (tel. 0171–380 7094). For further information on the existence and whereabouts of Nonconformist registers, see *Sources for Nonconformist Genealogy and Family History* (volume 2 of the *National Index of Parish Registers*).

Researchers seeking material on Roman Catholic or Jewish families should look at volume 3 of the same series, *Sources for Roman Catholic and Jewish Genealogy and Family History.*

Parish registers

Ministers in England were first ordered to keep records of all baptisms, marriages and burials in 1538; some registers therefore start in that year, but others were not commenced until a few years later or the earliest volumes have not survived. Not all parish registers have been deposited at the relevant local record office, but recent legislation provides that clergy who do not have adequate facilities for preservation and storage must deposit them within a reasonable time.

The best way to find out whether or not a particular parish register has been deposited is to telephone to the local record office; with new registers being deposited all the time, the situation is constantly changing. If the record office does not have what you require – and often they will not have registers of recent date – they will give you the name and telephone number of the incumbent in whose possession the relevant registers are, or you can look this up in the current *Crockford's Clerical Directory.* To obtain access to these registers, you must write or telephone to make an appointment, as either the minister or his parish clerk must be present. A fee is payable to the incumbent for this service: based either on the time spent or on the number of years searched, this is no longer standard, but you can expect to be asked for up to £5 per hour. If you are making a long search, you will normally be able to negotiate a special rate. To avoid any difficulty, it is wise to establish the fee before you make the appointment. (N.B. If you cannot get to the vestry yourself and the incumbent agrees to do the search for you, he is entitled to charge a higher fee.)

It is as well to remember that directories such as *Crockford's* go to press months ahead of publication and cannot therefore be totally up to date. (The same, alas, applies to this book.) To avoid your letter of enquiry being forwarded on to another parish, should the incumbent listed have moved (which at best will cause delay and may mean that you never receive a reply), it is wise to address it impersonally, i.e. to 'The Incumbent', 'The Rector' or 'Vicar'.

It is important for the novice researcher to remember that parish registers do not give the exact dates of birth or death, but only those of baptism and burial. (Some of the more diligent parish priests also noted the dates of births and deaths, but not often.) In some parishes there are separate registers for baptisms, marriages and burials; in others, the baptisms and burials may be recorded in the same book, starting at different ends, and where the incumbent ran out of space the entries are sometimes continued a few pages later or, worse, may be merged – be careful not to overlook these.

Many registers have been transcribed and/or printed, and the Society of Genealogists issues a very useful booklet: *Parish Register Copies in the Library of the Society of Genealogists*. The *National Index of Parish Registers*, a vast project started over twenty years ago, is now periodically revising or reprinting some of its earlier volumes. The first three volumes of the *Index* constitute a guide to the pre-1837 registers of all denominations in England, Scotland and Wales; the final two volumes deal with sources for Scottish genealogy and family history and the parish registers of Wales respectively. Seven regional volumes have been published so far; others are in progress. *The Phillimore Atlas and Index of Parish Registers* is the best quick reference tool.

Other useful sources, especially when it is difficult to gain access to the registers, are Bishop's Transcripts (copies of parish registers made by each minister and sent annually to the Bishop of his diocese). Unfortunately these are not altogether reliable and indeed are sometimes different, as entries were often copied wrongly, or even omitted. It is essential to make a double-check in the original registers.

Marriage indexes

Boyd's Marriage Index, compiled by Mr Percival Boyd from parish registers, Bishop's Transcripts and the marriage licences of

England, covers most of the English counties in the period 1538–1837. It contains more than 3½ million names and is housed at the Society of Genealogists in London; a booklet published by the Society and entitled *List of Parishes in Boyd's Marriage Index* gives the dates for each parish included. This is an important source for the researcher who already knows the place or county of the marriage he wishes to trace. However, it is neither complete nor infallible (Mr Boyd died in 1955), and entries should always be verified in the relevant parish register. This is a golden rule in genealogical research when using any printed or transcribed registers or indexes.

Another important marriage index is *Pallot's*, containing some 4½ million marriages between 1780 and 1837; this is held at the Institute of Heraldic and Genealogical Studies in Canterbury. Enquiries may be sent by post, and searches will be made on a fee-paying basis, currently (1995) £12 for one entry, £18 for up to twenty entries.

There are also a number of local marriage indexes compiled both by family history groups and by individuals, and more are in progress. Ask at your local record office, or consult the FFHS booklet, *Marriage, Census and Other Indexes for Family Historians*.

Marriage registers generally are separate from those of baptisms and burials; some are more informative than others. Supplementary information may be obtained from records of the intention to marry, such as banns, licences, marriage bonds and allegations. Advice on the availability of these will be given by staff on duty in the record office.

Divorce records

The Divorce Registry at Somerset House, Strand, London WC2R 1LP, holds records of all divorces since 1852 and will supply photocopies of decrees. These are useful to the researcher, as they give the date and place of the marriage.

Wills and administrations

Probate records constitute one of the most useful sources of genealogical information. Since 11 January 1858 copies of all wills and administrations in England and Wales have been centralised at the Principal Registry of the Family Division at Somerset House (address as above); they are calendared alphabetically under surnames in the year in which probate was granted (which may be the same as the year of death, but is sometimes later). The calendar volumes are on open shelves, and once you have traced the will or administration you need, the volume containing it will be produced on demand. Brief notes may be made (in pencil), or alternatively a photocopy ordered.

Prior to 1858 wills and administrations were proved by the courts which had general jurisdiction, of which the most important were the Prerogative Court of Canterbury (PCC) and the Prerogative Court of York (PCY). The PCC wills are likely to remain at the Public Record Office in Chancery Lane, London, during most of 1996 but will later be transferred to Kew. PCY wills are at the Borthwick Institute, York. Consult your local record office for details of other courts.

As a general guide the researcher should first consult J.S.W. Gibson's *Wills and Where to Find Them*, which discusses the availability of probate records in each English county and also explains the jurisdiction of the different courts, as well as the systems operating in Scotland, Ireland, the Channel Islands and the Isle of Man. For PCC wills the best tool is *An Index to the Wills proved in the Prerogative County of Canterbury 1750–1800* edited by Anthony J. Camp, Director of Research of the Society of Genealogists. The latter's *Wills and Their Whereabouts* is a standard guide and Eve McLaughlin's *Wills before 1858* is a useful introduction.

Census returns

The 19th-century census returns are a valuable source for the family historian and may be seen on microfilm in the Census Room of the Public Record Office, now in the basement of the Chancery Lane building. A decision has not yet (1995) been taken as to whether or not they will be transferred to Kew; because of their importance it is probable that in this event copies will be retained in central London. Returns exist from 1801, but individual names were not recorded until 1841. As census records are subject to a 101-year rule, the most recent return available for public inspection is that of 1891. Do not be misled by the CD-ROM on the market claiming to contain the 1991 census: it consists only of the statistics, *not* the names and addresses and occupations that are of such value to the family historian.

Any member of the public may have access to the census records. A PRO reader's ticket is not required.

The great value of the census to the genealogist is that he will usually find the whole family (or at least those living under the

131

same roof at the appropriate date) recorded together. The returns of 1851 onwards are the most informative, since they give exact ages and places of birth, and also each person's marital status and relationship to the household, whereas the 1841 census return states only their occupations, in what area of the country they were born and, for those over fifteen, ages to the lowest term of five.

It is of course essential to know, if not the exact address at which the family is believed to have been living at the date of the census, at least the parish. The relevant dates are:

    6 June 1841
    30 March 1851
    7 April 1861
    2 April 1871
    3 April 1881
    5 April 1891

Index books are on open shelves in the Census Room, in which you can look up the number of the book and the enumerator's district; this helps you to locate the precise place on the spool. Most towns are now street-indexed. There are pitfalls in that streets may appear half in one enumerator's district and half in another, and not all enumerators, especially in the earlier returns, were scrupulously accurate. It is a little complicated at first, but the PRO staff will assist anyone in difficulties over tracing the right entry or in deciphering the handwriting, which is often far from clear. As delving into census returns nearly always takes longer than one imagines it will, the wise researcher allows plenty of time for it. Excellent handbooks include E. Higgs' *Making Sense of the Census, Census Returns on Microfilm: 1841–91* by Jeremy Gibson and *Censuses 1841–1891: Use and Interpretation* by Eve McLaughlin.

Other records

The above-mentioned are but a few of the sources open to the genealogist/family historian. Searching these will enable you to draw up at least a skeleton family tree as a basis from which to work. The next stage will be to explore the various other classes of records likely to yield further information. Elucidation of the mysteries of Court rolls, Quarter Sessions records, poll books, service records, and so on, is best left to the expert. The classic study is Sir Anthony Wagner's *English Genealogy*. Recommended textbooks include *Genealogy for Beginners* by

A.J. Willis and M. Tatchell; *In Search of Ancestry* and *In Search of Scottish Ancestry*, both by G. Hamilton-Edwards; *A Genealogist's Bibliography* by C.R. Humphery-Smith; *Family Roots* by Stella Colwell; *Tracing Your Ancestors in the Public Record Office* by Amanda Bevan and Andrea Duncan; and *Tracing Your Scottish Ancestors* by Cecil Sinclair. *The Family Historian's Enquire Within* by Pauline Saul and F.C. Markwell should ideally be kept at the researcher's elbow. Terrick Fitzhugh's *Dictionary of Genealogy* has over a thousand entries: descriptions and locations of records by county, as well as explanations of obsolete terms and translations of those Latin phrases most likely to be encountered in ancestry research.

Use should also be made of the indexes to proceedings of local archaeological societies and to publications of local family history societies (see page 123). Most public libraries and county record offices possess complete sets of those relating to their districts. The standard works and guides mentioned above contain details of the records of special groups such as the Baptists, Huguenots, Methodists and Quakers.

The major printed biographical sources have been discussed under 'Biography and Autobiography' (pages 101–21), but special mention should be made here of the publications issued by Burke's Peerage Ltd. Publication of the long-awaited new (106th) edition of *Burke's Peerage and Baronetage* is still pending. *Burke's Family Index* has already been mentioned. Other titles include *Burke's Dormant and Extinct Peerages*, *Burke's Guide to the Royal Family*, *Burke's Irish Family Records*, *Burke's Landed Gentry* and, international in scope, *Ruvigny's Titled Nobility of Europe* (originally published in 1914, reprinted by Burke), *Burke's Presidential Families of the United States of America*, and *Burke's Royal Families of the World*.

Debrett's Peerage and Baronetage is up to date (1995), while the older, but more comprehensive, *Cockayne's Complete Peerage*, covering extant, extinct and dormant titles to 1938, and out of print for many years, has been reprinted, as has *Cockayne's Complete Baronetage*. *Boutell's Heraldry* and A.C. Fox-Davies' *A Complete Guide to Heraldry* are standard works, while for the amateur there is a useful booklet entitled *How to Read a Coat of Arms. Debrett's Guide to Heraldry and Regalia* is a new work. The best place to look up a coat of arms when you come across one and do not know to which family it belongs is Papworth's *Ordinary of British Armorials*. F.L. Leeson's *Directory of British Peerages*, which covers earliest times to the present day in one continuous alphabetical listing of titles and surnames, is an invaluable finding aid.

Local History

Local history writing may range from a short article in the local newspaper or county magazine to a full-length academic study. In all cases painstaking research and a good deal of detective work will be necessary; care must be taken to transcribe original documents accurately and to keep a note of all sources. References should normally be quoted in all but the shortest and most 'popular' articles.

There is a vast store of printed and manuscript material open to the local historian, much of it as yet untapped. Some of these sources have been discussed already under chapter 3, 'Basic Sources of Information and their Location' (pages 33–66). As with family history, before embarking on a project it is wise to check with the local record office whether the same ground has been covered by someone else; even if nothing has yet been published or deposited, archivists notoriously have their 'ears to the ground' and will usually be aware of any other writers, researchers or students working on parallel lines. A preliminary study of a work of similar nature, even if it deals with a totally different district, can be of considerable help to a writer wondering how to tackle the particular subject he has in mind. A useful tool is the *English Local Studies Handbook*, which lists local history resources county by county; it also contains some simple outline county maps showing the boundaries pre- and since 1974. (These boundary changes can be a headache for the researcher.) Anyone writing about London or Greater London will find the *Greater London Local History Directory* (a borough by borough guide to local history organisations, their activities and publications 1988–1992) invaluable. If you are seeking the location of manorial records, your first port of call should be the Royal Commission on Historical Manuscripts office (Quality House, Quality Court, Chancery Lane, London WC2A 1HP) to consult the *Manorial Documents Register*. Note that this is a location tool only; the Commission does not hold original manorial documents. Nor does it answer requests for information by telephone.

Difficulty may be encountered in reading early documents, and unless you have some knowledge of palaeography and Latin, you may need to use the services of an expert. If however you are serious about learning the necessary skills, plenty of guidance is at hand, ranging from E.E. Thoyts' *How to Read Old Documents* and F.G. Emmison's *How to Read Local Archives 1550–1700* to Eve McLaughlin's *Reading Old Handwriting* and a more recent publication, *Discovering Old Handwriting* by John Barrett and David Iredale.

The Latin of local records differs considerably from school Latin, and Eileen A. Gooder's *Latin for Local History* is an excellent textbook. C.T. Martin's *The Record Interpreter*, with its invaluable list of Latin abbreviations and glossary of Latin words used in English historical manuscripts and records, first published in 1892 and out of print for many years, became available again in a facsimile edition a few years ago. Another useful reference work is the *Revised Medieval Latin Word-List*.

C.R. Cheney's *Handbook of Dates for Students of English History* and Fryde's *Handbook of British Chronology* are indispensable aids to dating: they contain not only lists of rulers (with regnal years), popes, archbishops and other officers of state, but also include saints' days and tables that enable you to work out the day of the week of any date from AD 500 to the year 2000. A new edition of Cheney is in preparation for use after the year 2000.

As general introductions to the subject, David Dymond's *Writing Local History* and Robert Dunning's *Local History for Beginners* are highly recommended. Among numerous other titles on the subject, there are the classics by W.G. Hoskins, *Local History in England* and *Fieldwork in Local History*, and W.E. Tate's *The Parish Chest*. The *Victoria County Histories* (a varying number of volumes per county) are immensely detailed architecturally and topographically. Of more general interest will be the Historical Association's *British and National Archives and the Local Historian, The Batsford Companion to Local History*, and a revised edition of W.B. Stephens' *Sources for English Local History*. The Historical Association's two ongoing series, *Helps for Students of History* and *Short Guides to Records* are always worthwhile. The publications of many local record societies and the Index Library have been made available on microfiche by Chadwyck-Healey (a massive 5,136 microfiches) under the general title of *Publications of the English Record Societies, 1835–1972, and the Index Library*.

Depositing Papers

Every writer of family or local history, whether or not his work achieves publication, should consider depositing a copy of it, together with any original papers that may have come into his possession, and possibly also his research notes, at the appropriate local record office or, in the case of a family history, at the Society of Genealogists in London. By so doing he will be making a valuable contribution to the store of material on English social history and genealogy for the use of future generations of students and researchers.

The Batsford Companion to Local History, by Stephen Friar, Batsford, London, 1991

Boutell's Heraldry, rev. edn by J.P. Brooke-Little, Warne, London, 1983

British and National Archives and the Local Historian, by A. Morton and G. Donaldson, 'Helps for Students of History' series, Historical Association, London, 1980

Burke's Dormant and Extinct Peerages, Burke's Peerage, London, reprinted 1985

Burke's Family Index, Burke's Peerage, London, 1976

Burke's Guide to the Royal Family, Burke's Peerage, London, 1973

Burke's Irish Family Records, Burke's Peerage, London, 1976

Burke's Landed Gentry, 3 vols, Burke's Peerage, London, 1965–72

Burke's Peerage and Baronetage, Burke's Peerage, London, 105th edn, 1970; rev. edn pending

Burke's Presidential Families of the United States of America, Burke's Peerage, London, 1981

Burke's Royal Families of the World, 2 vols, Burke's Peerage, London, 1977, 1980

Census Returns on Microfilm: A Directory to Local Holdings, compiled by Jeremy Gibson, FFHS, Birmingham, 6th edn, 1994

Censuses 1841–1891: Use and Interpretation, by Eve McLaughlin, FFHS, Birmingham, 5th edn, 1992

[*Cockayne's*] *Complete Baronetage*, reprinted in 6 vols, Alan Sutton, Gloucester, 1982

[*Cockayne's*] *Complete Peerage of England, Scotland, Ireland, Great Britain and the United Kingdom, Extant, Extinct or Dormant*, 13 vols, London, 1910–59; reprinted in 6 vols, Alan Sutton, Gloucester, 1982

A Complete Guide to Heraldry, by A.C. Fox-Davies, rev. by J.P. Brooke-Little, Orbis, London, 1985

Computers in Genealogy, quarterly periodical published by the Society of Genealogists, London, 1982–

Crockford's Clerical Directory, first issued in 1858, now biennial; latest edition (1995–96), by Church House Publishing, London, 1995

Debrett's Guide to Heraldry and Regalia, by David Williamson, Webb & Bower, Exeter, 1992

Debrett's Peerage and Baronetage, published by Debrett's Peerage Ltd and Macmillan, London; latest edn, 1995

Dictionary of Genealogical Sources in the Public Record Office, by Stella Colwell, Weidenfeld & Nicolson, London, 1992

Dictionary of Genealogy, by Terrick Fitzhugh, 3rd edn, A & C Black, 1991

Directory of British Peerages from earliest times to the present day, ed. F.L. Leeson, Society of Genealogists, London, 1984

Discovering Old Handwriting, by John Barrett and David Iredale, Shire Publications, Princes Risborough, 1995

English Genealogy, by Anthony Wagner, Phillimore, Chichester, 3rd edn, reprinted 1990

English Local Studies Handbook, compiled by Susanna Guy, University of Exeter Press, Exeter, 1992

The Family Historian's Enquire Within, eds P. Saul and F.C. Markwell, FFHS, Birmingham, 5th edn, 1995

Family History News and Digest, published twice a year (April and September), by the Federation of Family History Societies (FFHS), Birmingham

Family Roots: Discovering the Past in the Public Record Office, by Stella Colwell, Weidenfeld & Nicolson, London, 1991

Family Tree Magazine, published monthly since 1984 (61 Great Whyte, Ramsey, Huntingdon, Cambs PE17 1HL); also *Family Tree Computer Magazine*, quarterly since 1992

Fieldwork in Local History, by W.G. Hoskins, Faber, London, 1982

Genealogical Research Directory, published in the USA annually since 1982; available from the UK agent, Mrs E. Simpson, 2 Stella Grove, Tollerton, Notts NG12 4EY

A Genealogist's Bibliography, by C.R. Humphery-Smith, Phillimore, Chichester, 1985

Genealogist's Magazine, published quarterly by the Society of Genealogists, London

Genealogy for Beginners, by A.J. Willis and M. Tatchell, Phillimore, Chichester, 1984

Greater London Local History Directory, compiled and published by Peter Marcan, London, 1993

Handbook of British Chronology, eds E.B. Fryde *et al.*, Royal Historical Society, London, 3rd edn, 1985

Handbook of Dates for Students of English History, by C.R. Cheney, Royal Historical Society, London, 1978; latest reprint 1995; new edition in preparation

Helps for Students of History series, Historical Association, London

How to Read a Coat of Arms, by Peter Summers, Alphabooks, Sherborne, rev. edn, 1986

How to Read Local Archives 1550–1700, by F.G. Emmison, Historical Association, London, 1967; latest reprint, 1988

How to Read Old Documents, by E.E. Thoyts, Phillimore, Chichester, 1980

How to Write a Family History, by Terrick Fitzhugh, A & C Black, London, 1988

In Search of Ancestry, by G. Hamilton-Edwards, Phillimore, Chichester, 1983

In Search of Scottish Ancestry, by G. Hamilton-Edwards, Phillimore, Chichester, 1983

An Index to the Wills proved in the Prerogative Court of Canterbury 1750–1800, ed. A.J. Camp, 6 vols, Society of Genealogists, London, 1976–93; some vols now out of print but on microfiche

Latin for Local History, by Eileen A. Gooder, Longman, Harlow, 1978; reprinted (8th impression of 2nd edn), 1992

List of Parishes in Boyd's Marriage Index, Phillimore, Chichester, for the Society of Genealogists, London, 6th edn, 1987; reprinted 1992

The Local Historian (formerly *The Amateur Historian*), published quarterly by Phillimore, Chichester, for the British Association for Local History (BALH)

The Local Historian's Encyclopedia, by John Richardson, Phillimore, Chichester, 2nd edn, 1986; reprinted 1993

Local History for Beginners, by Robert Dunning, Phillimore, Chichester, 1980

Local History in England, by W.G. Hoskins, Longman, Harlow, 3rd edn, 1984; 4th impression 1990

Making Sense of the Census, The Manuscript Returns for England and Wales 1801–1901, by E. Higgs, PRO handbook no. 23, HMSO, London, 1989; 3rd impression 1991

Marriage, Census and Other Indexes for Family Historians, by Jeremy Gibson, FFHS, Birmingham, 5th edn, 1994

National Index of Parish Registers, series ed. Cliff Webb, published by Phillimore, Chichester, for the Society of Genealogists, in progress (some vols revised/reprinted, some out of print, others in preparation): I, *Sources for Births, Marriages and Deaths before 1837*, 1968, reprinted 1976; II, *Sources for Nonconformist Genealogy and Family History*, 1973, reprinted 1981; III, *Sources for Roman Catholic and Jewish Genealogy and Family History*, 1974, reprinted 1986; IV, *South East*

England, 1980: Part 1, *Surrey*, reprinted 1990; V, *South Midlands and Welsh Border*, 1966, 3rd edn revised, 1976; VI, *North Midlands*: Part 1, *Staffordshire*, 1982, 2nd edn, 1992; Part 2, *Nottinghamshire*, 1988; VII, *Cambridgeshire, Norfolk, Suffolk*, 1983; VIII, Part 1, *Berkshire*, 1989, Part 2, *Wiltshire*, 1992; IX, Part 1, *Bedfordshire and Huntingdonshire*, 1991, Part 2, *Northamptonshire*, 1991, Part 3, *Buckinghamshire*, 1992, Part 4, *Essex*, 1993; X, in preparation; XI, *North-East England*: Part 1, *Durham and Northumberland*, 2nd edn 1984, rev. edn 1992; XII, *Sources for Scottish Genealogy and Family History*, 1970, reprinted 1980; XIII, *The Parish Registers of Wales*, 1986

Never Been Here Before?, by J. Cox, FFHS, Birmingham, 1993

One-Name Studies, quarterly journal of the Guild of One-Name Studies, London

Ordinary of British Armorials, by A.W.W. Papworth, 1874; facsimile edn, Tabard Publications, London, 1961

The Parish Chest, by W.E. Tate, Phillimore, Chichester, 3rd rev. edn, 1983; reprinted 1985

Parish Register Copies in the Library of the Society of Genealogists, booklet published by Phillimore, Chichester, for the Society of Genealogists, London; updated at intervals (latest, 10th edn, 1992)

The Phillimore Atlas and Index of Parish Registers, ed. C.R. Humphery-Smith, Phillimore, Chichester, rev. edn, 1994

Publications of the English Record Societies, 1835–1972, and the Index Library, on microfiche, Chadwyck-Healey, Cambridge

Reading Old Handwriting, by Eve McLaughlin, FFHS, Birmingham, 1987; reprinted 1991

The Record Interpreter, by Charles Trice Martin, originally published 1892; facsimile of 2nd edn (1910), Kohler & Coombes, Dorking, 1976; reprinted 1982, 1994

Record Offices: How to Find Them, by J.S.W. Gibson and P. Peskett, FFHS, Birmingham, 6th edn, 1993

Record Repositories in Great Britain: A Geographical Directory, Royal Commission on Historical Manuscripts, HMSO, London; updated regularly (latest, 9th edn, 1991; reprinted with revisions 1994)

Revised Medieval Latin Word-List from British and Irish Sources, ed. R.E. Latham, Oxford University Press, Oxford, 1965

Ruvigny's Titled Nobility of Europe, originally published 1914; reprinted by Burke's Peerage, London, 1980

St Catherine's House, by Eve McLaughlin, FFHS, Birmingham, 8th edn, 1991

Short Guides to Records series, Historical Association, London

Sources for English Local History, by W.B. Stephens, Phillimore, Chichester, rev. edn, 1994

Tracing Your Ancestors in the Public Record Office, by Amanda Bevan and Andrea Duncan, PRO handbook no. 19, HMSO, London, 4th edn, 1990

Tracing Your Scottish Ancestors: A Guide to Ancestry Research in the Scottish Record Office, by Cecil Sinclair, HMSO, Edinburgh, 1990

'Using the Library of the Society of Genealogists', leaflet published annually by the Society of Genealogists, London

Victoria History of the Counties of England (VCH), over 200 vols published since 1901 (approx. 160 vols in print); Institute of Historical Research, London (distributed by Oxford University Press, Oxford)

Whitaker's Almanack, published annually by Whitaker, London

Wills and Their Whereabouts, by A.J. Camp, Phillimore, Chichester, 1974

Wills and Where to Find Them, by J.S.W. Gibson, Phillimore, 1974

Wills before 1858, by Eve McLaughlin, FFHS, Birmingham, 4th edn, 1992

Writing Local History, by David Dymond, Phillimore, Chichester, for the British Association for Local History (BALH), 1988

Note: Publications of the Federation of Family History Societies are obtainable through local family history societies or from FFHS Publications, 2–4 Killer Street, Ramsbottom, Bury, Lancs BL0 9BZ.

As this edition goes to press, a new title, *Latin for Local and Family Historians* by Denis Stuart, Phillimore, Chichester, 1995, is published.

8

Specialist Research

While it is always more rewarding to undertake your own research, there are times when it pays to employ the expert. Books or records to be consulted may be accessible only at some distance; specialist knowledge of a subject may be required, or familiarity with local records which it would take the inexperienced researcher, or one from another district, months, if not years, to acquire – in these circumstances the employment of an expert will usually save time and money in the long term. If you have press deadlines looming, or other commitments, it may even pay you to off-load some of the more routine research as well.

The best advice I can give to anyone looking for a reliable professional researcher is to get a personal recommendation from another writer. Failing that, look in the *Writers' & Artists' Yearbook*, under 'Editorial, Literary and Production Services', in the Cassell and Publishers Association *Directory of Publishing*, under 'Trade and Allied Services: publishing consultancies and research services in Great Britain', and in *The Writer's Handbook*, under 'Editorial, Research and Other Services'. The British Library, the Public Record Office and some other libraries and local record offices maintain lists of researchers/record agents and will pass on names and addresses to enquirers (send a stamped addressed envelope); naturally, they do not accept any responsibility for the work undertaken by these people. Experts willing to do research may also sometimes be contacted through the secretaries or librarians of professional or trade societies or institutions; alternatively, an advertisement in a professional or trade journal may yield a suitable result. Some freelancers advertise their services in *The Times*, the *Times Literary Supplement*, *The Author* and similar papers. Teachers and university students often seek research assignments during the long vacation. For details of how to obtain the services of a qualified indexer, see pages 168–9.

Contacting a suitable researcher abroad is rather more difficult. You can write to the national library of the country concerned, or to the library or archives centre where you want the research to be done (always enclose a sufficient number of International Reply Coupons for airmail if writing overseas – one is not enough); or you can approach the cultural attaché of the relevant embassy, legation or high commission in London.

The most obvious occasions when a writer may need this kind of help are in the fields of genealogy, when a complicated ancestral search may be necessary for the first chapter of a biography; in local or family history, for which not only a knowledge of the classes of records available is required, but also some skill in reading Latin and in palaeography (transcribing old handwriting); in picture research; and in translation.

Genealogy

Experience in palaeography and genealogy is acquired only after considerable study, and there are many traps into which the unwary novice can fall. A working knowledge of Latin is essential for the study of medieval or earlier texts, while later source material demands the ability to read and transcribe both the 'secretary hand' (the script in use in England from the mid-16th to the mid-17th centuries) and the later 'court hand', each with distinctive forms of capital letters and contractions. Unless you are embarking on your family or local history as a hobby, therefore, and can afford the time to qualify yourself in these subjects, some professional assistance will be desirable.

It is wise to employ someone who lives in the area in which the relevant search is to be made, for he will be familiar both with the local records and with local family names, and thus can save the client time and money. Most local record offices maintain lists of recommended searchers; alternatively, names and addresses of professional genealogists and record agents who are members of the Association of Genealogists and Record Agents (AGRA) may be obtained from the Joint Secretaries, 29 Badgers Close, Horsham, W. Sussex RH12 5RU (enclose £2.50 to cover cost and postage or six International Reply Coupons for overseas). All AGRA members have satisfied their Council as to integrity, qualifications and experience, and they adhere to a strict professional code of practice.

The College of Arms (Queen Victoria Street, London EC4V 4BT) is open to enquiries of a genealogical and heraldic nature from members of the public (arms and pedigrees of English, Northern Irish and Commonwealth families). For personal visitors only a brief search will be made free of charge to ascertain whether or not a family tree has been drawn up; further research will be conducted on a fee-paying basis. Debrett Ancestry Research Ltd, P.O. Box 7, New Alresford, Hants SO24 9EN (tel. 01962 732676), which formerly catered only for royalty and the aristocracy, now offers a worldwide genealogical research service to the commoner. So does Burke's Ancestry Research Department, 209 St John's Hill, London SW11 1TH (tel. 0171–924 5132; fax 0171–924 3369); this firm, which has the reputation of being very competitive, will give free advice on a genealogical search or provide a detailed feasibility assessment for £48, the cost of which will be deducted if they are commissioned to do further research. Simple research queries (i.e. for specific information) are charged on an hourly basis. A full family search is likely to cost in the region of £350–£480 (figures quoted at 1995 rates). Other firms and individuals offering genealogical research services in various parts of the United Kingdom and abroad advertise in the *Genealogists' Magazine*, the quarterly journal of the Society of Genealogists. The Society itself will carry out research, on a fee-paying basis, for members and non-members. Enquiries, accompanied by a stamped addressed envelope, should be addressed to the Director of Research, The Society of Genealogists, 14 Charterhouse Buildings, London EC1M 7BA.

Picture Research

Picture research is immensely complicated and therefore beyond the scope of this book. Sometimes a writer will be expected to provide all the illustrative material for his book or article; in other cases the publisher will employ a professional picture researcher, who may be a member of his staff or a freelance, to locate and select pictures, commission photographers, and clear the copyright and reproduction fees on a particular project. Whether the author or the publisher foots the bill for the picture researcher is a matter for negotiation. A wise author makes sure that it is stipulated in his contract that it will be the publisher who bears responsibility for print and reproduction fees, since these can be very costly.

Writers wishing to obtain the services of a qualified picture researcher are recommended to contact the Society of Picture Researchers and Editors (SPREd): telephone Emma Krikler on 0171–431 9886 (mobile phone 0374 804 680), or write to SPREd at 5a Alvanley Gardens, London NW6 1JD.

Those who are tempted to undertake their own picture research should first read the excellent introductory article on the subject in the *Writers' & Artists' Yearbook*, published annually by A & C Black. Among a variety of practical manuals and useful source-books are the following:

Art Historians and Specialists, published by Peter Marcan, P.O. Box 3158, London SE1 4RA, 1995

BAPLA Directory, published annually by the British Association of Picture Libraries and Agencies, 18 Vine Hill, London EC1R 5DX (tel. 0171–713 1780; fax 0171–713 1711)

Dictionary of British Cartoonists and Caricaturists 1730–1980, compiled by M. Bryant and S. Heneage, Scolar Press, London, 1994

1995 Directory of Photographers, published by GHP Publishing, Freepost (HU593), Brough HU15 1BR

Index to Stock Libraries, booklet published annually by Creative Magazines Ltd, 35 Britannia Row, London N1 8QH

The Picture Researcher's Handbook, by Hilary and Mary Evans, 5th edn, Blueprint (Chapman and Hall), London, 1992 (new edition in preparation)

Picture Sources UK: A Guide to more than 1200 Public and Private Picture Collections, compiled by R. Eakins, Macdonald, London, 1985 (out of print but available in libraries)

Practical Picture Research: A Guide to Current Practice, Procedure, Techniques and Resources, by Hilary Evans, Blueprint (Chapman and Hall), London, 1992

Sources of Illustration 1500–1900, Adams & Dart, London, 1971 (out of print, but still a valuable source, available in libraries)

Translation

Translation is another field in which professional help may be required from time to time. For basic research purposes a rough translation or précis may be adequate to work on, but any passage to be quoted in print should be prepared by a qualified trans-lator. The best way to find one is to contact the Institute of Translation and Interpreting (ITI), 377 City Road London EC1V 1NA (tel. 0171–713 7600; fax 0171–713 7650). The languages and skills of qualified members of the Institute, together with those of some members of the Translators Association of the Society of Authors, will be found in the *ITI Directory*. Alter-natively, translation agencies are listed in the yellow pages of most telephone directories, but these normally handle commercial rather than literary texts.

The Translator's Handbook by Catriona Picken (2nd edn, Aslib, London, 1989) is an excellent introduction and source-book for all members of the profession; it will also be of use to writers who need to commission a translator.

Research Fees

Fees for professional freelance assistance are negotiable and depend on the nature and complexity of the task. Genealogists, record agents and researchers usually work on an hourly basis plus out-of-pocket expenses (travelling, search fees, photocopying, postages, telephone, etc.); short pieces of translation are charged per thousand words. Most freelance workers have a sliding scale of fees; the professional bodies to which the majority of them belong recommend standard rates for the job, and if you are asked to pay 'above the odds' it will be either because the assignment is very specialised or complicated, or is needed in a great rush (necessitating week-end and evening work), or because the person engaged has special qualifications.

It is normal practice for the client commissioning the work to pay a lump sum on account (up to 50 per cent of the total cost estimated) and the balance on completion, but in the case of long-term commissions accounts may be rendered monthly. Estimates will be given on request; but do not expect your researcher to give one with any accuracy – neither he nor you will know at the outset precisely how much time he will spend on the job.

Fees paid to researchers, genealogists, translators and other workers may be set against a writer's tax.

9

Information from and about Foreign Countries

The writer/researcher who needs to obtain information about foreign countries or to use published or unpublished material from abroad has few problems these days, thanks to the new technology. Twenty years ago you might have had to budget (or squeeze an advance out of your publisher) for an extended trip in order to look at some vital records lurking the other side of the world. Today you can search the catalogues of almost all the great national library and archive collections on screen from the comfort of your study or on the library computer; an enormous amount of material is available on CD-ROM and microform; and if you so wish you can exchange research information with fellow writers worldwide via the Internet without leaving home. What once took weeks, or sometimes months – and a great deal of money – is now more or less instantly accessible at a reasonable cost.

It is true that you may still have to travel to get at some of your material. But by doing your initial searching from the home base (which in the first instance normally involves extracting bibliographical information) you can discover precisely what exists and where, if necessary, you must go to examine it. Often you will find that the books or journals you need are held by some library or archive centre in the UK, or that they have been – or can be – microfilmed for you to use at home. In the case of private papers you will of course almost always have to go to the source in person.

When it is a question simply of finding some factual or background information on a foreign country that would hardly justify the expense of a computer search, the best place to start is the reference library. National encyclopedias, bibliographies and current works of reference are usually to be found on the open shelves; many are now available on CD-ROM and microfiche. If these do not provide what you are looking for, consult the subject index, first under the relevant country and then under the desired subject subheading. One of the best sources is the *World Bibliographical Series* published by Clio Press of Oxford. The use of bibliographies and how to trace books has been outlined in chapter 2.

All the copyright libraries and university libraries in the UK have substantial foreign language holdings, and you should experience little difficulty in obtaining most standard works. Use *Walford's Guide to Reference Material* and its US equivalent Sheehy's *Guide to Reference Books* (details in chapter 3) to find out, under each country, the principal encyclopedias, national bibliographies and major works (listed under subject).

Foreign newspapers and weeklies going back for many years are held at the British Library Newspaper Library in Colindale; there are some gaps during the two world wars. Today they are nearly all purchased on microfilm. You can trace the whereabouts of all foreign periodicals held in British libraries in *Serials in the British Library*. Current publications are listed in *Benn's Media, Ulrich's International Periodicals Directory* and *Willing's Press Guide* (see chapter 3, pages 44–5).

If you are thinking of subscribing to a foreign periodical you should contact Dawson UK Ltd, Cannon House, Park Farm Road, Folkestone, Kent CT19 5EE (tel. 01303 850101; fax 01303 850440). This firm offers a range of services including online access to a database of 90,000 journal titles and a huge stock of back issues; any enquiries that cannot be answered directly from the database are automatically passed on to the Dawson Bibliographic Research Service. The subscription division's *Guide to International Journals and Periodicals* lists publications alphabetically by title, with frequency of issue and prices in £ sterling; there is a detailed subject index. CD-ROMs are also available.

So far as books published abroad are concerned, the London booksellers Grant & Cutler, 55–57 Great Marlborough Street, London W1V 2AY (tel. 0171–734 2012; fax 0171–734 9272) hold a large stock of foreign language titles and will order on any subject. Bay Foreign Language Books, 19 Dymchurch Road, St Mary's Bay, Romney Marsh, Kent TN29 0ET (tel. 01797 364417; fax 01797 364539) import new books and will also search for out-of-print titles. For other bookfinding services, see chapter 3, pages 42–3.

A number of countries now have a Biographical Archive (see chapter 6, pages 105–6), and most have printed biographical dictionaries and/or *Who's Who* volumes. There is a *World Biographical Database*, on CD-ROM, from Saur, Munich. For quick factual reference look out for the single-volume encyclopedias such as *Le Petit Larousse* (French), *Der Brockhaus in einem Band* (German) and *Pequeño Larousse Ilustrado* (Spanish), as they contain information not always included in their English equivalents.

For up-to-date general information you should contact the relevant tourist information offices (listed in the London telephone directory) or the press offices of the particular embassy or high commission. A personal approach is often productive; you will find the addresses, and names of cultural attachés, in the current *London Diplomatic List* (published twice a year by HMSO and usually available at the library enquiry desk). For addresses of embassies and other diplomatic bodies worldwide look at *The World Directory of Diplomatic Representation*, published by Europa Publications. The same firm has recently brought out an *International Relations Research Directory* (December 1995) which contains information on every major research institute concerned with international relations, as well as an alphabetical list of relevant periodicals and journals. You should remember, too, that public relations officers of the major international companies are often able to provide useful source material and/or contacts; you will find their names and addresses in the current *Hollis Press & Public Relations Annual* and *Hollis Europe*.

Finally, and by no means least, you will find much first-class information about foreign countries in some of the quality travel guides. The *Blue Guides* published by A & C Black are excellent in this respect; there are volumes for most European countries, some for individual towns and regions, and they are regularly revised. For countries farther afield, look at the *Handbooks* produced by Trade & Travel; these contain a wealth of information and are very reliable.

Foreign libraries in the United Kingdom are listed in the *Aslib Directory*. *The World of Learning* is international. For information on libraries and the book trade generally, look at the two Bowker annuals, *Literary Market Place*, covering the United States and Canada, and *International Literary Market Place*, for the rest of the world. Other useful tools not already mentioned include the US *Public Affairs Information Service Index* (*PAIS*), which is worldwide in coverage, the *Regional Surveys of the World* series published by Europa Publications, and the *International Historical Statistics* series published by Macmillan. Do not forget old favourites such as the *Europa World Year Book*, the *International Who's Who* and the *Yearbook of International Organizations*. As with every other kind of research, you need only one book title, or one contact, to start you off.

Readers who live in or near London may be able to make use of the following:

Bibliothèque de l'Institut Français (French Institute), 15 Queensberry Place, London SW7 2DT (tel. 0171–589 6211; fax 0171–581 5127). Use of reference facilities is free; books may be borrowed on subscription. Open Mon, Tue, Wed, Fri, 11–7.

British Library Oriental and India Office Collections (formerly the India Office Library), 197 Blackfriars Road, London SE1 8NG (tel. 0171–412 7873). Mon–Fri, 9.30–5.45; Sat, 9.30–12.45; prints and drawings room by appointment only Mon–Fri, 2–5. *N.B.* These collections will move to the new British Library at St Pancras by the end of 1997.

Goethe-Institut (German Institute) Library, 50 Princes Gate, Exhibition Road, London SW7 2PH (tel. 0171–411 3452; fax 0171–584 0974). Open to the public, free of charge, for reference and study. Mon–Thu, 10–8; Sat, 10–1.

Institute of Commonwealth Studies Library, 27–28 Russell Square, London WC1B 5DS (tel. 0171–580 5876). Open (during term) Mon–Wed, 10–7; Thu, Fri, 10–6; (during vacations) Mon–Fri, 10–5.30.

Italian Institute Library, 39 Belgrave Square, London SW1X 8NX (tel. 0171–235 1461; fax 0171–235 4618). Mon–Fri, for reference only.

Polish Library, 238–246 King Street, London W6 0RF (tel. 0181–741 0474; fax 0181–746 3798). Mon, Wed, 10–8; Fri, 10–5; closed Tue and Thu. Reference only (loans to scholars).

School of Oriental and African Studies Library, Thornhaugh Street, Russell Square, London WC1H 0XG (tel. 0171–637 2388). Mon–Thu, 9–8.45; Fri, 9–7; Sat, 9.30–5; summer vacation, Mon–Fri, 9–5; Sat, 9.30–5. Reader's ticket required (letter of introduction).

Spanish Institute Library, 102 Eaton Square, London SW1W 9AN (tel. 0171–235 1484/5; fax 0171–235 4115). Mon–Thu, 9.30–1, 2.30–5; Fri, 9.30–2. For reference only.

United States of America Information Service Reference Center, American Embassy, 55/56 Upper Brook Street, London W1A 2LH (tel. 0171–408 8060). *N.B.* This is not a library open to the public. Telephone enquiry service only, Mon–Fri, 10–12.

Short List of Foreign Source-material (arranged alphabetically under area or country)

Africa

Sources of information in the UK:

African Studies Centre Library, University of Cambridge, Free School Lane, Cambridge CB2 3RQ (tel. 01223 334398; fax 01223 334396)

The School of Oriental and African Studies, University of London, Thornhaugh Street, Russell Square, London WC1H 0XG (tel. 0171–637 2388; fax 0171–436 3844)

Recommended books:

Africa South of the Sahara, published annually by Europa Publications, London

The African Book Publishing Record, published quarterly since 1975 by Bowker-Saur, East Grinstead

African Books in Print, 2 vols, Zell, Munich, 4th edn, 1993

African Studies Abstracts, quarterly by Bowker-Saur, East Grinstead

East African Handbook 1996, Trade & Travel, Bath, 1995

Guide to Documents in the British Isles relating to Africa, by J.D. Pearson, 2 vols, Mansell, London, 1993–4

International African Bibliography, published quarterly since 1971 by Bowker-Saur, East Grinstead

Morocco and Tunisia Handbook 1996, Trade & Travel, Bath, 1995

South African Bibliography, Mansell, London, 3rd edn, 1996

Arab States and the Middle East

Sources of information in the UK:

British Library Oriental and India Office Collections, Orbit House, 197 Blackfriars Road, London SE1 8NG (tel. 0171–412 7873). Moving to the new British Library at St Pancras by the end of 1997.

Centre for Arab Gulf Studies, Documentation Unit, University of Exeter Old Library, Prince of Wales Road, Exeter, Devon EX4 4JZ (tel. 01392 264041; fax 01392 264023)

Middle East Centre, St Anthony's College, Woodstock Road, Oxford OX2 6JF (tel. 01865 284764; fax 01865 311475)

(collections of papers of individuals involved in the Middle East from 1800 to the present day)

Recommended books:

Dictionary of the Middle East, Macmillan, London, 1995
Egypt and the Nile Handbook, Trade & Travel, Bath, 1996
Index Islamicus 1906–1955, with 5-year supplements to 1985, Mansell, London, 1958–91; published quarterly since 1977
The Middle East and North Africa, published annually by Europa Publications, London
Saudi Arabia: A Bibliography on Society, Politics and Economics from the 18th Century to the Present, Saur, Munich, 1984
Theses on Islam, the Middle East and NW Africa 1880–1978, Mansell, London, 1983
Who's Who in the Arab World 1995–96, Saur, Munich, 1994

Asia and the Far East

Sources of information in the UK:

Asian and Indian Studies Centre, St Anthony's College, Woodstock Road, Oxford OX2 6JF (tel/fax 01865 274559)
British Library Oriental and India Office Collections, Orbit House, 197 Blackfriars Road, London SE1 8NG (tel. 0171–412 7873). Moving to the new British Library at St Pancras by the end of 1997.
Centre of South Asian Studies, University of Cambridge, Laundress Lane, Cambridge CB2 1SD (tel. 01223 338094; fax 01223 316913).
School of Oriental and African Studies, University of London, Thornhaugh Street, Russell Square, London WC1H 0XG (tel. 0171–637 2388; fax 0171–436 3844)

Recommended books:

Asia: A Selected and Annotated Guide to Reference Works, Mansell, London, 1980
Australasian Biographical Archive, Saur, Munich, 1990–92
Cumulative Bibliography of Asian Studies 1941–1965, Association for Asian Studies Inc., Boston, Mass; now annually with cumulative volumes
The Far East and Australasia, published annually by Europa Publications, London
India Handbook 1996, Trade & Travel, Bath, 1995

The Commonwealth

Sources of information in the UK:

Commonwealth Institute Library, Kensington High Street, London W8 6NQ (tel. 0171–603 4535; fax 0171–602 7374)

Commonwealth Secretariat Library, 10 Carlton House Terrace, Pall Mall, London SW1Y 5AH (tel. 0171–747 6164; fax 0171–930 0827)

Foreign & Commonwealth Office Library, King Charles Street, London SW1A 2AH (tel. 0171–270 3925; fax 0171–930 2364)

Institute of Commonwealth Studies, University of London, 27–28 Russell Square, London WC1B 5DS (tel. 0171–580 5876)

Rhodes House Library, South Parks Road, Oxford OX1 3RG (tel. 01865 270909; fax 01865 270912)

Researchers should also contact the various high commissions in London, i.e. Australia House, Canada House, India House, New Zealand House, etc. (addresses and telephone numbers in *Whitaker's Almanack* under 'The Commonwealth' or in *Hollis Press & Public Relations Annual* under 'International and Overseas Information Sources in the UK', and the London telephone directory).

Recommended books:

General:
The Commonwealth Yearbook, HMSO, London; formerly published annually, now approx. every two years

Australia

Australian Books in Print, D.W. Thorpe, Melbourne

Australian Dictionary of Biography, Melbourne University Press, 12 vols to date plus index vol

Australian National Bibliography, National Library of Australia, Canberra (previously known as *Annual Catalogue of Australian Publications*, published 1936–60): since 1972 published weekly, with monthly and 4-monthly cumulations and annual volumes

The Concise Oxford Dictionary of Australian History, Oxford University Press, Oxford, 2nd edn, 1995

Official Year Book of the Commonwealth of Australia, published annually by the Government Printing Office, Canberra

Resources for Australian and New Zealand Studies: A Guide to Library Holdings in the United Kingdom, British Library, London and Australian Studies Centre, University of London, 1986

Who's Who in Australia, published triennially since 1906, now by Information Australia, Melbourne

Canada

Canadiana, national bibliography published monthly since 1951, with annual cumulations, National Library of Canada, Ottawa

Dictionary of Canadian Biography, University of Toronto Press, 1966– (in progress)

Encyclopedia Canadiana (standard national encyclopedia). A new *Canadian Encyclopedia* was published by Hurtig in 3 volumes in September 1985

Historical Statistics of Canada, Statistics Canada, Ottawa, 2nd edn, 1983

Statistics Canada, published annually by the Information Department of Canada, Ottawa

Who's Who in Canada, published annually since 1907, now by Global Press, Toronto

India

Index India, published quarterly by Rajasthan University, Jaipur, since 1967

India: A Reference Manual, published annually since 1953 by the Ministry of Information and Broadcasting, New Delhi

India Handbook 1996, Trade & Travel, Bath, 1995

India Who's Who, published annually since 1969 by INFA Publications, New Delhi

Indian National Bibliography, published monthly, with annual cumulations, since 1957 by the Central Reference Library, Calcutta

New Zealand

Encyclopedia of New Zealand, ed. A.H. McLintock, 3 vols, Owen, Wellington, 1966

New Zealand Books in Print, D.W. Thorpe, Melbourne

New Zealand National Bibliography, monthly since 1967, National Library of New Zealand, Wellington

New Zealand Official Year Book, published annually by the Department of Statistics, Wellington

Resources for Australian and New Zealand Studies, see page 152 under 'Australia'.

Regrettably, space does not permit the listing of other Commonwealth countries in this section.

Europe

Given the vast amount of material published each year, readers will understand that it is impossible to do more in the space of this chapter than to list some of the countries of Europe, with the location of their national libraries/archives and a selection of reference works. There are, however, a number of general guides which should first be mentioned. These include:

Directory of European Industrial & Trade Associations and *Directory of European Professional & Learned Societies*, both CBD Research, Beckenham; updated regularly

The Documentation of the European Communities, by Ian Thomson, Mansell, London, 1989

European Historical and Political Facts series, published by Macmillan, London

The European Union Encyclopedia and Directory, Europa Publications, London, 2nd edn, 1995

Hollis Europe, annually by Hollis Directories, Sunbury-on-Thames, Middx

Official Publications of Western Europe, ed. E. Johansson, 2 vols, Mansell, London, 1984, 1988

Statistics Europe, CBD Research, Beckenham; updated regularly

Western Europe, Europa Publications, London, 2nd edn, 1993

What's What and Who's Who in Europe, by Harry Drost, Cassell, London, 1994

Note: For purposes of this chapter, 'Europe' refers to Western Europe. The countries of Eastern Europe are included under the heading 'The Russian Federation (formerly the Commonwealth of Independent States) and Eastern Europe'.

Austria

The Österreichische Nationalbibliothek in Vienna is the national library, and there is also the Staatsarchiv (national archives) in the same city.

Austria, Facts and Figures
Dokumentation und Information in Österreich
Österreichische Bibliographie
Österreichisches Biographisches Lexikon 1815–1950
Österreich Lexikon
Who's Who in Austria

Belgium

The Bibliothèque royale Albert Iᵉʳ/Koninklijke Bibliotheek Albert
I and the Archives générales du Royaume, both in Brussels, are
the major library and archive sources.

Bibliographie de Belge/Belgische bibliografie
Biographical Archive of the Benelux Countries, Saur, Munich
*Documentation sur la Belgique: bibliographie selective et analy-
tique*
Inventaire des centres belges de recherche
Who's Who in Belgium and the Grand Duchy of Luxembourg

Denmark – see under 'Scandinavia'.

France

For the last 200 years or so the Bibliothèque Nationale (BN) (58
rue Richelieu, 75002 Paris, tel. (1) 47 03 81 26) has been the
national library of France. It is shortly to be replaced by a huge
new library, popularly known as the 'TGB' or *Très Grande
Bibliothèque*, due to open in 1997, on a site between the Pont
de Bercy and the Pont de Tolbiac, in the 13th arrondissement.
During 1996 books and documents will be transferred to the new
library, and the reading rooms at rue Richelieu will close in
October–November that year, when the new premises are scheduled to open. At the time of writing there is no guide to 'Tolbiac'.
The address of the new Bibliothèque nationale de France is 63
quai de la Gare, 75013 Paris (tel. (1) 44 23 03 70).

Among many other libraries in Paris is the Bibliothèque du Centre
National d'Art et de Culture Georges Pompidou, at the Centre
Beaubourg: 19 rue Beaubourg, 75191 Paris (tel. (1) 42 77 12 33).

The Archives Nationales are at 60 rue de Francs-Bourgeois,
75141 Paris (tel. (1) 40 27 61 31).

Recommended books:

Annuaire Statistique de la France, published annually by the
I.N.S.E.E., Paris
Archives Biographiques Françaises, covering the 18th to 20th
centuries, on microfiche with printed index vols, Saur, Munich,
1988–90
Le Bottin Administratif (yearbook of government departments and
public offices), Bottin, Paris, annually
Dictionnaire de biographie française, Letousey, Paris, in progress,
1929– (approximately one instalment per year)

French Biographical Archive, 2 series, Saur, Munich
French Biographical Index, 4 vols, Saur, Munich, 1993
Grand Larousse Encyclopédique, Larousse, Paris, 10 vols, 1960–64; supplements, 1968, 1975
Livres Hebdo: Bibliographie de la France, published weekly with monthly and quarterly supplements by Éditions Cercle de la Librairie, 30 rue Dauphine, 75006 Paris (who also publish *Les Livres Disponibles (French Books in Print)*
Qui est Qui en France/Who's Who in France, published biennially since 1953 by Éditions Jacques Lafitte, Paris

The Press Division of the Ambassade de France in London issues a most informative compact publication, approximately once a year, entitled *France: a journalist's guide*, which is available free on request. It is invaluable to any writer needing to do research in or about France: contact the Ambassade de France en Grande-Bretagne, Service Culturel, 23 Cromwell Road, London SW7 2EL (tel. 0171–838 2055; fax 0171–838 2088).

Germany

The three major libraries are the Deutsche Bibliothek, in Frankfurt and Leipzig; the Staatsbibliothek Preussischer Kulturbesitz, in Berlin; and the Bayerische Staatsbibliothek, in Munich.

Allgemeine Deutsche Biographie
Brockhaus Enzyklopädie
Deutsche Biographische Enzyklopädie
Deutsche Nationalbibliographie (since 1991 for the united Germany)
German Biographical Archive, 2 series, Saur, Munich
German Biographical Index, 4 vols, Saur, Munich, 1986
Neue Deutsche Biographie
Wer ist Wer? (includes some Austrian and Swiss entries)
Who's Who in Germany

Greece

The National Library is in Athens.

Greek Bibliography
Guide to Greek Libraries and Cultural Organizations
Hellenika Vivla (bibliography)
Modern Greece: A Bibliography
Mega Hellenikon Biographikon Lexikon (biographical dictionary), in progress

Italy

The major libraries are the Biblioteca Nazionale Centrale Vittorio Emanuele II in Rome and the Biblioteca Nazionale Centrale in Florence; there are also national libraries in Milan, Naples, Palermo, Turin and Venice.

Bibliografia Nazionale Italiana
Dizionario Biografico degli Italiani
Enciclopedia Italiana di Scienze, Lettre ed Arti
Guida delle Bibliothece Italiane
Italian Biographical Archive, 2 series, Saur, Munich
Italian Biographical Index, 4 vols, Saur, Munich, 1993
Italian Books in Print
Lui, Chi, E?
Who's Who in Italy

The Netherlands

The major collection is at the Koninklijke Bibliotheek (Royal Library) in The Hague.

Biographical Archive of the Benelux Countries, Saur, Munich
Brinkman's Cumulatieve Catalogus van Boeken (bibliography)
Digest of the Kingdom of the Netherlands (Government Information Service publication)
Grote Nederlandse Larousse Encyclopedie
Grote Winkler Prins Encyclopedie
Nieuw Nederlandsch Biografisch Woordenboek
Pythersen's Nederlandse Almanak
Who's Who in the Netherlands
Wie is Dat?

Norway – see under 'Scandinavia'.

Scandinavia

Two biographical dictionaries covering the region are the *Dictionary of Scandinavian Biography* and *Who's Who in Scandinavia*; the latter publication (1st edn, Bowker, New York, 1981) includes an appendix listing societies, associations and institutions. The *Scandinavian Biographical Archive* and the *Scandinavian Biographical Index*, both from Saur, contain entries for 150,000 individuals from Denmark, Finland, Iceland, Norway and Sweden.

Denmark

The Kongelige Bibliotek (Royal Library) in Copenhagen is the national library; the archive collection is at the Kobenhavns Stadsarkiv.

Bibliography of Books on Denmark 1900–1965
Dansk Biografisk Leksikon
Dansk Bogfortegnelse (national bibliography)
Denmark: An Official Handbook
Denmark: A Select Bibliography
Who's Who in Denmark

Norway

The national library is the Universitetsbiblioteket i Oslo (Royal University Library), and the national archives are at the Riksarkivet, also in Oslo.

Facts about Norway
Guide to Norwegian Statistics
Hvem or Hvem? (Norwegian who's who)
Norsk Biografisk Leksikon
Norsk Bokfortegnelse (national bibliography)
Norway Year Book

Sweden

The Kungliga Biblioteket (Royal Library), the Riksarkivet (National Record Office) and the Statistika Centralbyráns Biblioteket (Library of Statistics) are all in Stockholm.

Facts about Sweden
Svenskt Biografiskt Lexikon
Svensk Bokforteckning (national bibliography)
Vem är Det? (Swedish who's who)

Spain

The Biblioteca Nacional is in Madrid, as are the Archivo General de la Administración Civil del Estado (the General Archives of the Civil Administration of the State) and the Archivo Historico Nacional (the National Historical Archives). There is also the Real Biblioteca (Royal Library) at El Escorial, near Madrid. The Archivo de la Corona de Aragon (the Royal Archives of Aragon) are in Barcelona, where there is also the Biblioteca de Catalunya (the Library of Catalonia).

Bibliografia Española
Enciclopedia Universal Ilustrada Europeo-Americana
Gran Enciclopedia Rialp
Indice Cultural Español (Spanish cultural index)
Quién es quién (Spanish who's who)
Who's Who in Spain

See also the *Spanish, Portuguese, and Latin American Biographical Archive* and *Index* listed under 'Latin America'

Sweden – see under 'Scandinavia'.

Switzerland

The national library is the Schweizerische Landesbibliothek/ Bibliothèque Nationale Suisse in Berne; the Archives Fédérales (national archives) are in the same city. In Geneva there are the United Nations Library and the International Labour Office Library.

Das Schweizer Buch/Le Livre Suisse (national bibliography)
Who's Who in Switzerland

For the next two areas of the world – Latin America and the Caribbean, and Russia, the former USSR and Eastern Europe – space does not permit the listing of even major libraries in the different countries and states. The general works and bibliographies included should be useful to the researcher.

Latin America and the Caribbean

Bibliografia Latinoamericana, CERLAL, Bogotá, 1974–
Cambridge Encyclopedia of Latin America and the Caribbean, eds H. Blakemore, S. Collier and T. Skidmore, Cambridge University Press, 1985
Caribbeana, 1900–1965: A Topical Bibliography, by L. Comitas, University of Washington Press, Seattle and London, 1968
CARICOM Bibliography, Caricom Secretariat, Georgetown, Guyana, 1977–
Mexico and Central American Handbook 1996, Trade & Travel, Bath, 1995
South America, Central America and the Caribbean, Europa Publications, London, 5th edn, 1995
South American Handbook 1996, Trade & Travel, Bath, 1995

Spanish, Portuguese, and Latin American Biographical Archive, 2 series, Saur, Munich
Spanish, Portuguese, and Latin American Biographical Index, 4 vols, Saur, Munich, 1991

The Russian Federation (formerly the Commonwealth of Independent States) and Eastern Europe

Biographical Dictionary of the Former Soviet Union, Bowker-Saur, East Grinstead, 2nd edn, 1992

Eastern Europe and the Commonwealth of Independent States, Europa Publications, London, 2nd edn, 1994

The Great Soviet Encyclopedia (translation of *Bol'shaya Sovetskaya Entsiklopediya*, 3rd edn), 31 vols + 3 index vols, Macmillan, New York/Macmillan, London, 1973–83

Guide to Documents and Manuscripts in the United Kingdom relating to Russia and the Soviet Union, compiled by J.M. Hartley, Mansell, London, 1987

Guide to Russian Reference Books, in progress at Stanford University, California, 1962–

Official Publications of the Soviet Union and Eastern Europe 1945–1980: A Select Annotated Bibliography, ed. G. Walker, Mansell, London, 1982

Russian Books in Print Plus (with *Books Out of Print*), on CD-ROM, Bowker-Saur, East Grinstead, 1995 (includes forthcoming titles to 1997), to be updated annually

Who Was Who in the Soviet Union, 2 vols, Saur, Munich, 1992
Who's Who in Russia Today, Saur, Munich, 1993

United States of America

The Library of Congress, Washington, DC 20540 (tel. (202) 707 5000) is the national library, but it is not the exact equivalent of the British Library in that it does not automatically acquire a copy of every book published in the United States; it does, however, collect and catalogue books published in other countries. The *National Union Catalog*, which has replaced the old *Library of Congress Catalog*, will be found on open access at the British Library and in major libraries of the UK. The *Pre-1956 Imprints*, an impressive run of 755 volumes, are clear and easy to use; their great value to the researcher is that they provide in one alphabetical sequence, under authors, the holdings of the Library of Congress together with those of the principal libraries of North America. Another bonus is that the *NUC* gives dates of authors (otherwise sometimes difficult to obtain). The *NUC* from 1968 may be accessed through BLAISE-LINE (LC MARC).

The National Archives and Records Administration is at the National Archives Building, 8th Street at Pennsylvania Avenue NW, Washington, DC 20408 (tel. (202) 501 5000 (visitor information)).

Recommended books:

American Biographical Archive, 2 series, Saur, Munich

American Biographical Index, Saur, Munich, 4 vols, 1992

Books in Print. Books in Print Plus, Books in Print with Book Reviews Plus, Books Out of Print with Book Reviews Plus, Subject Guide to Books in Print, Bowker, New Providence, N.J.; some printed vols, some fiches, some CD-ROM, some online

Cambridge Dictionary of American Biography, ed. John S. Bowman, Cambridge University Press, Cambridge, 1995

Guide to Manuscripts relating to America in the United Kingdom, ed. J.W. Raimo, Mansell, London, 1979

Guide to Reference Books, by E.P. Sheehy, American Library Association, Chicago, 10th edn, 1986

Information Please Almanac, published annually since 1947, now by Houghton Mifflin, Boston, Mass.

National Inventory of Documentary Sources in the United States (*NIDS*), on microfiche in three parts: 1, *Federal Records*; 2, *Manuscript Division, Library of Congress*; 3, *State Archives, State Libraries, Historical Societies, Academic Libraries and Other Repositories*; by subscription, Chadwyck-Healey, Cambridge

Oxford Companion to American History, Oxford University Press, Oxford, 1966

Statistical Abstract of the United States, published annually since 1879 by the Government Printing Office, Washington, DC

Who's Who in America, Who Was Who in America, Who Was Who in American History, Marquis, Chicago, printed vols, fiches, CD-ROM and online. The same publisher issues regional volumes for the East, Midwest, South and Southwest, and West of the United States. There is a printed index vol. entitled *Index to Marquis Who's Who Publications*.

10

Preparation for the Press

The research is done, the text drafted and polished to the writer's satisfaction, on screen or in typescript, the length approximately right. (Some word processor owners will have a built-in word-count facility, but those less fortunate must do it the hard way, taking an average number of words per page and multiplying by the number of pages – remembering to allow for any short pages and inserts – and rounding up the total to the nearest hundred words.)

If the great work is an article, a short story, a novel or a play, all the author has to do now is to print it out, preferably on an inkjet or laser printer, or to type the fair copy himself electronically or manually, or – if he simply cannot face this task – to go to the expense of having it professionally typed. All typing agencies and most freelance typists today offer a word processing service. An ever-increasing number of publishers now accept – or even request, especially when commissioning new work – submission on disk. In either case a final check through the text should always be made before despatch to literary agent or publisher.

The non-fiction book requires a little extra attention. The prelims must be written, the notes and references section and the bibliography (if any) compiled, some thought given to the provision of an index, although this will not actually be prepared until later. None of these chores, strictly speaking, comes within the province of 'research', but their importance in giving the finished manuscript a professional look merits their mention here.

The word 'manuscript', abbreviated as MS (MSS in plural), which originally meant a handwritten document, in 20th-century literary jargon has become synonymous with 'typescript', a text that is either typed or prepared on a word processor. An 'electronic manuscript' is a text on disk.

There are some excellent works to help the writer with his final preparation. Godfrey Howard's *The Good English Guide* and the *Bloomsbury Good Word Guide* should resolve any problems as

162

to the use of particular words. G.V. Carey's *Mind the Stop*, first published some years ago and now a Penguin Reference paperback, is the layman's bible on punctuation. The *Writers' & Artists' Yearbook* carries a short article on 'Preparation of Typescripts', and Judith Butcher's *Copy-Editing*, although directed more at publishers than writers, contains many valuable hints on the final preparation of text for the printer. *The MHRA Style Book* is the standard work, not only for academics and editors, but for all authors writing for publication. Finally, the relevant *British Standards* are listed at the end of this chapter.

Prelims

These are the preliminary pages at the beginning of a book, known in the printing and publishing trade as 'prelims'. Normally they will consist of a title page, dedication, list of contents, list of illustrations, acknowledgments, abbreviations, preface or foreword. Not all of these will be required for every kind of book, and the publisher will have some say in the matter. It is up to the author to indicate, at this stage, what he intends to provide – i.e. if he wishes to include an 'Author's Note' or not. It will not matter if he cannot write the text of these as yet – it is quite sufficient to put a blank sheet in the typescript at the appropriate place or places, stating, for example, 'Acknowledgments' and below this, 'copy to follow'. The important thing is for the production manager and book designer to know that they are coming, so that they can allow for them in their calculations.

Notes and References

Consistency is the keyword here. If the book has been commissioned, the publisher may have sent the author a copy of the 'house style', or at least have stated a preference for the numbering and style of notes and references, such as whether they should appear at the foot of each page, after each chapter, or in a separate section at the end of the book. Failing such instruction, or if you do not yet have a publisher, it is advisable to study some published titles in a similar category of book and follow the same system.

Bibliography

Depending on whether the work is aimed at the popular or academic market, the bibliography may be selective or as comprehensive as you can make it. If the latter, it is usual to divide the entries into 'primary' and 'secondary' (or 'printed' and 'manuscript') sources, and to include not only books, but articles in periodicals and learned journals, as well as references to private papers consulted. Provided careful notes have been kept of all material used in the course of research, as suggested in chapter 2, the compilation of a bibliography should be quite straightforward. The normal arrangement of books and articles is in an alphabetical sequence, under the surname of the author. Care should be taken to list the particular editions used and to indicate any subsequent revised editions or reprints of each work, where possible.

The British Standard *BS 1629, Recommendations for references to published materials*, details an internationally accepted set of rules for the guidance of those compiling bibliographies in books.

Preparation of the Typescript

The cardinal rules for the presentation of material for publication, whether on disk or on paper, stipulate that the text should be typed on one side of the paper only, in double spacing, with good margins (at least 1½ inches (4 cm) on the left-hand side) and at top and bottom. It is helpful to the publisher if the same number of lines are typed per page; but try not to carry over onto the next page the last few words of a paragraph. With a word processor you will find that the page breaks are automatic: when you do your final check-through you should be able to insert page breaks where you wish, and to avoid a short line at the top of a page it is best to carry over the last two lines, even though it means that the previous page is one line short. A4 size paper is now standard. Headings should be consistent throughout, and quoted matter of more than a few lines should be indented, without the use of quotation marks. Indent five spaces at the beginning of each paragraph, unless the publisher's house style asks for anything different. Start each chapter on a new page.

New authors should aim to submit a pristine MS, especially if the work is going to a publisher unsolicited; first impressions are important. One of the joys of word processing is that corrections may be made right up to the last minute and the relevant pages printed out, without the need for laborious retyping. Established authors will find that their publishers adopt a more relaxed attitude and that they can get away with a modest number of handwritten additions, deletions or amendments. So long as these are absolutely legible and their place of insertion or deletion clear to the printer, it is unnecessary to go to the trouble of re-typing each amended page. Be very careful, however, about numbering pages: an insertion between pages 14 and 15, for example, would be numbered 14a, 14b and so on; but if page 15 is to be deleted altogether, the previous page should be numbered 14/15. Where an insertion does not take up the full page, always rule a line obliquely from left to right through the remaining part of the page to indicate that the text is continuous. It is far better to use white correcting fluid and to type the correction in than to risk an erasure and handwritten alteration that may be ambiguous to the typesetter. (A few publishers producing small runs of specialized books require what is known as 'camera-ready' copy, typed on electronic machines with carbon ribbon, variable spacing and justified lines, which is then photographed and reproduced lithographically; here, each page must of course be perfect, although pure spelling mistakes and punctuation may be corrected – very carefully – with the aid of correction fluid.)

If you use a typewriter, it is wise to make three copies of the final text, a top copy and two carbons; the publisher may ask for two, and the author should always retain one copy. Should additional copies be required later on, i.e. for an American or paperback publisher, photocopies can be made. There are on the market special packs of carbonless typing paper that produce one top and one copy without the need for a carbon; the quality of the copy is consistent and good (essential for photocopying purposes), but the cost so high at present that they are to be recommended only for short typescripts such as poems, articles or short stories. On the other hand, good film carbon is expensive too, and the sheets should be renewed every ten or fifteen pages when typing a full-length book so as to achieve some uniformity. (The discarded carbons can be used again for less important copies, such as correspondence.)

Never staple pages together. Short stories or features may be fastened with paper clips, and so may individual chapters of a book; but a full-length typescript is best put into a ring binder or packed loose into a box. (Use the boxes in which reams of bond typing paper are sold.)

Proof-correction

Book writers will normally see at least one, if not two, stages of proofs, which they are required to read and correct. It should be borne in mind that while printers' errors are not charged, any changes made by the author at this stage which amount to more than 10–15 per cent of the cost of composition will be payable by him (and deducted from royalties). The time to make last-minute amendments is *before* the copy editor passes the work to the printer.

Sometimes, where a work of topical interest is involved and some major event has taken place between the date of completion of the manuscript and delivery of proofs, the publisher will find the space to include a brief note to the effect that 'Since this book went to press [such and such] has occurred', but it cannot always be counted on.

A list of signs used in proof correction will be found in Judith Butcher's *Copy Editing*, in the *Writers' & Artists' Yearbook* and in the *British Standard BS 5261C: Marks for copy preparation and proof correction*. Other valuable guides for spelling, punctuation, division of words, and the use of capital and lower case, are *Hart's Rules for Compositors and Readers* and the *Oxford Writers' Dictionary*.

The Index

Every non-fiction book merits a good index, and reviewers these days are paying more attention than ever before to the quality of indexing and commenting unfavourably, where appropriate, on the lack of indexes.

Most authors' contracts stipulate that the author shall provide the index. It is however sometimes possible – and when, if ever, most publishers have accepted the Minimum Terms Agreement negotiated by the Society of Authors and the Writers' Guild it should become normal practice – for the publisher to contribute 50 per cent of the cost, especially if a professional indexer is to be employed. Some publishers have their own team of freelance indexers on whom they can call; others seek recommendations from the Society of Indexers, which was founded in 1957 to safeguard and improve indexing standards and which maintains a register of indexers suitably qualified in different subjects and types of indexing. To assist those seeking an indexer for their work, the Society now issues annually a booklet entitled *Indexers*

Available, which is distributed throughout the book trade; it lists practising members' names, addresses, telephone numbers and their specialist subjects. At the time of writing (1995) the Society's recommended minimum rate for indexing is £11 per hour for basic skills; specialist work commands more. Rates are revised annually.

There has long been controversy as to whether writers should or should not index their own books. Some people feel that an author is the ideal person, but others hold strongly to the view that he may be too close to his own work to be able to produce a truly objective index. Certainly, as a general rule, it will almost always take him longer than the trained professional. It is not generally realised that there is a great deal more to indexing than extracting the names of people and places and stringing them together in alphabetical order, so that when an author does decide to attempt it, he would be well advised to take the time and trouble to learn the basic rules.

Firstly, he must choose – and stick to – the form of alphabetical arrangement most suited to his book: either 'letter-by-letter' or 'word-by-word'. Then – and this is governed largely by space – he should give some thought to the layout and balance of the index and whether the sub-headings and sub-sub-headings (if any) will be indented or run on; both in layout and wording the sub-headings throughout must be consistent. There must be adequate cross-referencing of names and concepts, but not so much as to make the index unnecessarily long; care must be taken to avoid what is known as a 'wild goose chase', i.e. cross-references that never lead to the location of the subject-matter in the text, as in, for example, 'Indexers, Society of, *see* Society of Indexers' and 'Society of Indexers, *see* Indexers, Society of'. The main function of an index is to direct the user quickly to the place or places in the text where he will find precisely the information he seeks.

Indexing is normally undertaken at page proof stage and, for this reason, it nearly always has to be done at speed in order to meet the printers' deadline. Here the computer has really come into its own, and now that there is sophisticated software available that has been specially designed to meet the professional indexer's needs, two of the most time-consuming stages of the job – the sorting of entries into the required order, and the printing out of the edited index copy – can be accomplished very quickly. Beware, however, of the so-called 'automatic indexing' programs on offer, as these are inadequate for book indexing. Although a growing number of indexers now use computers, much manual indexing still goes on, the usual method being to mark on the page proofs (either with highlighter pen or by underlining) each name or concept to be indexed, and to write these on separate cards or slips which are filed alphabetically in a box as work proceeds; a certain amount of tightening up and editing of entries has to take place when all entries are assembled. It is a good plan for the author who intends to prepare his own index to start building it as he writes, making slips for the main entries and possible sub-headings; these can be edited later and the page numbers added. In the course of his work the indexer may come across inconsistencies or inaccuracies that both the author and the copy editor have missed; these should be telephoned through to the editorial office immediately. The index should be typed in double-spacing, with a maximum of 32 characters per line. The publisher will usually say that his tight production deadline does not permit him to send the indexer a proof for correction, but this should be insisted on wherever possible. Even the best printer can make a nonsense out of an index by failing to indent a sub-heading or by omitting or misprinting the occasional page reference – something that may not be spotted if the index is checked in the editorial office – and an index that is inaccurate is worse than no index at all.

These are but a few of the problems that confront the indexer. Authors interested in acquiring some basic training in indexing may take the Training in Indexing course administered by the Society of Indexers, successful completion of which entitles members of the Society to the status of 'Accredited Indexer' and, ultimately, to that of 'Registered Indexer' (details from the Course Administrator, Society of Indexers, Flat 4, 1 Ingleside Grove, Blackheath, London SE3 7PH; tel. 0181–858 9692). The course consists of five units, which may be purchased separately; you are not committed to taking the formal tests. Also available is a Book Indexing Postal Tutorials (BIPT) course (details from Ann Hall, The Lodge, Sidmount Avenue, Moffat, Dumfriesshire DG10 9BS; send a stamped addressed envelope).

The most comprehensive and up-to-date manual, recommended by and available from the Society, is Hans Wellisch's *Indexing A to Z*, published in the United States. The *British Standards BS 1749* and *BS 3700* (details at the end of this chapter) are the authoritative guides to current practice.

Names of suitably qualified indexers, general or specialist, may be obtained from the Registrar of the Society of Indexers, Mrs E. Wallis, 25 Leyborne Park, Kew Gardens, Surrey TW9 3HB (tel. 0181–940 4771). For a copy of *Indexers Available*, or other information about the Society, write to the Hon. Secretary, Mrs

H.C. Troughton, 38 Rochester Road, London NW1 9JJ, or telephone (answerphone only) 0171–916 7809.

A Last Word of Advice

Once the proofs have been corrected and returned to the publisher, the author may safely return all borrowed books and documents to their respective libraries and/or owners. He may also wish to parcel up and store his original notes and early drafts. *It is important not to throw these away.* When eventually his book is published, there is always the possibility that it may arouse unexpected interest and may even lead to other related commissions; almost certainly he will receive a number of readers' letters either asking him to justify certain statements or to give further information. Some of these enquiries may come from researchers working in the same field. Bearing in mind the enormous help he himself has derived from the work of others, would it not be churlish and ungenerous to refuse or not to be in a position to pass on the fruits of his own research – especially any information gathered but not used – to other *bona fide* writers?

It should not be forgotten that all writers feed to a lesser or greater extent on the work of other writers. As the Californian playwright Wilson Mizner put it, 'When you steal from one author, it's plagiarism; if you steal from many, it's research'.

British Standards (available from the British Standards Institution, Sales Department, 389 Chiswick High Road, London W4 4AL (tel. 0181–996 7000; fax 0181–996 7001):

BS 1629: 1989	*Recommendations for references to published materials*
BS 1749: 1985	*Recommendations for alphabetical arrangement and the filing order of numbers and symbols*
BS 3700: 1988	*Recommendations for preparing indexes to books, periodicals and other documents*
BS 5261 Part 1: 1983	*Recommendations for preparation of typescript copy for printing*
BS 5261 Part 2: 1976 (1995)	*Specifications for typographical requirements, marks for copy preparation and proof correction, proofing procedure*
BS 5261C: 1976	*Marks for copy preparation and proof correction* (extract from *BS 5261 Part 2*)
BS 5605: 1990	*Recommendations for citing and referencing published material*

Bloomsbury Good Word Guide, ed. M.H. Manser, Bloomsbury, London, 2nd edn, 1990; paperback edn, 1991

Copy-Editing, by Judith Butcher, Cambridge University Press, Cambridge, 3rd edn, 1992; reprinted 1994

The Good English Guide: English Usage in the 1990s, by Godfrey Howard, Macmillan, 1993

Hart's Rules for Compositors and Readers at the University Press Oxford, Oxford University Press, Oxford, 39th edn, 1983

Indexers Available, annual list of accredited and registered indexers, Society of Indexers, London

Indexing A to Z, by Hans Wellisch, H.W. Wilson, New York, 1991 (available from Thompson Henry Ltd, London Road, Sunningdale, Berks SL5 0EP, tel. 01344 24615, or from the Sales Manager of the Society of Indexers, Dorothy Frame, 26 Draycot Road, London E11 2NX, tel. 0181–530 2727)

The MHRA Style Book, eds A.S. Maney and R.L. Smallwood, Modern Humanities Research Association, London, 4th edn, 1991; new edition in preparation

Mind the Stop: A Brief Guide to Punctuation, by G.V. Carey, Penguin Books, Harmondsworth, 1971; reprinted 1993

Oxford Writers' Dictionary, Oxford University Press, Oxford, 1990

Writers' & Artists' Yearbook, published annually by A & C Black, London; article on 'Preparation of Typescripts'

Appendix I

Selective List of Major Sources in the United Kingdom

This list is limited by space and should be used as a guideline only, in conjunction with the *Aslib Directory*, the booklet *Record Repositories in Great Britain* and other reference source guides mentioned in earlier sections of this book. Unless otherwise stated, the libraries and record offices are open to the public without formality. Addresses, telephone numbers and hours of opening are subject to change with alarming frequency; most libraries and record offices have fax numbers, but some have asked for them not to be listed. In general, therefore, the fax number, where available, is stated only in the main text where a library or archive centre is first mentioned. While every effort has been made to bring information up to date at the time of going to press, it is advisable that researchers should check in advance before travelling any distance.

The Copyright Libraries

The British Library, Humanities and Social Sciences, Great Russell Street, London WC1B 3DG. Telephone nos: Reader Admissions Office, 0171–412 7677 (fax 0171–412 7794); Main Reading Room (general enquiries), 0171–412 2676; North Library and North Library Gallery, 0171–412 2673; Official Publications and Social Sciences Service, 0171–412 7536; Music Reading Room, 0171–412 7527; Map Library, 0171–412 7700. Admission by reader's ticket. Special pass required for admission to Manuscripts Students' Room (enquiries tel. 0171–412 7513). Mon, Fri, Sat, 9–5; Tue, Wed, Thu, 9–9. Most services are closed for one week at the end of October/beginning of November.

N.B. *The British Library is preparing to move to its new building at St Pancras, North London. During the transition period, from mid-1997 onwards, intending readers should telephone*

171

for information. The automated switchboard number is 0171–412 7000. There are two direct dial St Pancras 'help lines': for the humanities, 0171–412 7766; for science, business and technology, 0171–412 7915. The address of the new British Library is 96 Euston Road, St Pancras, London NW1 2DB.

Bodleian Library, University of Oxford, Broad Street, Oxford OX1 3BG (tel. 01865 277000). Admission by reader's ticket (fee payable). Mon–Fri, 9–10 (term), 9–7 (vacation); Sat, 9–1; closed last week in August.

Cambridge University Library, West Road, Cambridge CB3 9DR (tel. 01223 333000). Admission by reader's ticket. Mon–Fri, 9–7; Sat, 9–1; closed for one week in September.

National Library of Scotland, George IV Bridge, Edinburgh EH1 1EW (tel. 0131–226 4531). Admission by reader's ticket. Mon–Fri, 9.30–8.30; Sat, 9.30–1.

National Library of Wales, Aberystwyth, Dyfed SY23 3BU (tel. 01970 623816). Admission by reader's ticket. Mon–Fri, 9.30–6; Sat, 9.30–5.

N.B. Trinity College Library, College Street, Dublin 2, in the Republic of Ireland (tel. 003531 6772941) is also a copyright library.

Public Record Offices

Public Record Office, Ruskin Avenue, Kew, Richmond, Surrey TW9 4DU (tel. 0181–876 3444) and Chancery Lane, London WC2A 1LR (same tel. no.). Admission by reader's ticket. Mon–Fri, 9.30–5; closed for two weeks in October.

Scottish Record Office, H.M. General Register House, Edinburgh EH1 3YY (tel. 0131–556 6585). Admission by reader's ticket. Mon–Fri, 9–4.45.

Public Record Office of Northern Ireland, 66 Balmoral Avenue, Belfast BT9 6NY (tel. 01232 251318). Admission by reader's ticket. Mon–Fri, 9.15–4.45; closed first two weeks in December.

General Register Offices

General Register Office (The Office of Population Censuses and Surveys): indexes to registers of births, marriages and deaths at St Catherine's House, 10 Kingsway, London WC2B 6JP (tel. 0171–242 0262). Mon–Fri, 8.30–4.30. Postal applications tel. 0151–471 4200.

N.B. Census returns open for public inspection are in the basement of the Public Record Office, Chancery Lane, London WC2A 1LR. Admission without ticket.

Principal Registry of the Family Division, Somerset House, Strand, London WC2R 1LP (tel. 0171–936 6000). Mon–Fri, 10–4.30.

General Register Office for Scotland, New Register House, Edinburgh EH1 3YT (tel. 0131–334 0380). Mon–Thu, 9.30–4.30; Fri, 9.30–4.

General Register Office for Northern Ireland, Oxford House, 49–55 Chichester Street, Belfast BT1 4HL (tel. 01232 235000). Mon–Fri, 9.30–3.30.

N.B. The records for the whole of Ireland from 1864 to 1921 are at the office of the Registrar General, Joyce House, 8–11 Lombard Street East, Dublin 2, which houses the records of the Republic only since 1922.

Manuscript Collections/Registers of Archives

British Library, Department of Manuscripts, Great Russell Street, London WC1B 3DG (tel. 0171–412 7513). Admission to Students' Room by reader's ticket (applications at least 2 days in advance).* Mon–Sat, 10–4.45; closed first week in November.

British Library Oriental and India Office Collections (formerly the India Office Library), Orbit House, 197 Blackfriars Road, London SE1 8NG (tel. 0171–412 7873). Admission by reader's ticket. Mon–Fri, 9.30–5.45, Sat, 9.30–12.45.

N.B. *The above-mentioned collections will move to the new British Library at St Pancras by the end of 1997. During the transition period readers should telephone either the main British Library switchboard, 0171–412 7000, or the St Pancras 'help line' number for the humanities, 0171–412 7766, in advance of their visit, for up-to-date information.*

Royal Commission on Historical Manuscripts/National Register of Archives, Quality House, Quality Court, Chancery Lane, London WC2A 1HP (tel. 0171–242 1198). Mon–Fri, 9.30–5.

National Register of Archives (Scotland), West Register House, Charlotte Square, Edinburgh EH2 4DF (tel. 0131–556 6585). Mon–Fri, 9–5.

---

* The normal reader's ticket for the British Library does not admit to the Department of Manuscripts Students' Room. A higher level pass will also be required for access to the manuscript collections at St Pancras.

Large collections of manuscripts are also housed at the Public Record Offices (see page 172) and at the various County Record Offices and University Libraries (see pages 174–83).

County Record Offices/Regional Archives Centres

In this list opening times are not given for the individual offices: some are open all day throughout the working week, others close for lunch (or do not produce material during the lunch period), some are open late one evening in the week (but material must be ordered beforehand), others are shut either on Mondays or Saturdays. It is advisable to check prior to making a visit, as these opening hours are subject to change, and to reserve a seat.

Avon

Bath City Record Office, Guildhall, Bath BA1 5AW (tel. 01225 477421)

Bristol Record Office, B Bond Warehouse, Smeaton Road, Bristol BS1 6XN (tel. 0117 922 5692)

Bedfordshire

Bedfordshire Record Office, County Hall, Bedford MK42 9AP (tel. 01234 228833)

Berkshire

Berkshire Record Office, Shire Hall, Shinfield Park, Reading RG2 9XD (tel. 01734 233182)

Buckinghamshire

Buckinghamshire Record Office, County Hall, Aylesbury HP20 1UA (tel. 01296 382587)

Cambridgeshire

Cambridge County Record Office, Shire Hall, Castle Hill, Cambridge CB3 0AP (tel. 01223 317281); also at Grammar School Walk, Huntingdon PE18 6LF (tel. 01480 425842)

Cheshire

Cheshire Record Office, Duke Street, Chester CH1 1RL (tel. 01244 602559)

Chester City Record Office, Town Hall, Chester CH1 2HJ (tel. 01244 324324, ext. 2108)

Cleveland

Cleveland County Archives Department, Exchange House, 6 Marton Road, Middlesbrough TS1 1DB (tel. 01642 248321)

Cornwall

Cornwall County Record Office, County Hall, Truro TR1 3AY (tel. 01872 73698)

Royal Cornwall Museum, River Street, Truro TR1 2SJ (tel. 01872 72205)

Cumbria

Cumbria County Record Office, The Castle, Carlisle CA3 8UR (tel. 01228 812416); also at County Offices, Kendal LA9 4RQ (tel. 01539 814330) and at Duke Street, Barrow-in-Furness LA14 1XW (tel. 01229 831269)

Derbyshire

Derbyshire Record Office, New Street, Matlock DE4 3AG (tel. 01629 580000, ext. 7347). Postal address: DRO, c/o Education Dept., County Offices, Matlock DE4 3AG.

Devon

Devon Record Office, Castle Street, Exeter EX4 3PQ (tel. 01392 384253)

West Devon Record Office, Clare Place, Coxside, Plymouth PL4 0JW (tel. 01752 385940)

Dorset

Dorset Record Office, Bridport Road, Dorchester DT1 1RP (tel. 01305 250550)

Durham

Durham County Record Office, County Hall, Durham DH1 5UL (tel. 0191–383 3474)

Essex

Essex Record Office, P.O. Box 11, County Hall, Chelmsford CM1 1LX (tel. 01245 430067); and Central Library, Victoria Avenue,

Southend-on-Sea SS2 6EX (tel. 01702 612621); Colchester and NE Essex Branch, Stanwell House, Stanwell Street, Colchester CO2 7DL (tel. 01206 572099)

Gloucestershire

Gloucestershire Record Office, Clarence Row, Alvin Street, Gloucester GL1 3DW (tel. 01452 425295)

Hampshire

Hampshire Record Office, Sussex Street, Winchester SO23 8TH (tel. 01962 846154)
Portsmouth City Records Office, 3 Museum Road, Portsmouth PO1 2LE (tel. 01705 829765)
Southampton City Records Office, Civic Centre, Southampton SO9 4XL (tel. 01703 832251)

Hereford and Worcester

Hereford and Worcester Record Office, County Hall, Spetchley Road, Worcester WR5 2NP (tel. 01905 766351)
Hereford Record Office, The Old Barracks, Harold Street, Hereford HR1 2QX (tel. 01432 265441)
St Helen's Record Office, Fish Street, Worcester WR1 2HN (tel. 01905 765922)

Hertfordshire

Hertfordshire Record Office, County Hall, Hertford SG13 8DE (tel. 01992 555105)

Humberside

Humberside County Archives Office, County Hall, Beverley, North Humberside HU17 9BA (tel. 01482 885007)
South Humberside Area Record Office, Central Library, Town Hall Square, Grimsby DN31 1HX (tel. 01472 353481)
Kingston upon Hull City Record Office, 79 Lowgate, Kingston upon Hull HU1 2AA (tel. 01482 595102)

Kent

Centre for Kentish Studies, County Hall, Maidstone ME14 1XQ (tel. 01622 694363)
South-East Kent Record Office, Folkestone Library, 2 Grace Hill, Folkestone CT20 1HD (tel. 01303 850123)

Lancashire

Lancashire Record Office, Bow Lane, Preston PR1 2RE (tel. 01772 263039)

Leicestershire

The New Leicestershire Record Office and Local Studies Centre, Long Street, Wigston Magna, Leicester LE8 2AH (tel. 0116 257 1080)

Lincolnshire

Lincolnshire Archives Office, St Rumbold Street, Lincoln LN2 5AB (tel. 01522 525158)

London

Greater London Record Office, 40 Northampton Road, London EC1R 0HB (tel. 0171–332 3822). Tue–Fri, 9.30–4.45. Archives section, late night Tue to 7.30. Closed third and fourth weeks of October.

Manchester

Greater Manchester Record Office, 56 Marshall Street, New Cross, Ancoats, Manchester M4 5FU (tel. 0161–832 5284)

Merseyside

Merseyside Record Office, Cunard Building (4th floor), Pier Head, Liverpool L3 1EG (tel. 0151–236 8038). Tue only, 9–5
Liverpool Record Office, City Libraries, William Brown Street, Liverpool L3 8EW (tel. 0151–225 5417)
Wirral Archives Service, Birkenhead Reference Library, Borough Road, Birkenhead L41 2XB (tel. 0151–652 6106/7/8)

Midlands

Birmingham Local Studies, Central Library, Chamberlain Square, Birmingham B3 3HQ (tel. 0121–235 4220)
Coventry City Record Office, Mandela House, Bayley Lane, Coventry CV1 5RG (tel. 01203 832418)
Modern Records Centre, University of Warwick Library, Coventry CV4 7AL (tel. 01203 524219)

Norfolk

Norfolk Record Office, Gildengate House, Anglia Square, Upper Green Lane, Norwich NR3 1AX (tel. 01603 761349)

Northamptonshire

Northamptonshire Record Office, Wootton Hall Park, Northampton NN4 9BQ (tel. 01604 762129)

Northumberland

Northumberland Record Office, Melton Park, North Gosforth, Newcastle-upon-Tyne NE3 5QX (tel. 0191–236 2680)

Nottinghamshire

Nottinghamshire Archives Office, County House, Castle Meadow Road, Nottingham NG2 1AG (tel. 0115 950 4524)

Oxfordshire

Oxfordshire Archives, County Hall, New Road, Oxford OX1 1ND (tel. 01865 815203)

Shropshire

Shropshire Records and Research Centre, Castle Gate, Shrewsbury SY1 2AQ (tel. 01743 255350)

Somerset

Somerset Record Office, Obridge Road, Taunton TA2 7PU (tel. 01823 278805)

Staffordshire

Staffordshire Record Office, Eastgate Street, Stafford ST16 2LZ (tel. 01785 278380)
Lichfield Joint Record Office, Lichfield Library, The Friary, Lichfield WS13 6QG (tel. 01543 256787)

Suffolk

Suffolk Record Office, Gateacre Road, Ipswich IP1 2LQ (tel. 01473 264541)
Suffolk Record Office, Bury St Edmunds Branch, 77 Raingate Street, Bury St Edmunds IP33 2AR (tel. 01284 722522)

Suffolk Record Office, Lowestoft Branch, Central Library, Clapham Road, Lowestoft NR32 1DR (tel. 01502 503308)

Surrey

Surrey Record Office, County Hall, Penrhyn Road, Kingston-upon-Thames, KT1 2DN (tel. 0181–541 9065); Guildford Muniment Room, Castle Arch, Guildford GU1 3SX (tel. 01483 573942)

East Sussex

East Sussex Record Office, The Maltings, Castle Precincts, Lewes BN7 1YT (tel. 01273 482349)

West Sussex

West Sussex Record Office, Sherburne House, 3 Orchard Street, Chichester PO19 1DD (tel. 01243 533911). Postal enquiries to WSRO, County Hall, Chichester, West Sussex PO19 1RN

Tyne and Wear

Tyne and Wear Archives Department, Blandford House, West Blandford Square, Newcastle-upon-Tyne NE1 4JA (tel. 0191–232 6789); Local Studies Collection, Gateshead Central Library, Prince Consort Road, Gateshead NE8 4LN (tel. 0191–477 3478)

Warwickshire

Warwick County Record Office, Priory Park, Cape Road, Warwick CV34 4JS (tel. 01926 412735)

Isle of Wight

Isle of Wight County Record Office, 26 Hillside, Newport PO30 2EB (tel. 01983 823821/20)

Wiltshire

Wiltshire Record Office, County Hall, Trowbridge BA14 8JG (tel. 01225 713138)

North Yorkshire

North Yorkshire County Record Office, Malpas Road, Northallerton DL7 8TB (tel. 01609 777585)

York City Archives, Art Gallery Building, Exhibition Square, York YO1 2EW (tel. 01904 551879)

South Yorkshire

Barnsley Archive Service, Central Library, Shambles Street, Barnsley S70 2JF (tel. 01226 773950)

Doncaster Archives Department, King Edward Road, Balby, Doncaster DN4 0NA (tel. 01302 859811)

Sheffield Archives, 52 Shoreham Street, Sheffield S1 4SP (tel. 0114 273 4756)

West Yorkshire

West Yorkshire Archive Service, Wakefield Headquarters, Registry of Deeds, Newstead Road, Wakefield WF1 2DE (tel. 01924 295982)

Scotland

Argyll and Bute District Archives, Kilmory, Lochgilphead, Argyll PA31 8RT (tel. 01546 602127)

Borders Regional Archive, Regional Library HQ, St Mary's Mill, Selkirk TD7 5EW (tel. 01750 20842)

Central Regional Council Archives Department, Unit 6, Burghmuir Industrial Estate, Stirling FK7 7PY (tel. 01786 450745)

Dumfries Archives Centre, 33 Burns Street, Dumfries DG1 2PS (tel. 01387 69254)

Dundee District Archive and Record Centre, 21 City Square, Dundee DD1 3BY (tel. 01382 23141, ext. 4494)

City of Edinburgh District Archives, City Chambers, High Street, Edinburgh EH1 1YJ (tel. 0131–225 2424, ext. 5196)

Grampian Regional Archives, Old Aberdeen House, Dunbar Street, Aberdeen AB2 1UE (tel. 01224 481775)

The Highland Regional Library and Archive Service, Inverness Public Library, Farraline Park, Inverness IV1 1NH (tel. 01463 220330)

Orkney Archives, Orkney Library, Laing Street, Kirkwall KW15 1NW (tel. 01856 3166)

Perth and Kinross District Archives, A.K. Bell Library, 2–8 York Place, Perth PH2 8EP (tel. 01738 444949)

Shetland Archives, 44 King Harald Street, Lerwick ZE1 0EQ (tel. 01595 3535, ext. 269)

Strathclyde Regional Archives, Mitchell Library, North Street, Glasgow G3 7DN (tel. 0141–227 2405)

Wales

Clwyd Record Office, The Old Rectory, Hawarden, Deeside CH5 3NR (tel. 01244 532364) and 46 Clwyd Street, Ruthin LL15 1HP (tel. 01824 703077)

Dyfed Archives Service, Carmarthenshire Area Record Office, County Hall, Carmarthen SA3 1JP (tel. 01267 233333, ext. 4182)

Glamorgan Record Office, County Hall, Cathays Park, Cardiff CF1 3NE (tel. 01222 780282)

Gwent County Record Office, County Hall, Cwmbran NP44 2XH (tel. 01633 832214)

Gwynedd Archives Service: Caernarfon Area Record Office, Victoria Dock, Caernarfon (tel. 01286 679095); Dolgellau Area Record Office, Cae Penarlag, Dolgellau LL40 2YB (tel. 01341 422341, ext. 3300/3302); Llangefni Area Record Office, Shire Hall, Llangefni LL77 7TW (tel. 01248 750262, ext. 269)

University Libraries (other than Oxford and Cambridge) with Important Manuscript Collections

Students, undergraduates and graduates of other universities are normally admitted without formality; temporary tickets will be issued to other *bona fide* researchers at the Librarian's discretion. At some libraries there are slightly amended opening hours during vacations. Please note that opening times and telephone extensions, where stated, are for the departments of manuscripts and archives. In all cases you should write in advance of your visit.

The main libraries of the University of Cambridge and the University of Oxford are listed under 'Copyright Libraries' (pages 171–2).

England

Birmingham University Library, Edgbaston, Birmingham B15 2TT (tel. 0121–414 5816). Mon–Fri, 9–5. Closed Christmas and Easter vacations.

Durham University Archives and Special Collections, 5 The College, Durham DH1 3EQ (tel. 0191–374 3610). Mon–Fri, 9–1, 2–5. During term 5–8, by arrangement.

Exeter University Library, Stocker Road, Exeter EX4 4PT (tel. 01392 263869/70). Mon–Fri, 9–5.30.

Hull University, Brynmor Jones Library, Cottingham Road, Hull HU6 7RX (tel. 01482 346311). Mon–Fri, 9–1, 2–5.

Keele University Library, Keele ST5 5BG (tel. 01782 621111, ext. 3741. Mon–Fri, 9.30–5.

Leeds University, Brotherton Library, Leeds LS2 9JT (tel. 0113 243 1751). Mon–Fri, 9–1, 2.15–5.

Liverpool University, Sydney Jones Library, P.O. Box 123, Liverpool L69 3DA (tel. 0151–794 2679). Mon–Fri, 9–5.

University of London Library, Senate House, Malet Street, London WC1E 7HU (tel. 0171–636 8000). Mon–Fri, 10–5. Also the Institute of Historical Research (tel. 0171–636 0272).

John Rylands University Library of Manchester, Deansgate, Manchester M3 3EH (tel. 0161–834 5343). Mon–Fri, 10–5.30; Sat, 10–1.

Newcastle-upon-Tyne University, Robinson Library, Newcastle-upon-Tyne NE2 4HQ (tel. 0191–222 6000). Mon–Fri, 9.15–5.

Nottingham University Library, University Park, Nottingham NG7 2RD (tel. 0115 951 4555). Mon–Fri, 9–5.

Reading University Library, Whiteknights, Reading RG6 2AE (tel. 01734 318770). Mon–Fri, 9–1, 2–5.

Sheffield University Library, Western Bank, Sheffield S10 2TN (tel 0114 276 8555, ext. 4334). Mon–Thu, 9–9.30; Fri, 9–5 (term); Mon–Fri, 9–5 (vacation); Sat, 9–12.30.

Southampton University Library, Highfield, Southampton SO17 1BJ (tel. 01703 593007). Mon–Fri, 9–1, 2–5.

Sussex University Library, Falmer, Brighton BN1 9QL (tel. 01273 606755). Mon–Thu, 9–1, 2–5.

Warwick University Modern Records Centre, University Library, Coventry CV4 7AL (tel. 01203 523523). Mon–Thu, 9–1, 1.30–5; Fri, 9–1, 1.30–4.

York University, Borthwick Institute of Historical Research, St Anthony's Hall, Peasholme Green, York YO1 2PW (tel. 01904 642315). Mon–Fri, 9.30–12.50, 2–4.50.

Scotland

Aberdeen University Library, Queen Mother Library, Meston Walk, Aberdeen AB9 2UE (tel. 01224 272579). Mon–Fri, 9.30–4.30.

Dundee University Library, Dundee, Tayside DD1 4HN (tel. 01382 23181, ext. 4087). Mon–Wed, 9–5; Thu, 9–1.30; Sat a.m. by appointment (term only).

Edinburgh University Library, 30 George Square, Edinburgh EH8 9LJ (tel. 0131–650 3384). Mon–Fri, 9–5.

Glasgow University Library, Department of Special Collections, Hillhead Street, Glasgow G12 8QE (tel. 0141–339 8855). Mon–Fri, 9–9.30, Sat, 9–12.30 (term); Mon–Fri, 9–5, Sat, 9–12.30 (vacation).

St Andrews University Library, North Street, St Andrews KY16 9TR (tel. 01334 462280). Mon–Fri, 9–12, 2–5; Sat, 9–12 (term only).

Wales

University College of North Wales Library, Department of Manuscripts, Bangor LL57 2DG (tel. 01248 351151). Mon–Fri, 9–1, 2–5; Wed to 9 (term only).

Cathedral Archives and Libraries

Canterbury Cathedral Archives, The Precincts, Canterbury, Kent CT1 2EH (tel. 01227 463510). Mon–Thu, 9–5; 1st and 3rd Sat of each month, 9–1. Reader's ticket required (take 2 passport-size photographs and means of identification).

Durham Dean and Chapter Library, The College, Durham DH1 3EH (tel. 0191–386 2489). Mon–Fri, 9–1, 2.15–5. Closed in August.

Exeter Cathedral Library and Archives, Old Bishop's Palace, Diocesan House, Palace Gate, Exeter EX1 1HX (tel. 01392 72894). Mon–Fri, 2–5.

Salisbury Cathedral Chapter Archives, 6 The Close, Salisbury SP1 2EF (tel. 01722 326107), by appointment (written application required).

York Minster Library, Dean's Park, York YO1 2JD (tel. 01904 625308), by appointment.

Westminster Abbey Library and Muniment Room, Westminster Abbey, London SW1P 3PA (tel. 0171–222 5152, ext. 228). Written application to Librarian or Keeper of the Muniments required.

Westminster Diocesan Archives (Roman Catholic), 16a Abingdon Road, London W8 6AF (tel. 0171–938 3580), by appointment.

Winchester Cathedral Library, 5 The Close, Winchester SO23 9LS (tel. 01962 853137). Written application required, opening times vary.

Other Major Reference Libraries

Belfast: Irish and Local Studies Department, Central Library, Royal Avenue, Belfast BT1 1EA (tel. 01232 243233)

Birmingham Reference Library, Central Library, Chamberlain Square, Birmingham B3 3HQ (tel. 0121–235 4511)

Cardiff Arts and Social Studies Library, University of Wales College of Cardiff, Corbett Road, P.O. Box 430, Cardiff CF1 3XT (tel. 01222 874000)

Edinburgh City Libraries, George IV Bridge, Edinburgh EH1 1EG (tel. 0131–225 5584)

Glasgow: Mitchell Library, North Street, Glasgow G3 7DN (tel. 0141–221 7030)

Liverpool City Libraries, William Brown Street, Liverpool L3 8EW (tel. 0151–225 5429/5435)

London: City of Westminster Central Reference Library, 35 St Martin's Street, London WC2H 7HP (tel. 0171–798 2034/2036)

Manchester: Central Library, St Peter's Square, Manchester M2 5PD (tel. 0161–234 1900)

Private Subscription Libraries

Highgate Literary and Scientific Institution Library, 11 South Grove, Highgate Village, London N6 6BS (tel. 0181–340 3343). Tue–Fri, 10–5; Sat, 10–4. £33 per year (£51 family subscription).

London Library, 14 St James's Square, London SW1Y 4LG (tel. 0171–930 7705). Mon–Sat, 9.30–5.30; Thu to 7.30. £120 per year.

Space does not permit the listing of the few other surviving private subscription libraries in the provinces, but these will be well known to readers living locally; or consult the yellow pages of the local telephone directories. A descriptive leaflet is available from the Secretary of the Association of Independent Libraries: Geoffrey Foster, Leeds Library, 18 Commercial Street, Leeds LS1 6AL (tel. 0113 245 3071).

Short List of Subjects and Sources

Advertising

Advertising Association Library, Abford House, 15 Wilton Road, London SW1V 1NJ (tel. 0171–828 2771). Mon–Fri, 9.30–1, 2–5. Non-members by appointment only, Tue–Fri, 2–4.

History of Advertising Trust, Unit 6, The Raveningham Centre, Raveningham, Norwich NR14 6NU (tel. 01508 548623). Mornings only.

Agriculture

Institute of Agricultural History and Museum of English Rural Life, University of Reading, Whiteknights, Reading RG6 2AG (tel. 01734 318660). Mon–Fri, 9.30–1, 2–5, by appointment.

Air Force

Royal Air Force Museum, Department of Aviation Records, Grahame Park Way, Hendon, London NW9 5LL (tel. 0181–205 2266). By appointment only.

See also Ministry of Defence Whitehall Library under '*Military*', and under '*World Wars I and II*'.

Architecture

British Architectural Library, Royal Institute of British Architects, 66 Portland Place, London W1N 4AD (tel. 0171–580 5533). Mon, 1.30–5; Tue, 10–8; Wed, Thu, Fri, 10–5; Sat, 10–1.30. Closed in August.

Art

Art and Design Library (incorporating the Preston Blake Library), City of Westminster Central Reference Library, 2nd floor, 35 St Martin's Street, London WC2H 7HP (tel. 0171–798 2038). Mon–Fri, 10–7; Sat, 10–5.

British Museum, Department of Prints and Drawings, Great Russell Street, London WC1B 3DG (tel. 0171–636 1555). Admission by ticket (apply in advance). Mon–Fri, 10–1, 2.15–4; Sat, 10–12.30.

Cartoon Art Trust, Baird House, 15–17 St Cross Street, London EC1N 8UN (tel. 0171–405 4717). Mon–Fri, 12–6.

Courtauld Institute of Art Library, Somerset House, London WC2R 2LS (tel. 0171–873 2526). Mon–Fri, 10–7 (term); 10–6 (vacation). Closed in August.

National Portrait Gallery Heinz Archive and Library, 2 St Martin's
Place, London WC2H 0HE (tel. 0171–306 0055). Tue–Sat,
10–5, by appointment only.
Victoria & Albert Museum Library, Cromwell Road, London SW7
2RL (tel. 0171–938 8315). Tue–Sat, 10–5. N.B. A specially
endorsed reader's ticket is required for access to certain MSS
and reserved material in the National Art Library.

Recommended titles:
Allgemeines Lexikon der bildenden Künstler, by U. Thieme and
F. Becker, 37 vols; photographic reprint of original 1907 edition
published by Seeman Verlag, Leipzig, 1978
The Dictionary of British Cartoonists and Caricatures 1730–1980,
compiled by Mark Bryant and Simon Heneage, Scolar Press,
London, 1994
Dictionnaire des peintres, sculpteurs, dessinateurs et graveurs, ed.
E. Benézit, new edn, 10 vols, Gründ, Paris, 1976

Banking and Commerce

Bank of England Library and Information Services, Threadneedle
Street, London EC2R 8AH (tel. 0171–601 4715). Telephone
or written enquiries only. The Bank of England and other
major banks will grant access to historical records only when
applications are supported by a university or other centre of
research.
City of Westminster Central Reference Library, 35 St Martin's
Street, London WC2H 7HP (tel. 0171–798 2034/2036).
Computer search and information for business services available.

Births, Marriages and Deaths

See under 'General Register Offices' (pages 172–3) and
'*Genealogy*'.

Broadcasting and Television

BBC Written Archives Centre, Caversham Park, Reading RG4
8TZ (tel. 01734 472742, ext. 281/282). Open to *bona fide*
researchers, Wed–Fri, 9.45–1, 2–5.15, by appointment only.
British Universities Film and Video Council (BUFVC), 55 Greek
Street (1st floor), London W1V 5LR (tel. 0171–734 3687).
Bona fide researchers may use library for reference purposes
and on payment of small fee consult the Slade Film History
Register (newsreels 1896–1979).

National Sound Archive, 29 Exhibition Road, Kensington, London SW7 2AS (tel. 0171–589 6603). Mon–Fri, 10–5; Thu to 9. Listening service by appointment 3–4 days in advance. Northern listening service at British Library Document Supply Centre, Boston Spa, W. Yorks (tel. 01937 546060). There will also be NSA listening facilities at the new British Library at St Pancras.

Business

British Library Business Information Service, Science Reference Library, 25 Southampton Buildings, Chancery Lane, London WC2A 1AW (tel. for basic enquiries, 0171–412 7454, for priced research service, 0171–412 7457). Mon–Fri, 9.30–5. Will be moving to the new British Library at St Pancras by the end of 1997.

Business Archives Council, The Clove Building, 4 Maguire Street, London SE1 2NQ (tel. 0171–407 6110). Will assist in tracing business histories and business archives. By appointment.

City Business Library, 1 Brewers Hall Garden, London EC2V 5BX (tel. 0171–638 8215). Mon–Fri, 9.30–5.30.

Companies House (Department of Trade and Industry), 55–71 City Road, London EC1Y 1BB (tel. 0171–253 9393) and Companies Registration Office, Crown Way, Maindy, Cardiff CF4 3UZ (tel. 01222 388588). Mon–Fri, 9.30–3.45. Microfilm copies of company records in London, files in Cardiff. In Scotland, 102 George Street, Edinburgh EH2 3DJ (tel. 0131–225 5774).

Census Returns

Public Record Office, basement, Chancery Lane, London WC2A 1LR (tel. 0181–876 3444 ext. 2630). Mon–Fri, 9.30–5. Open to public without ticket.

Children's Books

Bethnal Green Museum of Childhood, Cambridge Heath Road, London E2 9PA (tel. 0181–980 3204). Renier Collection of Historic and Contemporary Children's Books; also Young Book Trust Collection (after two years) and some smaller collections. Computerized catalogue in preparation; postal and telephone enquiries only.

Young Book Trust, Book House, 45 East Hill, London SW18 2QZ (tel. 0181–870 9055). Reference library and information service, membership by subscription.

Costume

Costume and Fashion Research Centre, 4 Circus Road, Bath, Avon BA1 2EW (tel. 01225 477752). Enquiries to Keeper of Costume.

European Commission

European Commission Information Unit and Library, Jean Monnet House, 8 Storey's Gate, London SW1P 3AT (tel. 0171–973 1992). Mon–Fri, 10–1. Not open to students.

Films and Cinema History

British Film Institute Library (BFI), 21 Stephen Street, London W1P 1PL (tel. 0171–255 1444). Mon, Fri, 10.30–5.30; Tue, Thu, 10.30–8; Wed, 1–8. *Note.* An annual subscription to the BFI including library membership is £26.95; library membership only £25.00; a one-day reader's pass is £5.00. There are various subscriptions, with or without handbook, discounts to students, the unemployed and senior citizens (for details tel. 0171–815 1374).

British Universities Film and Video Council (BUFVC), 55 Greek Street (1st floor), London W1V 5LR (tel. 0171–734 3687). By appointment to *bona fide* researchers; contact Head of Information.

Folklore

English Folk Dance and Song Society, Cecil Sharp House, 2 Regent's Park Road, London NW1 7AY (tel. 0171–485 2206). Library Mon–Fri, 9.30–5.30; sound library closed 12–2.

The Folklore Society, c/o University College, Gower Street, London WC1E 6BT (tel. 0171–387 5894)

Recommended title: *Larousse Dictionary of World Folklore*, Larousse, London, 1995

Genealogy and Heraldry

College of Arms, Queen Victoria Street, London EC4 4BT (tel. 0171–248 2762). Mon–Fri, 10–4; Sat by appointment.
N.B. There are no public search rooms. Research is undertaken only by the Heralds and their staff, on a fee-paying basis (brief preliminary search is free).

Hyde Park Family History Center of the Church of Jesus Christ of Latter-Day Saints (of Salt Lake City, Utah, USA), 64–68 Exhibition Road, London SW7 2PA (tel. 0171–589 8561). Mon,

9–6; Tue–Fri, 9–8; Sat, 9–3. Appointment necessary to reserve computer.

Institute of Heraldic and Genealogical Studies Library, 79–82 Northgate, Canterbury, Kent CT1 1BA (tel. 01227 768664). Mon, Wed, Fri, 10–5, by appointment.

Religious Society of Friends, Friends House, Euston Road, London NW1 2BJ (tel. 0171–387 3601). Tue–Fri, 10–5; closed for one week before Spring Bank Holiday and one week at end of November. *Bona fide* researchers providing suitable introductions/letters of recommendation may use the Library on payment of a search fee, or searches will be carried out by staff at a fee.

Society of Genealogists' Library, 14 Charterhouse Buildings, Goswell Road, London EC1M 7BA (tel. 0171–251 8799). Tue, Fri, Sat, 10–6; Wed, Thu, 10–8; closed on Mondays. Nonmembers pay search fees (currently £3.00 for one hour; £7.50 for half day (4 hours); £10.00 for a day or a day and an evening). Closed for one week in February and on Friday afternoons and Saturdays prior to bank holidays.

Geography and Maps

British Library Map Library, British Museum (King Edward Building), London WC1B 3DG (tel. 0171–412 7700). Mon–Sat, 10–4.30 or from 9.30 with reader's pass; closed for the week following the last complete week in October. Moving to St Pancras by the end of 1997.

Royal Geographical Society, Kensington Gore, London SW7 2AR (tel. 0171–589 5466). Mon–Fri, 10–5. Library open to *bona fide* researchers by arrangement; map room open to general public (closed 1–2).

Government and Official Information

British Library Official Publications and Social Sciences Service, Great Russell Street, London WC1B 3DG (tel. 0171–412 7536). Admission by reader's ticket. Mon–Fri, 9.30–4.45, closed for the week following the last complete week in October. Moving to St Pancras by the end of 1997.

Central Office of Information, Hercules Road, Westminster Bridge Road, London SE1 7DU (tel. 0171–928 2345). Telephone or written enquiries only.

Foreign & Commonwealth Office Library, King Charles Street, London SW1A 2AH (tel. 0171–270 3925). Open to *bona fide* researchers only, by appointment.

Oriental and India Office Collections (formerly India Office
    Library), 197 Blackfriars Road, London SE1 8NG (tel.
    0171–412 7873). Mon–Fri, 9.30–5.45; Sat, 9.30–12.45.
    Moving to St Pancras by the end of 1997.
Public Record Office, Ruskin Avenue, Kew, Richmond, Surrey
    TW9 4DU (tel. 0181–876 3444) and Chancery Lane, London
    WC2A 1LR (same tel. no.). Admission by reader's ticket.
    Mon–Fri, 9.30–5; closed first two weeks in October.
See also under '*Parliament*'.

International Affairs

Royal Institute of International Affairs Library, Chatham House,
    10 St James's Square, London SW1Y 4LE (tel. 0171–957 5700).
    Open to non-members by arrangement with the librarian. *Note*:
    The press cuttings collection for period 1940–71 has been trans-
    ferred to British Newspaper Library, Colindale (indexes at
    Chatham House).

Law

Use of the law libraries in London is limited to members of the
    legal profession, but *bona fide* researchers may be able to obtain
    information by telephone or written enquiry. For other law
    libraries, see the *Aslib Directory*.
Inner Temple Library, Inner Temple, London EC4Y 7DA (tel.
    0171–797 8218)
Institute of Advanced Legal Studies, University of London, 17
    Russell Square, London WC1B 5DR (tel. 0171–637 1731)
The Law Society, 113 Chancery Lane, London WC2A 1NB (tel.
    0171–320 5946). (Holds records of solicitors from 1907, also
    LEXIS index to newspaper law reports.)
Lincoln's Inn Library, Lincoln's Inn, London WC2A 3TN (tel.
    0171–242 4371)
Middle Temple Library, Middle Temple Lane, London EC4Y 9BT
    (tel. 0171–353 4303)
Royal Courts of Justice Library, Strand, London WC2A 2LL (tel.
    0171–936 6000)
Recommended title: *Legal Information – What it is and where to
    find it*, by Peter Clinch, Aslib, London, 1995

London

City of Westminster Archives Centre, 10 St Ann's Street, London
    SW1P 2XR (tel. 0171–798 2180). Mon–Fri, 9.30–7; Sat, 9.30–5.

Corporation of London Records Office, Guildhall, London EC2P 2EJ (tel. 0171–260 1251). Mon–Fri, 9.30–4.45.

Greater London Record Office and History Library, 40 Northampton Road, London EC1R 0HB (tel. 0171–332 3822). Tue–Fri, 9.30–4.45. Closed last two weeks in October.

Guildhall Library, Aldermanbury, London EC2P 2EJ (tel. 0171–332 1868/1870). Mon–Sat, 9.30–5.

N.B. A number of London borough public libraries hold sizeable local history collections. Consult current edition of *Record Repositories in Great Britain*, HMSO, London, and *Greater London Local History Directory*, Peter Marcan, London, 1993.

Medicine

Marylebone Public Library Health Information Library, Marylebone Road, London NW1 5PS (tel. 0171–798 1039). Mon–Fri, 9.30–7; Sat, 9.30–5. Reference and lending facilities (tickets from other public libraries are accepted).

Royal College of Physicians of London Library, 11 St Andrew's Place, London NW1 4LE (tel. 0171–935 1174). Mon–Fri, 10–5. *Bona fide* researchers not members of the profession may use the reference facilities. Holds *Munk's Roll* (lives of Fellows of the Royal College of Physicians from the 16th century to the present day).

Royal College of Surgeons of England Library, 35–43 Lincoln's Inn Fields, London WC2A 3PN (tel. 0171–405 3474). Admission by introduction from a graduate of the College. Mon–Fri, 10–6. Closed in August.

Wellcome Institute for the History of Medicine Library, 183 Euston Road, London NW1 2BE (tel. 0171–611 8582). Mon, Wed, Fri, 9.45–5.15; Tue, Thu, 9.45–7.15; Sat (except prior to bank holidays), 9.45–1.

For further information see the *Directory of Medical and Health Care Libraries in the British Isles*, Library Association, London (latest edition, 9th, 1994).

Military

Liddell Hart Centre for Military Archives, King's College, Strand, London WC2R 2LS (tel. 0171–873 2187/2015). Mon–Fri, 9.30–5.30 (term); 9.30–4.30 (vacation), by written application. N.B. 20th-century records only.

Ministry of Defence Whitehall Library, 3–5 Great Scotland Yard,

London SW1A 2HW (tel. 0171–218 4445). Telephone or written enquiries only.

National Army Museum, Department of Archives, Photographs, Film and Sound, Royal Hospital Road, London SW3 4HT (tel. 0171–730 0717). Admission by reader's ticket. Tue–Sat, 10–4.30. Now handles research enquiries for Society for Army Historical Research.

Public Record Office, Ruskin Avenue, Kew, Richmond, Surrey TW9 4DU (tel. 0181–876 3444) and Chancery Lane, London WC2A 1LR (same tel. no.). Admission by reader's ticket. Mon–Fri, 9.30–5; closed for two weeks in October.

See also under '*World Wars I and II*'.

Music

British Library Music Reading Area, Great Russell Street, London WC1B 3DG (tel. 0171–412 7527). Mon–Fri, 9.30–4.45. Will be moving to St Pancras by the end of 1997.

Central Music Library (Westminster), Victoria Library, 160 Buckingham Palace Road, London SW1W 9UD (tel. 0171–798 2192). Mon–Fri, 1–7; Sat, 10–5.

Royal College of Music Reference Library, Prince Consort Road, London SW7 2BS (tel. 0171–589 3643). Admission by reader's ticket. Mon–Fri, 10–5; closed late July to early September, also for two weeks at Christmas and at Easter.

Royal Opera House Archives, Covent Garden, London WC2E 7QA (tel. 0171–212 9353). Mon, Tue, Thu, Fri, 10.30–1, 2.30–5.30. By appointment only.

Vaughan Williams Memorial Library, English Folk Dance and Song Society, Cecil Sharp House, 2 Regent's Park Road, London NW1 7AY (tel. 0171–284 0523). Open to the general public for reference (fee payable).

Recommended title: *The New Grove Dictionary of Music and Musicians*, ed. Stanley Sadie, 20 vols, Macmillan, London, 1981; paperback edn, 1995.

Natural History

Natural History Museum Library, Cromwell Road, London SW7 5BD (tel. 0171–938 9191). Mon–Fri, 10–4.30.

Royal Botanic Gardens Library and Archives, Kew, Richmond, Surrey TW9 3AE (tel. 0181–940 1171). Mon–Thu, 9–4.30; Fri, 9–5. Prior application to consult the archives is necessary.

Naval

National Maritime Museum Library, Romney Road, Greenwich, London SE10 9NF (tel. 0181–312 6673/6712). Mon–Fri, 10–4.45.

Royal Naval Historical Library, at Ministry of Defence Whitehall Library, see under '*Military*' on pages 191–2.

Newspapers and Periodicals

British Library Newspaper Library, Colindale Avenue, London NW9 5HE (tel. 0171–323 7353). Admission by reader's ticket. Mon–Sat, 10–4.45; closed for the week following the last complete week in October.

British Library Humanities and Social Sciences, Great Russell Street, London WC1B 3DG, for periodicals (monthly or quarterly), to be seen in the main Reading Room (tel. 0171–412 7676) or North Library Gallery (tel. 0171–412 7763). Mon, Fri, Sat, 9–5; Tue, Wed, Thu, 9–9; closed for the week following the last complete week in October. Will be moving to St Pancras by the end of 1997.

Parliament

House of Lords Record Office, House of Lords, Palace of Westminster, London SW1A 0PW (tel. 0171–219 3074). Mon–Fri, 9.30–5. Intending searchers should write to the Clerk of the Records in advance, giving at least one week's notice and details of the nature of their research and/or specific documents they wish to consult.

See also under '*Government and Official Information*'.

Politics (20th-century)

British Library of Political and Economic Science (London School of Economics), 10 Portugal Street, London WC2A 2HD (tel. 0171–955 7223), by appointment.

Churchill Archives Centre, Churchill College, Cambridge CB3 0DS (tel. 01223 336168). Mon–Fri, 9.30–12.30, 1.30–5, by appointment with the Archivist. N.B. Certain collections are subject to special conditions of access.

Printing and Publishing

St Bride Printing Library, Bride Lane, London EC4Y 8EQ (tel. 0171–353 4660). Mon–Fri, 9.30–5.30.

Recorded Sound

National Sound Archive, 29 Exhibition Road, Kensington, London SW7 2AS (tel. 0171–589 6603). Mon–Fri, 10–5, with late opening Thu, to 9. Listening service by appointment 3–4 days in advance. Northern listening service at British Library Document Supply Centre, Boston Spa, W. Yorks (tel. 01937 546060). There will also be NSA listening facilities at the new British Library at St Pancras.

Religion

Catholic Central Library, 47 Francis Street, London SW1P 1QR (tel. 0171–834 6128). Non-members for reference and research only. Mon–Fri, 10.30–5; Sat, 10.30–1.30.

Church of England Record Centre, 15 Galleywall Road, South Bermondsey, London SE16 3PB (tel. 0171–222 7010). Mon–Fri, 9.30–5, by appointment.

Dr Williams's Library, 14 Gordon Square, London WC1H 0AG (tel. 0171–387 3727). Mon, Wed, Fri, 10–5; Tue, Thu, 10–6.30; closed first half of August. Admission by recommendation; subscription rate for borrowers (details on application to Librarian).

Lambeth Palace Library, London SE1 7JU (tel. 0171–928 6222). *Bona fide* students, others by special permission. Mon–Fri, 10–5. Closed for ten days at Christmas and at Easter.

Methodist Archives and Research Centre, formerly at Epworth House, London, are now housed at the John Rylands University Library of Manchester, Deansgate, Manchester M3 3EH (tel. 0161–834 5343). Mon–Fri, 10–5.30; Sat, 10–1.

Parkes Library (Jewish studies), University of Southampton Library, Highfield, Southampton SO17 1BJ (tel. 01703 593007).

Religious Society of Friends (Quakers) Library, Friends House, Euston Road, London NW1 2BJ (tel. 0171–387 3601). Tue–Fri, 10–5. Closed one week before Spring Bank Holiday and one week at end of November. Letter of introduction required for non-members.

Sion College Library, Victoria Embankment, London EC4Y 0DN (tel. 0171–353 7983). Mon–Fri, 10–5. Annual subscription rates and temporary membership available.

See also under '*Cathedral Archives and Libraries*'.

Recommended title: *Keyguide to Information Sources on World Religions*, compiled by Jean Holm, Mansell, London, 1991

Royal Archives

By special permission of the Keeper of the Queen's Archives, Windsor Castle, Berks SL4 1NJ. Apply in writing.

Science and Technology

British Library Science Reference and Information Service: 25 Southampton Buildings, Chancery Lane, London WC2A 1AW (tel. 0171–412 7494), Mon–Fri, 9.30–9; Sat, 10–1. Also at 9 Kean Street, London WC2B 4AT (tel. 0171–412 7288), Mon–Fri, 9.30–5.30. Moving to St Pancras by the end of 1997.

City of Westminster Central Reference Library, Ground Floor, 35 St Martin's Street, London WC2H 7HP (tel. 0171–798 2034). Mon–Fri, 10–7; Sat, 10–5.

Imperial College of Science and Technology Archives, Sherfield Building, Imperial College, London SW7 2AZ (tel. 0171–589 5111, ext. 3022). Mon–Fri, 10–12, 2–5, by appointment. Letter of introduction required.

Royal Society of London Library, 6 Carlton House Terrace, London SW1Y 5AG (tel. 0171–839 5561). Mon–Fri, 10–5. Admission on introduction by a Fellow: *bona fide* researchers on written application.

Science Museum Library, Exhibition Road, London SW7 5NH (tel. 0171–938 8234). Mon–Fri, 9.30–9; Sat, 9.30–5.30.

See also the Highgate Literary and Scientific Institution, listed under '*Private Subscription Libraries*'.

Recommended titles: *ISIS Cumulative Bibliography* and the *History of Technology* series, both published by Mansell, London

Science Fiction

Science Fiction Foundation Research Library, Liverpool University Library, P.O. Box 123, Liverpool L69 3DA (tel. 0151–794 2733/2696). By appointment.

Recommended title: *Encyclopedia of Science Fiction*, compiled by John Clute and Peter Nicholls, Orbit, London, rev. edn, 1993

Theatre

Mander and Mitchenson Theatre Collection, The Mansion, Beckenham Place Park, Beckenham BR3 2BP (tel. 0181–658 7725). Open to *bona fide* researchers by appointment.

Society for Theatre Research, c/o Theatre Museum, 1e Tavistock Street, Covent Garden, London WC2E 7PA. Written enquiries only.

Theatre Museum, 1e Tavistock Street, London WC2E 7PA (tel. 0171–836 7891). Study Room open Tue–Fri, 10.30–4.30, strictly by appointment. Entrance to the Study Room is not the Museum entrance, but round the corner in Tavistock Street at basement level, approached by a ramp. The collection includes that of the Enthoven Collection, previously at the Victoria & Albert Museum, and the library of the former British Theatre Association.

Recommended books:

Biographical Dictionary of Actors, Actresses, Musicians, Dancers, Managers and Other Stage Personnel in London 1660–1800, by P.H. Highhill, K.A. Burnim and E.A. Langhans, Southern Illinois University Press, USA, in progress since 1973 and nearing completion (15 vols to date)

A *Directory of Theatre Research*, ed. Diana Howard, Society for Theatre Research/Library Association, London, 2nd edn, 1986; new edition in preparation

International Dictionary of Theatre, St James Press, Detroit, 3 vols, 1992–4

The London Stage, series published by Scarecrow, Metuchen, N.J., consisting of a day-by-day calendar of plays produced at the major London theatres 1890–1959; 16 vols to date, continuing

Transport

CAA Central Library, Aviation House, South Area, Gatwick Airport, West Sussex RH6 0YR (tel. 01293 573901). Mon–Fri, 9.30–4.30.

Leicester University Library, Transport History Collection, University Road, Leicester LE1 9QD (tel. 0116 252 2042). Mon–Fri, 9–5.

London Transport Museum Library, Covent Garden, London WC2E 7BB (tel. 0171–379 6344). Mon–Fri, 10–5.

United Nations

United Nations Information Centre Library, Ship House, 20 Buckingham Gate, London SW1E 6LB (tel. 0171–630 1981). Mon, Wed, Thu, 9.30–1, 2–5.30. Reference library only open to public.

Weather

Meteorological Office Library, London Road, Bracknell, Berks RG12 2SZ (tel. 01344 420242). *Bona fide* researchers admitted, preferably by appointment; otherwise written enquiries only. Mon–Fri, 8.30–4.30.

Wills

Borthwick Institute of Historical Research (York University), St Anthony's Hall, Peaseholme Green, York YO1 2PW (tel. 01904 642315). Mon–Fri, 9.30–12.50, 2–4.50, by appointment; closed for one week at Easter and part of Christmas vacation (PCY wills).

Principal Registry of the Family Division, Somerset House, Strand, London WC2R 1LP (tel. 0171–936 6000). Mon–Fri, 10–4.30 (wills and administrations since 1858).

Public Record Office, Chancery Lane, London WC2A 1LR (tel. 0181–876 3444). Admission by reader's ticket. Mon–Fri, 9.30–5; closed two weeks in October (PCC wills).

Women's Studies

Fawcett Library, London Guildhall University, Old Castle Street, London E1 7NT (tel. 0171–247 5826). Term-time, Mon, 11–8.30, Wed–Fri, 10–5; vacation, Mon, Wed, Fri, 10–5. Annual subscription or one-day pass for non-members.

Feminist Library, 5 Westminster Bridge Road, London SE1 7XW (tel. 0171–928 7789). Tue, 11–8; Sat, Sun, 2–5.

Recommended title: *Women's Studies: A Guide to Information Sources*, by Sarah Carter and Maureen Ritchie, Mansell, London, 1990.

World Wars I and II

Churchill Archives Centre, Churchill College, Cambridge CB3 0DS (tel. 01223 336168). Mon–Fri, 9–12.30, 1.30–5, by appointment with the Archivist. Letter of introduction required. (Papers of military and naval commanders, politicians and scientists; certain collections subject to special conditions of access.)

Imperial War Museum Library, Lambeth Road, London SE1 6HZ (tel. 0171–416 5000). Mon–Fri, 10–5, preferably by appointment. Closed last two full weeks in October.

Wiener Library, Institute of Contemporary History, 4 Devonshire Street, London W1N 2BH (tel. 0171–636 7247/8). Letter of introduction required. Subscription payable for extensive research, but short-term use of reference facilities free. Mon–Fri, 10–5.30. N.B. The collection of books was mostly transferred to Tel Aviv University in 1980, but the bulk of the material has been retained on microfilm in London.

Appendix II

Reference Books for the Writer

Good reference books, microfiches and CD-ROMs are expensive, and the average writer cannot afford to compete with a library in keeping his personal collection fully up to date. He would be foolish even to try. What he buys, therefore, must be related to his own pocket, mobility and access to a well-stocked reference library, as well as to the special nature of his work.

Some basic suggestions for a writer's bookshelf are listed below. It is recommended that a plan for systematic renewal should be worked out, whereby you replace the essential yearbooks annually and other books in rotation. Sell those which you discard to a secondhand book-dealer and put the proceeds towards the purchase of new editions. Excellent reference works may often be picked up in secondhand bookshops for a fraction of their original cost and are a good buy for those not engaged on highly topical work; the information they contain can be supplemented or updated by the occasional visit to the library or, in case of urgent need, by a telephone call to the reference librarian. Remainder dealers also frequently sell reference books at substantial discounts, and you should also keep an eye open for special offers advertised by book clubs. Paperbacks are by no means to be scorned. Naturally they will not stand up to as much handling as hard-covers, but you will be less reluctant to offload them when revised editions become available – and less guilty about giving them the full 'working tool' treatment, annotating and marking them as your research proceeds.

At the end of a major project you may decide to dispose of a number of books in order to create shelf space for a new set related to your next work, and here again the secondhand book-seller with whom you are in the habit of dealing should give you a fair price. Do not however be *too* ruthless! (How to locate specialist booksellers will be found on page 34, and details of bookfinding services on page 42.)

Suggested Basic Reference Library for the Writer

The essential items are:

1 A good English dictionary.

   The Oxford English Dictionary (OED), 2nd edition, 20 volumes, 1989, is obviously ideal, but probably beyond the pocket (and shelf-space) of the average writer for home use. There is a second edition of the *Compact OED*, in slipcase with magnifying glass (1991). The *OED* (2nd edn), the *New Shorter OED* and the *Concise OED* are also marketed in electronic form (CD-ROM and magnetic tape). *Note*: a third edition of the *OED* is in preparation and scheduled for publication in 2005. Among single-volume dictionaries recommended are the *Oxford Paperback Dictionary* (4th edn, 1994), *Collins English Dictionary* (3rd edn, 1991) and the *Chambers Dictionary* (now also on CD-ROM). For American meanings and spellings you will need *Webster's New World Dictionary* (3rd edn, 1988). It is a good idea to keep a smaller dictionary handy for quick reference, even if your word processor has a spell-checker, and there are many to choose from. Especially valuable to writers is the *Oxford Writers' Dictionary* (1990), mentioned in chapter 10. If you have a CD-ROM drive you may like to consider the Oxford University Press's *Writers' Shelf* CD-ROM, consisting of the *Pocket Oxford Dictionary*, the *Oxford Dictionary for Writers and Editors*, the *Oxford Guide to English Usage*, the *Oxford Minidictionary of Quotations* and *A Compact Encyclopedia*, available for Windows, Macintosh and DOS systems.

2 An encyclopedic dictionary.

   Again, there are many to choose from. Recommended up-to-date editions include the *Chambers Encyclopedic English Dictionary* (1995) and the *Oxford Encyclopedic Dictionary* (1991).

3 An up-to-date biographical dictionary.

   Who's Who, if you can afford it. The 3-volume *Concise Dictionary of National Biography* is not cheap, but invaluable. The best inexpensive buy is *Chambers Biographical Dictionary*, 5th edn, 1990 (available in hardback and paperback). Other compilations include the *Cambridge Biographical Encyclopedia* (1994) and *A Dictionary of Twentieth-Century World Biography* (OUP edn, 1992).

4 A good atlas, plus, if possible, a world gazeteer.
The Times Comprehensive Atlas of the World (latest edn, 1995) is the best. There is a cheaper version, *The Times Concise Atlas of the World*. Also recommended is the *Oxford–Hammond Atlas of the World* (1993) and its concise edition (1994). *The Statesman's Year-Book World Gazeteer* (4th edn, 1991) is the best of its kind.
N.B. Atlases are brought up to date every few years, and it is wise to buy the latest edition and the best you can afford. Take the advice of a firm like Stanford's, 12–14 Long Acre, London WC2E 9LP (tel. 0171–836 1321; fax 0171–836 0189). If you have a PC with a 386 SX processor or above you will be able to use *The Times Electronic World Map and Database* pack of four 3.5 inch floppy disks plus user's guide, produced by HarperCollins.

5 A road atlas/gazeteer of the British Isles.
These also go out of date very quickly, and you should replace them regularly. The *AA Big Road Atlas Britain* (scale 3 miles to 1 inch) (1994) is currently excellent value. An up-to-date copy of *London AZ* is also a good investment.

6 An encyclopedia (or two).
Here the choice depends very much on your needs and the money you have to spend. The newest state-of-the-art versions are 'multimedia', presenting information not only in print but with the accompaniment of sound and video. Supreme among the traditional compilations, *The New Encyclopedia Britannica* runs into thirty-two volumes in printed form but is now (1995) available on CD-ROM. Also on CD-ROM is the new world English edition of the US multimedia encyclopedia *Microsoft Encarta 1996*. Outstanding among the single-volume encyclopedias are *The Macmillan Encyclopedia*, *The Hutchinson Encyclopedia* and *The Cambridge Encyclopedia*. Unless you live a long way from a good reference library, where you can consult the multi-volume encyclopedias, it makes sense to buy one of these concise editions and renew them frequently; most are now updated annually. However, if you have the chance to acquire a secondhand set of the 9th (the so-called 'scholars' edition) or the 11th *Britannica* (with supplements, the most extensive), do not pass it by, as these contain much information not included in modern editions. That said, one word of warning: do not be tempted to acquire too many different encyclopedias, or when you come to look things up, you will be driven crazy by conflicting facts!

7 A dictionary of quotations (or more than one).
  Standard works are *The Oxford Dictionary of Quotations* (4th edn, 1992), *The Oxford Dictionary of Modern Quotations* (1991, reprinted 1992) and *Bartlett's Familiar Quotations* (15th edn, 1985). There are a number of paperback editions for quick reference, including *The Concise Oxford Dictionary of Quotations* (1993), *The Little Oxford Dictionary of Quotations* (1994), the *New Penguin Dictionary of Quotations* (1991) and the *New Penguin Dictionary of Modern Quotations* (1991). Also useful are *The Oxford Dictionary of English Proverbs* (3rd edn, 1970) and *The Concise Oxford Dictionary of Proverbs* (2nd edn, 1992). In recent years there have been numerous compilations of quotations on specialist subjects ranging from the biographical and the humorous to war, too numerous to list here. Buy a standard work and one or two others that best reflect your writing interests.

8 A dictionary of dates and/or chronology of historical events.
  One of the most up to date is the *Chronology of World History: Compact Edition* (Helicon, 1995). The Oxford University Press paperback, *A Dictionary of Dates* (1993), *Everyman's Dictionary of Dates* (7th edn, rev. 1987) and S.H. Steinberg's *Historical Tables 58 BC–AD 1990* (Macmillan, 12th edn, 1991) are also recommended. *The Wall Chart of World History* (Studio, 1991) is useful for quick reference.

9 A concise world history.
  Chambers Dictionary of World History (Larousse, rev. edn, 1994) is an excellent reference tool. The 4-volume *Chronology of World History*, published by Helicon, mentioned above, is now also available on CD-ROM.

10 A thesaurus.
  Roget's Thesaurus of English Words and Phrases is the standard work; revised and brought up to date by E.M. Kirkpatrick, it is available in hardback (Longman, 1987) and as a Penguin paperback. A different style of compilation is *The Oxford Thesaurus* (Oxford University Press, 1991). This is also available in concise form as *The Little Oxford Thesaurus* and *The Oxford Minireference Thesaurus*, and as *The Oxford Paperback Thesaurus*. There is also the *Chambers Combined Dictionary Thesaurus* (Larousse, 1995).

11 A guide to English usage.
  Fowler's *A Dictionary of Modern English Usage*, revised by Sir Ernest Gowers (Oxford University Press, 2nd edn, 1965;

paperback edn, 1983) has long been the standard. A highly recommended modern work is Godfrey Howard's *The Good English Guide: English Usage in the 1990s* (Pan Macmillan, 1993).

12 *Brewer's Dictionary of Phrase and Fable*, originally published in 1870 (15th edn, Cassell, 1995) is now available in a concise edition, revised by Betty Kirkpatrick (Helicon, 1995). A recent compilation is Adrian Room's *Brewer's Dictionary of Names: People & Places & Things* (Helicon, 1995).

13 A current yearbook.
   Whitaker's Almanack is a classic. *Hutchinson Info*, published by Helicon, was the first UK yearbook to be marketed on floppy disk (March 1995). *Info '96* (October 1995) was published simultaneously in hardback, paperback and on CD-ROM, also by Helicon, Oxford.

14 *Writers' & Artists' Yearbook*, published annually by A & C Black. Every writer should possess a current edition. This is one reference book that should be renewed each year.

15 One or more other directories reflecting the writer's chief interests. For example, *Cassell Directory of Publishing* (Cassell, The Publishers Association and the Federation of European Publishers); *Benn's Media*; *Willing's Press Guide*. The radio and television writer will want Barrie Macdonald's *Broadcasting in the United Kingdom* (Mansell, rev. 2nd edn, 1994) and *The Media Guide*, published annually by Fourth Estate, London.

The above titles form a first-class nucleus reference library, which can be built up over the years according to the dictates and fluctuations of the bank balance and work requirements. Some further suggestions (many of which have been mentioned in various chapters of this book) are:

Britain: An Official Handbook, published annually by HMSO, London
Debrett's Correct Form, Headline, London, 1992
Dictionary of Information Technology, by Tony Gunton, Penguin, Harmondsworth, 2nd edn, 1994
Europa World Year Book, published annually by Europa Publications, London
Hollis Press & Public Relations Annual, published annually by Hollis Directories, Sunbury-on-Thames, Middx

International Authors' & Writers' Who's Who, Melrose Press, Cambridge; updated every few years (14th edn, 1995)

International Who's Who, published annually by Europa Publications, London

Oxford Companion to English Literature, Oxford University Press (5th edn, edited by Margaret Drabble, 1985); concise edition (paperback), edited by Margaret Drabble and Jenny Stringer, 1987; reissued 1992

Pears Cyclopaedia, Pelham Books, London, 104th edn, 1995

Record Repositories in Great Britain, HMSO, London, updated every few years (9th edn, 1991; reprinted with revisions, 1994)

The Statesman's Year-Book, published annually by Macmillan, London

Walford's Concise Guide to Reference Material, compiled by A. Chalcroft *et al.*, Library Association, London, 2nd edn, 1992

Who Was Who, 8 vols to date, covering the years 1897–1990, plus cumulative index volume, A & C Black, London

The Writer's Handbook, ed. Barry Turner, published annually by Macmillan, London

Index

Note. It would be impossible to include in this index every library, institution and book or newspaper title referred to in the text. Entries are therefore confined to those of major importance and those with special mention in the book. Users will quickly locate other material by looking up the relevant subject entry and by consulting the bibliographies at the end of the various chapters.

Personal Notes